The First Book of

Paradox 3.5

The First Book of

Paradox 3.5

Jonathan Kamin

A Division of Macmillan Computer Publishing

11711 North College, Carmel, Indiana 46032 USA

To
DR. JOHN
MACK REBBENACK
with Laurie's blessing

International Standard Book Number: 0-672-27370-5
Library of Congress Catalog Card Number: 91-60986

Publisher: *Richard K. Swadley*
Publishing Manager: *Marie Butler-Knight*
Managing Editor: *Marjorie Hopper*
Manuscript Editor: *Joe Kraynak*
Editorial Assistant: *Tracy Kaufman*
Book Designer: *Scott Cook*
Cover Designer: *Dan Armstrong*
Technical Editors: *Corinne Cottle and Joe Kraynak*
Production Assistance: *Scott Boucher, Brad Chinn, Martin Coleman, Sandy Grieshop, Bob LaRoche, Sarah Leatherman, Howard Peirce, Cindy L. Phipps, Tad Ringo*

Printed in the United States of America

Contents

V

vi

ix

Introduction

Simplify, simplify.

> *—Henry David Thoreau*

How wonderful that we have met with Paradox. Now we have some hope of making progress.

> *—Niels Bohr*

Paradox is a powerful tool for managing information. Indeed, it is one of the most powerful record management systems available for the PC and PS/2 families of computers. Normally, such power carries a price tag: harnessing it requires learning myriad commands—perhaps even a programming language. But the paradox of Paradox is its ease of use. Using simple menu commands, you can set up sophisticated data-management systems with no programming whatsoever.

The First Book of Paradox 3.5 is your first step toward harnessing the power of Paradox. It guides you step-by-step from the most basic through many of the more advanced features. Keystroke guides and "Quick Steps" take you through the common procedures you'll use every day. Each chapter builds on the information in previous chapters, so that by the end of this book, you'll be quite comfortable with all of Paradox's main features. You'll be creating data tables and sophisticated presentation tools with ease.

You don't need to know anything about data management to use this book. Chapter 1 explains the most basic principles, and others are introduced as needed. All you need is a basic knowledge of your computer and a willingness to learn.

How to Use This Book

The best way to use this book is to be seated at your computer with Paradox running. Then you can try out each new technique as it's introduced and gain proficiency as you read. If you're new to database management, begin with Chapter 1 "What is Paradox?" to learn what database management software is; what it can and cannot do; and what Paradox, in particular, can do for you.

If you have experience with database management, but have never used Paradox, begin with Chapter 2, "Getting Started." You'll learn about Paradox's menus and how to use them. Paradox's screen layout is described so you'll know where to look for various types of useful information. You'll learn how to get help and how to get into and out of Paradox. You'll also learn how Paradox relates to DOS, your computer's operating system.

Chapter 3, "Your First Table," guides you through the creation of database tables and introduces the various categories of data that Paradox can handle. In the process, you'll set up a simple database application and lay the groundwork for a more complex one to be developed later in the book.

In Chapter 4, you begin "Entering and Editing Data." You'll learn three different ways to enter data and many ways to alter the data you have already entered. By the time you finish, you'll have an almost-usable address and phone number file.

There's no point to storing information you can't find. Sorting your data makes it easier to find what you're looking for. In addition, database management programs such as Paradox have built-in safeguards that help ensure that your data is valid. You'll learn how to use the features that accomplish these ends in Chapter 5, "Sorting and Key Fields."

Designing a data management system is a complex task. Virtually everyone makes some design decisions they later regret. Paradox makes it easy to redesign your system. You'll learn how in Chapter 6, "Modifying and Fine-Tuning Tables." You'll also learn how to exercise precise control over the items of data that appear in your system.

The reason for setting up a data-management system is to be able to get information from the data you have stored in it. Chapters 7 through 9 introduce you to the many ways of using your data to answer questions. You'll learn how to find specific items and groups of items with something in common. You'll find out how to create new values from the data you have gathered and to use these new values to change the data you have stored. Chapter 8 also provides your first introduction to scripts—Paradox's powerful tool for creating programs from the keystrokes you type.

The strength of a high-level database-management system such as Paradox is its ability to deal with bodies of data that involve complex interrelationships. Paradox makes it especially easy to do so. In Chapter 10, "Creating Relationships Between Tables," you'll set up the beginnings of an application that uses such complex relationships—an order entry application. In the process, you'll learn the basic principles of organizing data in multiple tables.

Chapters 11 through 14 continue the development of this application, while at the same time introducing you to many ways of presenting your data for review and consideration. Chapter 11, "Creating and Editing Forms," shows you new methods of presenting data on the screen. It also shows you how to enter data into several tables at once. Chapter 12, "Creating and Using Reports," shows you how to design presentation-quality reports. Chapter 14 shows you how to create and use "Graphs and Crosstabs."

Chapter 13 deviates from that path. You learn a bit more about how to use scripts to tie together a complex application.

If you do not have Paradox already running on your computer, Appendix A will tell you how to install it.

If you're relatively new to computers, Appendix B will give you an overview of DOS, your computer's operating system, and Paradox's relationship to it.

Appendix C provides a diagram of Paradox's menus for reference.

When you have finished with *The First Book of Paradox 3.5*. you'll have a basic mastery of all the major components of Paradox. You can continue to develop your skills with the help of the menus and the help screens, or seek further guidance from more advanced books. Two I can recommend highly are *The Best Book of Paradox 3* by Celeste Robinson (Howard W. Sams & Company, 1989) and *Understanding Paradox* by Alan Simpson (Sybex, 1991).

Conventions Used in This Book

Several typographical elements are used to set off various types of information. What you see on the screen is set off from the body of the text in this manner:

```
This is part of a screen display
```

When you are instructed to type text at the keyboard, the text you type is set off from the instructions like this:

```
Enter this text
```

Most Paradox commands are entered by pressing the key corresponding to the first letter of the command name. Hence, commands are shown or appear in boldface type like this: **C**reate. Many Paradox commands display menus of subcommands. Instructions to enter a subcommand will generally list all the commands to enter, separated by slashes, like this: **T**ools/**M**ore/**A**dd. When you see a command such as this, you press T M A in succession.

Other keys on the keyboard are simply referred to by name—for example, Enter, Escape, F? (function key). When you see key names that are hyphenated, hold down the first key and then press the second. Thus, for example, if you see Ctrl-F, hold down the Ctrl key and then press the F key, releasing both at once. Keys to be pressed one after the other are shown in boldface and are separated by slashes, like this: **T/M/A**.

DOS file names and commands are shown in all capital letters. Paradox operators appear in italics, for example *changeto*.

Acknowledgments

No book is ever the work of a single individual, no matter what the title page says. It would have been completely impossible for me to complete the first edition of this book without the advice and guidance of Celeste Robinson. Celeste helped me conceptualize many issues, drew my attention to the essentials, and was always patient with my numerous questions. Although my familiarity with Paradox had increased considerably before I completed the current edition, Celeste's contributions were no less essential.

Martin Waterhouse and Enrique LaRoche gave me some general pointers on database design. Nan Borreson of Borland International kept me abreast of developments in Paradox and kindly supplied the software.

Others who contributed to the first edition included Marie Butler-Knight, Jim Rounds, Martin Brown, and Marj Hopper of SAMS; Corinne Cottle and Chris Kelsay of Borland International; and Jennifer Garske. Thanks to Laurie Langer for moral support, and Mary Lyn Sorenson for administrative assistance.

The current issue owes a great deal to the work of Joe Kraynak, of SAMS. Joe patiently tested everything I submitted to make sure it worked, often made things work that didn't, and worked hard to banish the murk and smooth many rough edges.

The manuscript was created with WordStar Release 5.5. Screens were captured using Inner Media's Collage Plus. Other illustrations were prepared using Digital Research's GEM Draw Plus and Delrina Technology's Per:FORM.

XV

Trademarks

All terms mentioned in this book that are known to be trademarks or service marks are listed below. In addition, terms suspected of being trademarks or service marks have been appropriately capitalized. SAMS cannot attest to the accuracy of this information. Use of a term in this book should not be regarded as affecting the validity of any trademark or service mark.

Paradox and Quattro are registered trademarks of Borland International.

PAL and Personal Programmer are trademarks of Borland International.

PS/2 is a registered trademark of International Business Machines Corp.

MS-DOS is a registered trademark of Microsoft Corp.

Lotus and 1-2-3 are registered trademarks of Lotus Development Corp.

Zenith is a registered trademark of Zenith Data Systems.

SuperSport is a trademark of Zenith Data Systems.

OS/2 is a trademark of Microsoft Corp.

WordStar is a registered trademark of Wordstar International.

Inset is a trademark of Inset System Inc.

GEM and GEM DrawPlus are trademarks of Digital Research, Inc.

Per:Form is a trademark of Delrina Technology, Inc.

Rolodex is a trademark of Rolodex Corp.

What is Paradox?

What You Will Learn

- ▶ The Structure of a Database
- ▶ Database-Management Functions
- ▶ Planning Your Databases
- ▶ The Components of Paradox

Paradox is a *relational database management* program. If you're new to the world of database-management software, that sentence probably doesn't mean a thing to you right now. By the end of this chapter, however, it will. You'll learn what a database is, and learn some fundamental terms and concepts. You'll also learn something about what makes Paradox special in the world of database-management software, and what it can do for you.

If you've just obtained a copy of Paradox 3.5, and you're anxious to get it up and running, you may be tempted to skip this chapter. I urge you not to. (All right. If you must, go on to Chapter 2 and install the program. but after you're through, come back and read this chapter.) Although Paradox is a relatively easy program to learn and use, you will be better prepared if you understand what it's designed to do and how it does it.

What Is a Database?

A database is a collection of information that's organized in some systematic way. You probably use databases every day, without thinking of them as such. For example, your telephone directory is a database, as is your Rolodex. A mail-order catalog may be thought of as a database. The card catalog in the library is a particularly complex database. (Indeed, you might even think of the library itself as a database.)

The key factor, as noted, is that the information in a database is *organized*. While you may have a pile of business cards containing the same information that you keep in your Rolodex, that pile of business cards is not a database. Your personal library is probably not a database.

Why Use Database Software?

2

Since you already use databases every day, and they work perfectly well on paper, you may wonder what advantage you'd gain by using database software on a computer. Depending on the data you want to manage, database software may not help you at all. After all, the telephone directory, for example, is a reasonably accurate guide to addresses and telephone numbers.

However, the telephone directory is updated only once a year, and it's organized by only one criterion: the alphabetical order of the last names of telephone-service subscribers. If you maintain extensive telephone contacts in your business, you'll want your phone directory to be up-to-the-minute. ("But that's what my Rolodex is for," you may protest. True enough, but read on.) And what do you do if you remember someone's first name, but not their last name? Or if you've filed an entry by the name of your contact person, and you remember only the name of the company he or she works for?

Here's where database software can really help you. Database software can arrange your information so that you can get to any item quickly and easily. If you set up your database correctly, it's equally easy to find somebody's first name, company affiliation, or last name.

Moreover, database software can provide you with many perspectives on your data that would be difficult to get when you manage your records by hand. Suppose, for example, that you wanted to sort the names of your customers by Zip code, to find out whether there was a relationship between their addresses and the merchandise they ordered, or simply to create a bulk-mailing list to take advantage of reduced postal rates. If all the data were on index cards, and you had many customers, it might take you several days to get the information you wanted. Database software, however, can produce the information almost instantly. Good database software can even provide you with a detailed—and good-looking—report summarizing the information in many different ways.

In addition, with a little effort, the information in your database can always be up-to-date. Database software allows you to add new information to a database, provided it's of the same type that the database already contains. It also lets you delete outdated information, or make whatever changes are needed to keep your information current.

In sum, some of the biggest advantages of database software are:

▶ It can find any information contained in your database quickly and easily.

▶ It can provide you with many different views of your information.

▶ It allows you to maintain the information so that it's always current.

In addition, most database software also allows you to perform mathematical calculations on the stored information and to view the results.

3

The Parts of a Database

Although you may think otherwise, computers actually aren't very smart. (If they were, they'd be able to figure out what you mean when you mistype a command and do what you want in spite of the error.) Therefore, you have to be very careful about the information you give them and the questions you want them to answer. However, computers *are* very fast and very precise. Hence, given properly arranged information, they can perform complex and tedious tasks (such as sorting all your alphabetized customer addresses by Zip code) quite quickly and easily.

For this reason, databases must be designed to conform to a very strict structure. They are generally set up in rows and columns. All the items in a given row have something in common, and all the items in a given column have something in common. Each column represents a different *category* of data. Each row represents a single object about which you have information. For example, if you were to turn your Rolodex into a database, you might want separate columns for Names, Addresses, and Phone Numbers. As a result, each row would represent a separate card.

In database lingo, these columns are called *fields*, and the rows are called *records*. Fields represent categories of information about the items in the database, and records represent the items to which the information pertains. Collectively, the set of matched records sharing the same fields make up a *table* or a *file*. Sometimes a table is referred to as a *relation*, because it relates the categories of data—the fields—to the real-world items represented by the records. (This is where the term *relational* database comes from, about which more shortly.)

One important feature of databases is that fields have *field names* and records have *record numbers*. If you think about some of the everyday databases mentioned earlier, it's easy to think of names for the various fields. For example, a library's card catalog always includes at least the following fields:

Author's name
Book title
Publisher
Place of publication
Publication date
Subject
Library of Congress Catalog Number

Many libraries include even further information, such as cross-references, alternative subject headings, author's date of birth and death, and so on. This is quite a complex database.

Much simpler is the database represented by a residential telephone directory. You can expect to find information that would fall into the following categories, or field names:

Last name
First name
Street address
City (if your directory covers more than one city)
Telephone number

The field names, along with some other information, make up what is called the *structure* of a database. In addition to the names of the fields, which tell you what kind of information appears in each, the structure also contains:

▶ Information about *how much* data can be stored in each field—generally expressed as a number of characters.

▶ Information about the *kind* of information represented by each field: text, numbers, dates, currency, and so on.

Additionally, the structure may include information about how the data is to be entered into each field—for example, whether the first character should be capitalized, and whether punctuation marks are allowed.

These examples again suggest one of the great advantages of a computerized database over a paper database. The library generally has three card catalogs—one each for titles, authors, and subjects. If the card catalog were computerized, it would be possible to record the information for each book only once. You could use the database software to select information by title, author, or subject from the same set of records.

What Is Database Management?

5

Any time you use your database software to rearrange the information in your database to get a new viewpoint, you are *managing* your database. You are also managing your database when you add information to it, change the information in it, or rearrange its organization (which is *not* the same as rearranging or editing the information).

Most important, you are managing your database when you extract useful information from it. In addition to browsing through a table record by record, or searching a table for specific values, there are two other ways to get information from your database. First, you can construct a *query*, where you ask Paradox to show you all the records that have certain characteristics in which you're interested. Second, you can print a *report*, showing either all of the information in a table, all the information in selected fields, or only the information generated by a query. Moreover, while querying or producing a report, you can ask Paradox to *calculate* values based on any numeric quantities that appear in your database. You can even save the calculated results to use again later.

In summary, database management includes the following functions:

► *Adding* information to the database.
► *Editing* the data in the database—making changes to the information in specific fields and records.
► *Deleting* information from the database.
► *Searching* for various items of information in the database.
► *Sorting* the information into a usable order.
► *Querying* the database to get answers to questions about the relationships between items in your database.
► *Reporting* on the data in your database, and the relationships it represents.
► *Calculating* values based on numeric quantities.

6 What Is a Relational Database?

OK, folks, it's time to bite the bullet. You already know that a database is a table, or relation, consisting of rows called records and columns called fields. So what's a relational database? Basically, a relational database is a *collection* of interconnected tables. Paradox, as a relational database manager, allows you to:

► Store information about the same items in several tables, and link the tables together meaningfully.
► Ask questions, or construct *queries*, about several tables at once.
► Create and manage *one-to-many* relationships—such as all the books by a given author, or all the orders taken by a given salesperson. It can even manage yet-more-complex *many-to-many* relationships—an issue we won't deal with in this book.

Because the relationships between the tables in a relational database are carefully defined, and controlled by the software, the software can do a great deal to maintain the *integrity* of your data. That is, it can discover whether the data in a table is properly linked to that in another table, and delete entries that are not so linked, or warn you so that you can make the necessary corrections. Paradox is especially friendly in this regard. It always gives you several chances to make corrections. In addition, when you perform complex operations that may change the structure of your data, Paradox generally creates a separate table to preserve the original form of any data that you alter or delete. Thus, you can correct it and add it back into the original table if you wish.

The Importance of Planning

Paradox is called Paradox because it allows you to deal with complicated data-management problems using simple means. Where other relational database managers require extensive programming to get answers to complex questions, you can generally get similar answers from Paradox just by filling out forms selected from menus. Moreover, if you find that the way you've set up your database doesn't permit you to answer the questions you want to ask, Paradox makes it relatively easy to restructure your tables to do so.

However, "relatively easy" is not the same as "a snap." Therefore, it's important to think about the kinds of questions you might want to ask before you set up your tables, The more accurately you anticipate what information you will need, the less trouble you will have later on. Nonetheless, no one can anticipate all contingencies.

Consider the Rolodex example. Suppose, as suggested, you created the following fields:

Name
Address
Phone number

These are, after all, the categories in which you think of the information in your paper Rolodex. But remember, computers aren't smart. They can't anticipate the way you think. Consider the Name field. Will you enter the names last name first, such as

```
Jones, Harry
```

or first name first, such as

```
Harry Jones
```

or will you leave it discretionary?

7

Now consider what happens when you try to sort the names in your database. Suppose it contains the following entries:

```
Diane Smith
Fred
J. Jonah Jameson
Jones, Harry
Oscar T. Grouch
```

If you asked your database management software to sort these names, they would always come out in that order. Paradox—or virtually any other database management program—will sort the data in a field character by character, starting from the left. It doesn't understand the difference between a first name and a last name—something that's intuitive to you—unless you tell it there's a difference. So instead of a name field, you'd be better off with two, or possibly three, name fields:

8

Last name

First name

(possibly) Middle initial

With separate last and first name fields, you can ask Paradox to search for Diane Smith by looking for Diane in the first name field, or for Smith in the last name field.

Now, what about that middle initial field? If you use it, J. Jonah Jameson will have to become J. J. Jameson, unless you want to put Jonah in the first name field. So do you include middle initials in the first name field or not? Basically, it depends on what you want to do with the data. Paradox is smart enough to find "Jonah" when one field of a record contains the data.

```
J. Jonah
```

but you have to know how to ask for it. (Don't worry, you'll learn. It's not hard.)

You'll run into similar problems with the address field. An address normally contains several discrete items, each of which might be in a separate field:

Street address

Apartment or Suite number

City
State
Zip code

If you remembered the state, but not the city, that a person lives in it would be a lot easier to find the address you're looking for if these items were treated separately. And you couldn't possibly sort by Zip code for mass mailing unless the Zip code were in a separate field.

With multiple tables, you add another dimension of complexity to your planning. But you also become able to handle much more complex data. Suppose you wanted to create a database containing information about a collection of record albums. In a *flat-file manager*—a program that handles only one table at a time—you would have to have a separate record for each song on each album. This creates a rather unwieldy—and large—file. If, however, you can *link* several tables, you can have a table containing a single entry for each album, and a second table listing the songs on all the albums, linked to the names of the albums in the first table.

This has many advantages. First, you don't have to type all of the information about each album over and over for each song. Second, proper linking of the two tables can make it easier to find the information you want. Third, because you don't have the *redundancy* created by multiple entries for each album, it's much easier to manage the data. If you get rid of an album, for example, in a flat-file database, you have to take extra care to be sure you've deleted all the records pertaining to it. With a relational database, you need perform the deletion only once, and everything depending on the main entry—called the *master record*—can be deleted automatically. This is true, however, only if you have constructed your individual tables—and the links between them—in a manner that makes that possible. To be able to do so, you must *normalize* your database. This is the name for the process of eliminating redundancy in a relational database. Normalization is a complex topic, and we won't be getting to it for a while.

In the course of this book, we're going to develop an order-entry application requiring multiple tables. However, we'll start simple, with a single, flat-file database, and work up to it gradually. By the time we deal with multiple tables, you'll already have mastered the fundamentals, and it will be relatively easy. In the meantime, keep these principles in mind:

9

▶ If you're creating a computerized version of information that's already on paper, use the paper forms and reports as the starting point for planning the structure of your database.

▶ Carefully consider how you will use your database. Try to anticipate future as well as present uses. This can help to ensure that you include all the fields you will need in the future as well as in the present.

▶ Give your fields a logical relationship to the data you expect them to hold. The clearer your picture of how your data is structured, the more likely you'll be to create categories that support, rather than hinder, your search for meaningful information. Treating a name as two fields (First and Last) and an address as five or more fields (Company, Department, Street address, Suite, City, State, Zip code) are examples.

▶ If you find yourself contemplating tables with huge numbers of fields, you probably need several additional linked tables. Keep the structure of your tables manageable.

10

▶ Your fields should be large enough to hold the data you want to put into them. On the other hand, if they are too large, they waste your computer's resources.

Under the best of circumstances, designing a database is an iterative process. It's virtually inevitable that as you use your database, you'll come across variations in the data that you didn't plan for, and you'll have to change the structure of a field, a table, or even an entire series of linked tables. Again, Paradox is flexible enough to let you add fields to a table, break tables up into a series of related tables, and change the size of your fields, all without losing any data. However, the less of this type of reorganization you have to do, the happier you'll be with the results.

Views of a Database

In addition to the various types of information in a database, there are several different ways of viewing that information. One, obviously, is through the table of rows and columns, which is called an *image* in Paradox. This view makes it easy to look at the data for each field in a given record.

A second way to view a database is through a *form*. A form is simply an arrangement of information on the screen that lets you view all—or any selected group—of the fields in a single record at one time. Paradox will create a form automatically for any image the first time you ask to see a *form view* of your database. However, if your company uses any kind of standard forms, you can easily re-create those forms in Paradox, so you can view the information in a way that you're already familiar with.

A third way to look at the information in a database is through a *report*. When you create a report, you specify exactly what information you want to include, and how and where it should appear on the printed form, including calculated values, if you wish. As with forms, Paradox will generate an instant report from any table at the press of a key, presenting all the data in the selected table. You can, however, customize report forms to your heart's desire, as easily as you can customize forms. Paradox makes it especially easy to customize reports and forms. You simply use the keyboard to "paint" a picture of the report or form on the screen, and show Paradox where you want the data from each field to appear. You'll learn how to create customized forms in Chapter 11, and how to create customized reports in Chapter 12.

In addition to these three standard ways of viewing a database, Paradox gives you a fourth—*graphs*. You can instantly create a graph of any numeric data in your database.

11

The Parts of Paradox

When you first load Paradox, you see the Main menu shown in Figure 1.1. (You'll learn how to load Paradox in the next chapter.) As you can see, the Main menu commands are displayed across the top of the screen. When a command is selected, a brief explanation of its function appears on the line below. Many of the commands you see display submenus of other commands. If you've ever used Lotus 1-2-3, you'll be quite familiar with this arrangement.

```
View  Ask  Report  Create  Modify  Image  Forms  Tools  Scripts  Help  Exit
View a table.
```

Figure 1.1: The Paradox Main menu.

The Main Menu

It may not immediately be clear what each of the commands does. Don't worry about that for now. You'll learn what commands to use and when to use them in the course of this book. Just think for a moment about what you've already learned. In using Paradox, you create several types of *objects:* tables (images), forms, reports, and graphs. There's another type of object I haven't mentioned—*scripts*. Paradox lets you record a series of keystrokes as you type them, and play them back with a single keystroke. In addition, Paradox includes a powerful programming language called PAL (Paradox Application Language) with which you can create extremely complex and efficient scripts. However, since you can do so much in Paradox without programming, you'll be using simpler means to create scripts. (There are several ways besides recording at the keyboard.)

You'll explore the menu options in greater detail in the next chapter. For now, let's just look at the relationship between Paradox objects and the menu choices.

Obviously, before you can work with Paradox objects, you must have something to work with. Thus you start with the **C**reate command. This command is used to create a table. More specifically, it creates a *structure diagram* for a table. This is simply a list of the fields in your table, the size of each field, and the kind of data each will contain.

Having created your table, you can view or edit it using the **V**iew command. You can also modify it using the **M**odify command. This command is also used to change the structure of tables.

In addition, you can change the way a table appears on the screen through the **I**mage menu. This changes the width of columns and the number of records displayed at a time, without affecting the actual structure of the table.

The **I**mage menu is also used to design and view graphs, and to create the cross-tabulations from which graphs are derived.

As noted, Paradox will create forms or reports instantly at the press of a key. However, when you want to design your own forms or reports, or change those that you have already created, you use the **F**orms and **R**eport menus, respectively.

The **A**sk command is used, as you might suspect, for asking questions about your database. Paradox features a sophisticated, yet easy-to-use, method of asking questions, called *query by example* (QBE). You simply use a mock-up of the table or tables from which you want

12

to get information, and enter the guidelines for selecting the information in them. Paradox will quickly find the information you want.

The **S**cripts menu is used, not surprisingly, to deal with scripts. You can save scripts, play scripts, and edit scripts from this menu.

There are three more commands on the Main menu that don't relate quite so directly to specific Paradox objects. The **T**ools menu is a catch-all containing a welter of subcommands. You'll use this menu more often than you think. Besides allowing you to temporarily leave Paradox to execute operating system commands, it allows you to copy, rename, and delete Paradox objects. In addition, it gives you several other ways to enter new data into your tables or edit existing data. Finally, it gives you a means to create copies of Paradox data that can be read by other programs and to have Paradox read files created by other programs.

The **H**elp command gives you access to Paradox's on-line help system. The help system is *context-sensitive*—that is, it normally displays information about whatever you're currently working on. In addition, it includes an index, so you can search for other topics.

Finally, the **E**xit command takes you out of Paradox entirely, so that you can run other programs.

13

The Power of Paradox

Now that you have some idea of what Paradox is, you may be interested in how much data it can handle. You'll be surprised and pleased to know the answers.

The number of tables you can create is limited only by the hardware in your computer. You can use up to 24 tables at one time.

Each table can have up to two billion records. Each record can have up to 255 fields, and each field can have up to 255 characters.

You can create up to 15 different forms for each table. Each form can have up to 15 pages. Moreover, you can create forms that automatically link up to five different tables, so you can enter data into as many as five different tables at once. When you include several tables in a single form, you can browse through the data in each of the tables while using the form.

As with forms, each table can have up to 15 reports. There is no limit to the number of pages a report may contain, and you may have reports as wide as 2,000 characters, and as long as 2,000 characters per page. Reports can display information from up to five tables at once.

Another aspect of Paradox that makes it especially powerful is that it almost always gives you more than one way to complete a task. There are several different keys that move the cursor in the same way. Many of the special keys are duplicated on the main keyboard, so that, for example, you can use either a function key or a Ctrl-key combination to execute many commands. In addition, there are many ways to enter and edit data in Paradox tables. This flexibility makes it easy to find a way to use Paradox that conforms to your habits and predilections.

In order to use Paradox, you must have a computer in the PC or PS/2 family that has a hard disk and at least 512K of memory and runs MS-DOS or PC-DOS release 2.0 or later. Paradox can run on any type of monitor, but to view graphs, you must have a monitor capable of displaying graphics. Paradox can be configured to use any type of printer, but you may have to do a bit of digging in your printer manual to get your printouts to look the way you want them to.

Chapter 2

Getting Started

What You Will Learn

- ► Using Paradox Menus
- ► Responding to Prompts
- ► Getting Help
- ► Exiting from Paradox
- ► Paradox and DOS

Now that you know what kind of program Paradox is, it's time to get started. You'll start up the program, take a tour of the menus, and learn a bit about the special keys you'll use regularly in Paradox.

Starting Paradox

If Paradox is not already installed on your computer, see Appendix A for instructions for doing so. Once you've installed Paradox, you can run it immediately by typing two commands:

```
CD\PDOX35
PARADOX
```

Press Enter after each command. (From now on, press Enter after any text you are told to type in this fashion unless directed otherwise.)

These two commands make Paradox's directory current, and invoke the program, respectively. Now you're ready to start using the program.

> ▶ If Paradox fails to appear on your screen, you will see a message giving you the reason for the failure. The most likely reason for the program to fail to load is that either you don't have enough memory available in your system when you invoke Paradox, or that your CONFIG.SYS file isn't set up correctly. See Appendix A for details and remedies.

The Main Paradox Screen

16

While Paradox loads, you'll see the title screen as shown in Figure 2.1. In a little while, you'll see the main Paradox screen. It appears again in Figure 2.2. You'll note that the screen is divided into three separate areas. (If you have a color monitor, the areas may appear in different colors.)

The Menu Area

At the top of the screen is the *menu area*. The top line is a series of commands. One command is always *selected*, a condition indicated by a reverse-video highlight. The second line briefly explains what the selected command does. For example, when you first load Paradox, the **View** command is selected. The legend on the second line reads

```
View a table.
```

The legend changes as you select different commands.

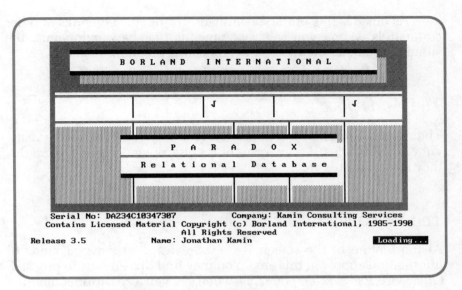

Figure 2.1: The Paradox title screen.

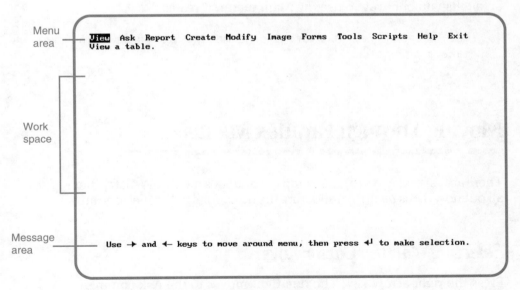

Figure 2.2: The main Paradox screen.

As noted, some of these commands bring up submenus of other commands. When you select commands that have submenus, the submenus appear on the top line, replacing the Main menu.

The Workspace

The central portion of the screen is the *workspace*. When you create, view, or edit tables, design forms or reports, or view reports or graphs, they appear in this area.

The Message Area

At the bottom of the screen is the *message area*. Several kinds of information appear in this area. You may find tips on how to proceed. Otherwise, Paradox lets you know when you've asked it to do something that it doesn't know how to do, or tells you when it can't carry out a command you've entered for some other reason. At present, the message area tells you one way to use the Main menu. It reads:

```
Use → and ← keys to move around menu, then press ↵ to
make a selection.
```

Moving Through Paradox Menus

There are several ways to get around in Paradox's menus. We'll try them all out now. Let's begin by following the directions in the message area.

Selecting with the Cursor Keys

Press the right-arrow key. The highlight moves to the **Ask** command, and the command explanation now reads

```
Get a query form to ask questions about a table.
```

Obviously, you can't ask any questions about a table because you haven't created one yet. As the message at the bottom of the screen still notes, you can move back and forth among all the commands on the menu with the right-arrow and left-arrow keys. Take a few minutes to do so now. You'll notice that the legend changes as each command is selected.

Selecting by First Letter

There are several other ways to move among the commands on a menu when it is displayed. Perhaps the most convenient is to press the key representing the first letter of the command. Thus, to select the **C**reate command, you can just press **C**, and Paradox immediately executes the **C**reate command. Get into the habit of entering commands by letter. Doing so helps you learn the commands and also is faster.

There may sometimes be more than one choice beginning with a given letter—especially when you're selecting one of several Paradox objects you have created. If several objects have names beginning with the same letter, Paradox will present you with a shorter list of selections, all beginning with that letter. You then select the item you want with the cursor keys or by typing the second letter of the command.

19

Other Ways to Move Through Menus

Additionally, the Home and End keys on the cursor keypad move the highlight to the first and last visible items on the menu. (I say "visible items" rather than "commands" because, as you'll soon see, you'll sometimes select items other than commands from the menus, and there may be too many to fit on the screen at once. However, Paradox menus themselves are never more than one screen across.) When there are too many items to fit on the width of the screen, the combination of the Ctrl key and the right- and left-arrow keys moves the list of items one screen to the right or to the left, respectively. The highlight will initially appear on the rightmost selection of the previous screen when you move to the right, and on the leftmost item of the previous screen when you move to the left.

Selecting and Unselecting Commands

Now that you know how to move around the menu, try selecting some commands. Press Escape. Move the cursor back to the View command, and press Enter. As you'll see in Figure 2.3, the legend now reads

```
Enter the name of a table to view, or press ⌐ for a list
of tables.
```

You dutifully press Enter, but of course, since you haven't created any tables yet, no list appears. Paradox points out this fact in the message area, with the highlighted message

```
None found
```

at the lower-right corner of the screen.

In the upper-right corner of the screen, the word

```
Main
```

appears in a highlight. This indicates that you are still working in the Main menu—you haven't actually begun using one of Paradox's other functions. You'll always see such a *mode indicator* when a menu is not on display.

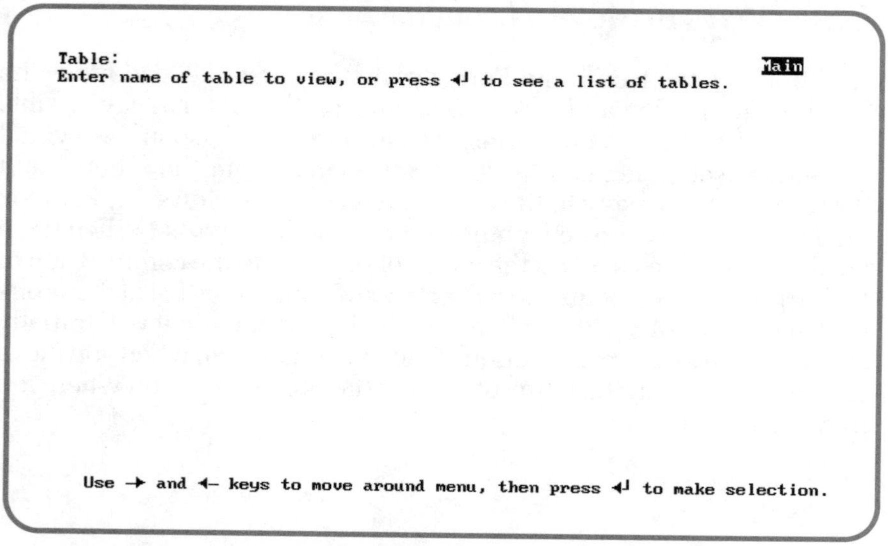

```
Table:                                                              Main
Enter name of table to view, or press ◄┘ to see a list of tables.




Use → and ← keys to move around menu, then press ◄┘ to make selection.
```

Figure 2.3: Selecting a command from the Main menu.

So now that you can't proceed, where do you go from here? Press Escape, and the Main menu will reappear. You can always move back up one level in the menus by pressing Escape. Try the same thing with any of the other commands except **T**ools, **H**elp, and **E**xit, and you'll quickly find that you're asked for the name of a table after either one or two levels. Don't worry. You'll create your first table in Chapter 3, and then you'll be able to try out more of the commands to see what they do.

The Menu Key

You'll use function keys extensively in Paradox. Some simply provide shortcuts to menu commands that otherwise would require several keystrokes. Others do things you can't do any other way. One essential key is the Menu key, F10. No matter what you're doing in Paradox, F10 always displays the highest-level menu in the current mode. Thus, if you are several levels deep into one of the Main menu's submenus, pressing F10 will always bring you back to the Main menu. If you're, say, editing a table or designing a report, F10 will display the most general commands that you can execute while performing that function.

Try it now. Press the following keystrokes:

T   To select the **T**ools menu.
M   To select the **M**ore command, which displays a secondary Tools menu.
D   To select the **D**irectory subcommand.

You'll see a display similar to Figure 2.4. The top line should read something like

```
Directory: c:\pdox35\
```

and you'll have a chance to enter a new directory path. Now press F10 to return to the Main menu, bypassing all the intermediate menus. You'll see that the mode indicator at the upper-right corner of the screen says

```
Main
```

as soon as you enter the first submenu, and stays there until you press F10, when the Main menu reappears.

21

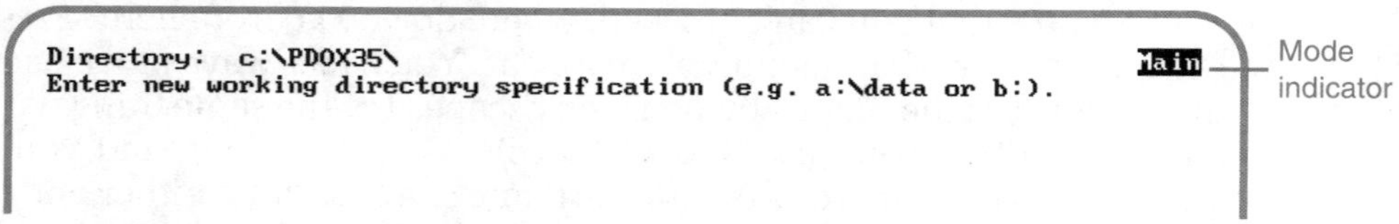

```
Directory:  c:\PDOX35\                                         Main     Mode
Enter new working directory specification (e.g. a:\data or b:).         indicator
```

Figure 2.4: Moving through several levels of menus.

Entering Text in Response to a Prompt

Sometimes you are asked to enter text in response to a menu prompt. For example, the **T**ools/**M**ore/**D**irectory command asked you to enter a directory path. (I'll use this shorthand notation to refer to submenu commands that have already been introduced.) To do so, simply type the requested text.

22

But what if, as in the **T**ools/**M**ore/**D**irectory command, default text is already present? There are several ways to deal with it. To accept the default text, just press Enter. The most obvious way to change the text is to erase it character-by-character by pressing the Backspace key. However, you can erase all of the text at once by pressing Ctrl-Backspace.

By default, you can't edit text that appears on the screen—you can only delete characters, or delete everything in the entry area. However, pressing Ctrl-F (or pressing Alt-F5) allows you to move the cursor through the entry area. The keyboard will be in insert mode, but you can toggle between insert and overtype modes by pressing the Ins or Insert key.

This mode of entry, where you can move the cursor over existing text, is called *field view* in Paradox, because it restricts the cursor to only the current field, whether that field is an entry field for a prompt or an actual database field. Whenever you can enter text, you can use field view to edit text that's already on the screen. However, you must press Enter to return to Paradox's normal entry mode before you can go on to do anything else. A warning in the message area will remind you if you forget.

Getting Help

One very useful command in Paradox is **H**elp. Help is always available no matter what you're doing in Paradox. At the Main menu, the **H**elp command shows you the screen illustrated in Figure 2.5. As you can see, it's an introduction to the help system. The help system has a menu that works just like the menus in Paradox proper.

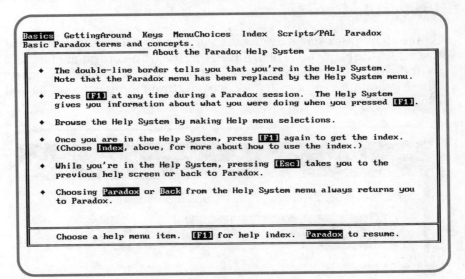

Figure 2.5: The opening help screen.

The Help Index

Get to know the Help menu's Index command. You can see it on the top-line menu in Figure 2.5. As you can see at the bottom of the screen, pressing F1 while in the help system always takes you to the Help Index, which is shown in Figure 2.6. The current help selection is highlighted, and you can search for a topic by pressing Ctrl-Z and entering the text you want to search for. Because Ctrl-Z "zooms" you to the item you ask for, it's called the Zoom key. If the Help Index doesn't contain an entry matching what you typed, Paradox honks.

Figure 2.7 shows an example of searching for an entry in the help system.

Using Wild-Card Characters in a Search

As the Help Index screen indicates, you can search for something that resembles the text you want to find, using the wild-card characters and to find groups of characters that might match what you're looking for. These techniques work with the Zoom key throughout Paradox, as well as in the help system.

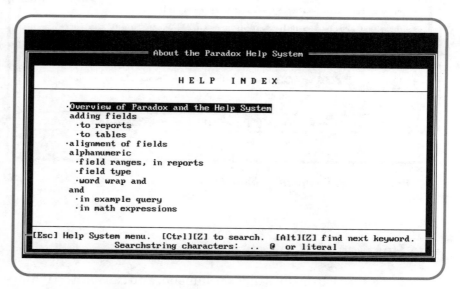

Figure 2.6: The Help Index.

Search
Entry

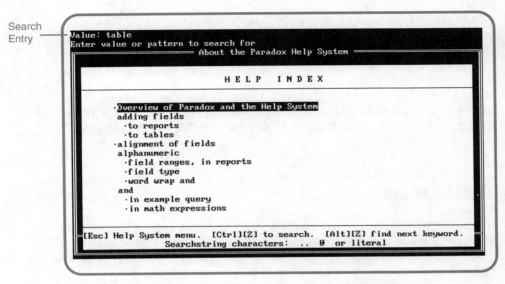

```
Value: table
Enter value or pattern to search for
                    About the Paradox Help System

                        H E L P   I N D E X

           ·Overview of Paradox and the Help System
            adding fields
             ·to reports
             ·to tables
           ·alignment of fields
            alphanumeric
             ·field ranges, in reports
             ·field type
             ·word wrap and
            and
             ·in example query
             ·in math expressions


 [Esc] Help System menu.  [Ctrl][Z] to search.  [Alt][Z] find next keyword.
                Searchstring characters:  ..  @ or literal
```

Figure 2.7: Searching for an item in the Help Index.

25

Try out the wild-card characters. In Figure 2.7, I searched for the word *table*, and Paradox found the entry

```
edit
.table
```

The wild-card characters, .., represent any characters preceding or following the literal characters you type (somewhat similar to the DOS wild-card character *, but with more flexibility). The @ symbol represents any single character (like the DOS wild-card character, ?).

Now, as you can see, in Figure 2.8 I've entered

```
..table..
```

as the pattern to search for. This tells Paradox to search for the characters

```
table
```

preceded or followed by any other characters. Given this additional information, it found the index entry

```
adding fields
.to tables
```

instead. As the screen also indicates, if the first result isn't what you're looking for, you can search again for the same pattern by pressing Alt-Z instead of Ctrl-Z.

The Help Key

No matter where you are in Paradox, you can always get help. Pressing the F1 key takes you immediately to the help system. The help screen you'll see will represent Paradox's best guess as to what you want to know, based on what you were doing before you pressed F1.

Leaving the Help System

To keep the menus simple, the help system uses heavily nested menus, with only a few items appearing on each. You might have to select from three or four levels of menus before you reach the specific item for which you're looking. The Escape key always takes you to the previous menu. To return to Paradox, however, you must select the **P**aradox command from the current menu. As with the rest of Paradox, you can do so either by pressing the **P** key or by moving the highlight to the command and pressing Enter. In the only exception to an otherwise general rule, the F10 key has no effect in the help system.

Executing DOS Commands

Another pair of special keys lets you temporarily exit from Paradox to enter a DOS command—or even to run another program. Pressing Ctrl-O gives you a small area of memory, above that used by Paradox, to issue a command. You may find it useful for checking a directory to find the exact spelling of a file name, or using the DOS TYPE command to view the contents of a file.

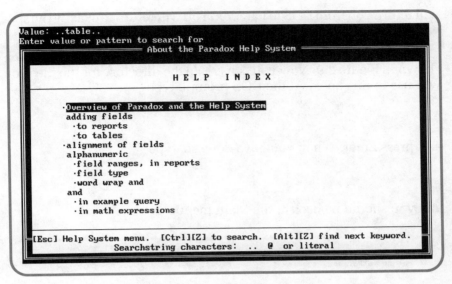

Figure 2.8: Searching using wild-card patterns.

For more elaborate DOS operations, you can press Alt-O. This key combination not only gives you access to DOS commands, but writes most of Paradox, including any open files, to a temporary file on disk, freeing a considerable amount of memory.

A third way to execute DOS commands is included in the menus. To execute the **T**oDOS command, press

T	To display the **T**ools menu.
M	To show the secondary Tools menu (**M**ore).
T	To execute the **T**oDOS command. This is equivalent to the Ctrl-O key combination.

When you go to DOS from Paradox using any of these means, you'll see the DOS prompt, preceded by the following warning:

```
WARNING! Do not delete or edit Paradox objects, or load
RAM-resident programs. To return to Paradox, type exit.
```

Heed this advice. If you make any changes to Paradox files, you may find you have lost information when you return to Paradox. If you load RAM-resident programs, you may not be able to run Paradox, and you risk losing any work you haven't saved. Typing

```
EXIT
```

will return you from DOS to Paradox. You will return to exactly the spot where you left off.

Let's try going to DOS. Press Ctrl-O. You should see the screen shown in Figure 2.9. Now you can create the directory for the files you will use in this book. At the DOS prompt, type

```
MD \LEARNPDX
```

and press Enter. When you have done so, type

```
EXIT
```

and you should be back at the Main menu.

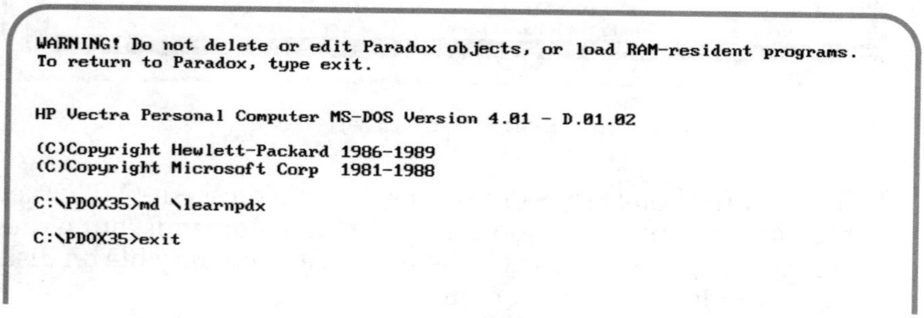

```
WARNING! Do not delete or edit Paradox objects, or load RAM-resident programs.
To return to Paradox, type exit.

HP Vectra Personal Computer MS-DOS Version 4.01 - D.01.02

(C)Copyright Hewlett-Packard 1986-1989
(C)Copyright Microsoft Corp   1981-1988

C:\PDOX35>md \learnpdx

C:\PDOX35>exit
```

Figure 2.9: Entering DOS commands from within Paradox.

Leaving Paradox

Now that you've found your way around Paradox's Main menu, you should learn how to get out of Paradox. To do so, use the **E**xit command. Press **E** select the **E**xit command. You'll see the screen shown in Figure 2.10. As you'll notice, the choice **N**o is selected, meaning, as the legend explains,

```
Do not leave Paradox.
```

As a rule, when Paradox gives you a choice between doing something and not doing something, the default is not to complete the action, but to continue doing what you were doing previously. This may help to keep you from making mistakes by accident.

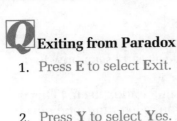

Exiting from Paradox

1. Press **E** to select **Exit**.

   Paradox presents a secondary menu with the choices No Yes.

2. Press **Y** to select **Yes**.

   Paradox saves any changes you have made, deletes any temporary working files it has created and returns you to the operating system.

3. If you press Enter or **N**, you return to Paradox's Main menu.

☐

```
No  Yes                                              Main
Do not leave Paradox.
```

Figure 2.10: Exiting from Paradox.

29

How Paradox Finds Files

Paradox itself comprises at least 40 files, depending on your configuration. It may include several subdirectories of other files if you have installed any auxiliary programs. If you store your data files among your program files, you won't be able to find them. Furthermore, if you set up more than one Paradox application, you'll probably want to keep each in its own subdirectory, or else the lists of Paradox objects that appear on your Paradox menus will become hopelessly cluttered. So give a little thought to how Paradox finds the files it uses.

Unless you explicitly tell it otherwise by one of several means, Paradox always looks in the current directory of the current drive when you ask for a data file. When you create a new data file, it creates that file in the current directory of the current drive. As I've just noted, the PDOX35 directory is probably not the best place to keep your data files. There are three ways you can tell Paradox where to create and to look for data files:

▶ By using the **Tools/More/D**irectory command to set a directory for your current work session. (You've already seen how to do this.)

▶ By installing a default data directory in Paradox itself. (This is probably the simplest course while you're learning, and developing the application you'll be creating in this book).

▶ By placing Paradox's directory on the search path and making your data directory current before invoking Paradox.

If you don't place Paradox's directory on your search path, it will be easier to start Paradox if you create a batch file. Now you'll see how to accomplish all of these steps.

Installing a Default Directory

Paradox has a customization system that allows you to select defaults for many conditions, choose screen colors, install an editor to use in creating PAL scripts, and otherwise tailor Paradox to your needs and habits. It's quite a complicated system, and we won't go into it in depth. Moreover, although its menus look exactly like those of Paradox itself, many keys don't function the way you'd expect them to.

For now, we'll go through the few steps needed to install a default directory. This directory will be where Paradox automatically looks for, or creates, data files and other objects until you tell it to look elsewhere with the **Tools/More/D**irectory command.

Q **Installing a Default Directory**

1. Press **S** to select **S**cripts from the Paradox Main menu.	Paradox displays the Scripts submenu with the **P**lay command highlighted.
2. Press Enter to select the **P**lay command.	Paradox displays the prompt `Script:`
3. Press Enter to display a list of available scripts.	If you haven't changed the working directory from C:\PDOX35, you should see only `Custom`.
4. Press Enter to select the Custom script.	Paradox executes the Custom script.

5. If you have changed the working directory from C:\PDOX35, type **C:\PDOX35\CUSTOM** and press Enter.

Paradox executes the Custom script and displays the Customization menu, with **V**ideo selected. Press **D** to select the **D**efaults command.

6. When the menu appears, press Enter to select the **D**efaults command again.

Paradox displays the Defaults submenu, with the **S**etDirectory command selected.

7. Press Enter to select the **S**etDirectory command.

Paradox displays the prompt `Directory:` with the current directory path displayed as the default.

8. Press Backspace or Ctrl-Backspace to delete the name of the displayed directory path.

9. Type the letter of the drive on which your desired default directory appears.

Paradox automatically inserts the characters : \

31

10. Type the name of your desired default path and press Enter. (This should be **pdox35\learnpdx** if you want to install the directory for the sample files in this book.)

11. Press **R** to execute the **R**eturn command.

Paradox returns you to the previous menu.

12. Press F2 to record the changes.

F2 executes the command **D**o-It! You'll learn more about this command in later chapters.

13. You will be asked whether to record the changes on your hard disk or on a network drive. (I'm assuming that you're not using Paradox on a network.) **H**ardDisk is selected, so press Enter.

Paradox records your changes and returns you to the DOS prompt.

□

Chapter 3

Your First Table

What You Will Learn

▶ Creating and Naming Tables
▶ Naming Fields
▶ Viewing Tables
▶ Navigating Through the Workspace
▶ Paradox Data Types

Now that you know how to find your way around Paradox's menus, it's time to get to work. In this chapter, you'll create, modify, and edit a "Rolodex" table. Later, when you'll begin developing your application, you'll modify it again so you can use it as a customer database.

The Structure of a Table

As you may remember, a database table has a strict structure. It is defined by three items:

▶ The *names* of its fields.
▶ The *size* of each field—the number of characters each field can hold.
▶ The *data type* of each field—the kind of information it can contain.

To create a table, naturally enough, you use the **C**reate command. The **C**reate command has a submenu, but you won't have access to it until you begin creating a table. At this point, Paradox prompts you with:

```
Table:

Enter new table name.
```

Rules for Table Names

Table names will also become DOS file names. Therefore, they must follow the rules for file names. DOS file names are limited to eight characters in length, and may consist of alphanumeric characters plus any of the special symbols on the keyboard except *, ?, <, >, =, +, /, \, |, and the comma, period, and space.

Paradox, however, restricts you further. Table names must also:

► Start with a letter.
► Be eight or fewer characters (Paradox will add a file name extension).
► Contain no characters other than alphanumeric characters and the underscore.

It's also helpful to use a name that gives you some idea of the kind of data you'll find in the table.

You cannot add a file name extension because Paradox creates "families" of files based on a table: forms, reports, graphs, and other special files. The files in a family all have the same name as the table on which they are based. However, Paradox uses different extensions for the various types of files in a family.

Entering Create Mode

Continue creating your table. Enter

```
Rolodex
```

and you will see the screen shown in Figure 3.1. Notice that the mode indicator changes from `Main` to `Create`. This tells you that a menu other than the Main menu will appear when you press F10.

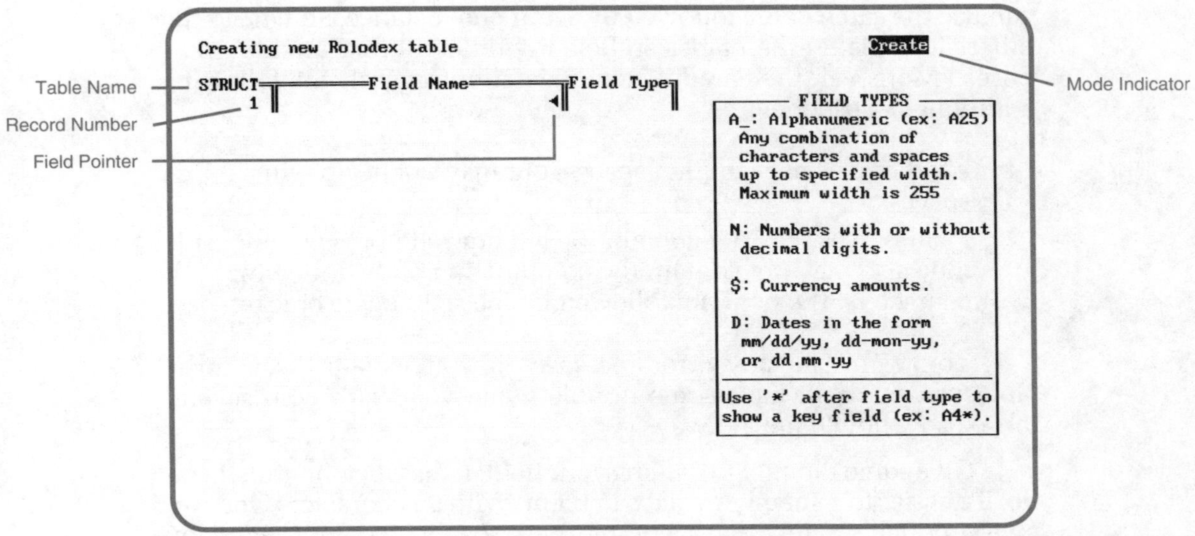

Figure 3.1: Creating a table.

35

As you can see, Paradox has created a table called STRUCTure. This table is set up exactly the same way as the database tables you will create in Paradox. The STRUCTure table has three columns. The first is headed by the name of the table, STRUCT, in uppercase letters. As you would expect in a database table, this table has field names and record numbers. The number 1 in the first column, below STRUCT, is a record number. The other columns represent the fields of the database. In this instance, Field Name and Field Type are the field names.

Creating the Structure

This is a *structure table*, not a database table, but you fill it the same way as you do a database table. Notice the pointer at the right end of the first field of the first record. This is the *field pointer*. It tells you which field is current—that is, the field in which you are working. You are now ready to enter information into the Field Name field of record number 1.

The field names you enter in the Field Name field will become the column headings—the field names—of the table you are creating. As with table names, there are restrictions governing a field name. First, field names cannot be longer than 25 characters. Second, no two fields can have the same name. (If you need two fields with similar names, you can use the same name followed by a **1** in one instance, and a **2** in the other. This makes the names sufficiently different for Paradox's purposes.) Moreover, the Paradox documentation suggests the following additional restrictions:

▶ Field names may contain spaces, but may not begin with spaces.

▶ Field names may not contain the left bracket [or right bracket]; they also may not contain the combination of the following characters: the hyphen, followed by the right angle bracket –>.

You won't get any error messages if you violate these rules. However, you will have some trouble when you work with several tables, so follow them anyway.

Give some thought to making your field names meaningful. If you do, it's easier to remember what's in them. With 25 characters, you can give your fields names that accurately describe their contents. Paradox won't care what you call your fields as long as they conform to the rules.

Since you're creating a Rolodex file, type the field name

    Last name

You don't have to capitalize the first letter—Paradox does it for you. (If you don't want your field name to begin with an uppercase letter, you can edit the field name later.) As in responding to prompts, there are three ways to make corrections if you make typing errors:

▶ Press the Backspace key to delete a character at a time.
▶ Press Ctrl-Backspace to clear the field and start over.
▶ Press Ctrl-F or Alt-F5 to switch to field view. Field view, as you remember, lets you move through the entry field using the left-arrow, right-arrow, Home, and End keys. While in field view, you can toggle between insert and overtype mode by pressing the Ins or Insert key. (Table 3.1 summarizes these keys.) Remember to press Enter when you are through editing.

The last method is also the means you use to change the initial capital in a field name to a lowercase haracter.

Table 3.1: Keys used in field view.

Key	Effect
Backspace	Deletes the character to the left of the cursor.
Del or Delete	Deletes the character at the cursor.
Ctrl-Backspace	Clears the entry field.
←	Moves the cursor one character to the left.
→	Moves the cursor one character to the right.
Home	Moves the cursor to the beginning of the entry field.
End	Moves the cursor to the end of the entry field.
Ins or Insert	Toggles between insert (the default) mode and overtype mode.
Enter	Ends field view.

When you've finished entering text, press Tab or Enter to move the cursor to the next field. Notice that both the cursor and the field pointer move at the same time. They always move together when both are visible, except when you're in field view.

Soon you'll be able to experiment with the various movement keys. At present, note that you are in the Field Type field. Remember, a field is defined by three elements: its name, its size, and its data type. The help box on the right side of the Create screen, indicates that you enter both the data type and the field size—also called the field width, in the Field Type field.

You'll also see that Paradox has four data types:

▶ *Alphanumeric,* which can contain any combination of characters and spaces.

▶ *Numeric,* which can contain only numbers.

▶ *Currency,* which also can contain only numbers.

▶ *Date,* which can contain only dates.

In the present example, you'll use only Alphanumeric fields. You'll get a closer look at the other data types before this chapter is over. To define a field as Alphanumeric, type an `A` in the `Field Type` column. Notice that there isn't a separate column for field size or field width. You determine the size of an Alphanumeric field by entering its width—the maximum number of characters it can hold—in the `Field Type` field. In this field, for example, type

```
A15
```

(You don't have to enter the A in uppercase, but Paradox will display it in uppercase regardless.) When you type this information, you have completed the definition of the first field. Press Tab or Enter to continue.

Paradox creates a new record below the first, with the record number 2.

Continue with this table, entering the following field names and field types:

Field name	Field type
First name	A15
Company	A30
Address 1	A30
Address 2	A20
City	A20
State	A2
Zip code	A10
Phone number	A14

When you're finished, your screen should look like Figure 3.2.

Why use only Alphanumeric fields? After all, Zip codes and phone numbers are numbers. But consider what would happen with numbers such as nine-digit Zip codes, phone numbers formatted with parentheses and hyphens, or Social Security numbers. The only characters that can be entered into Numeric fields are digits and arithmetic operators. Neither Paradox nor your computer makes any distinction between a hyphen and a minus sign. They are, to all intents and purposes, the same character. Paradox would let you enter a set of parentheses in a phone number, or the first hyphen in a Social Security number, because it would interpret these symbols as indicating a negative number. However, if you tried to enter a phone number in the form *(408)555-0830*, Paradox would honk and refuse to accept any keystrokes after the closing parenthesis. It wouldn't know how to interpret the result as a number. Also, Paradox routinely strips off leading zeros. Thus, you'd have trouble with Zip codes and Social Security numbers beginning with 0. (You'd have even more trouble with British Commonwealth postal codes such as *J8W 1C4*.)

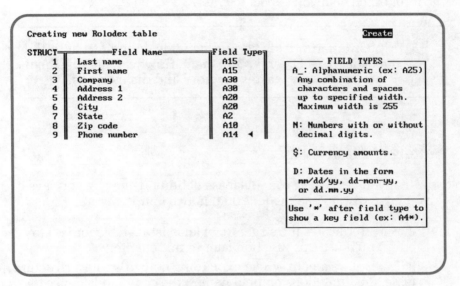

Figure 3.2: Completing the definition of the Rolodex table.

39

> ▶ *Use Numeric data types only for numbers on which arithmetic will be performed.* Use Alphanumeric data type for numbers such as Social Security numbers, Zip codes, and phone numbers.

How were the widths of our Alphanumeric fields chosen? If Paradox will allow Alphanumeric fields of up to 255 characters, why not make them all the maximum length? Why impose any limitation at all? The reason is that Paradox allocates storage space, both in your computer's memory and on disk, for the number of characters you specify. Even if a field contains only two characters, Paradox still reserves space for the number of characters specified in the field type definition. Thus, you have to balance your computer's resources against the form of the data you expect to enter.

> ▶ Alphanumeric fields should be wide enough to hold the data you expect to enter into them. However, making them wider than necessary wastes memory and disk storage.

40

Saving the Table Structure

Now that you've created your database definition, how do you save it? Press F10 to display the menu. You'll notice four items:

▶ Borrow duplicates the structure of an existing table for you to edit. You'll use this function later in this chapter.

▶ Help displays a help screen explaining how to create a structure table, the limitations on field names, the commands to use to change a table's structure, and the commands to save your work.

▶ DO-IT! is Paradox's equivalent of a "save" command. Under most circumstances, Paradox saves changes you make in a temporary file, and doesn't make them permanent until you select this command from the current menu. You can also select this command by pressing F2, the "DO-IT!" key, bypassing the menu.

▶ Cancel returns you to the Main menu without saving any changes you have made.

To save your structure table, either select **DO-IT!** by pressing the **D** key, or by pressing F2. Your workspace will clear, leaving you at the Main menu.

> ▶ You'll find the **H**elp, **D**O-IT!, and **C**ancel commands on virtually every Paradox menu.

Q Creating a Table

1. Press **C** to execute the **C**reate command.

   Paradox displays the prompt `Enter new table name.`

2. Type the name of the new table. The name must be a legal DOS file name.

3. Press Enter to record your entry.

   Paradox creates a STRUCT table in which you define the fields by name, data type, and size.

4. If you wish, you can borrow the structure of an existing table by pressing F10/**B** to invoke the **B**orrow command, and selecting, from the displayed list, the name of the table whose structure you want to borrow.

   Paradox displays the structure of the table you selected. You can insert fields with the Ins or Insert key, delete fields with the Del or Delete key, and edit existing fields using field view by pressing Alt-F5 or Ctrl-F. Press Enter to leave field view.

5. Type a field name and press Tab or Enter.

6. Type a data type: **A** for Alphanumeric, **N** for Numeric, **$** for Currency, or **D** for Date. If the field is Alphanumeric, enter a field width of no more than 255 characters. Press Tab or Enter.

7. Repeat Steps 5 and 6 until all fields are defined.

41

8. Press F2, the "DO-IT!" key.

Paradox creates a table meeting the specifications you have entered, temporarily saves the structure table under the name STRUCT, and clears the workspace. □

Viewing Tables

Press **V** to select the **View** command. Press Enter. As Figure 3.3 shows, you have a choice of two tables, Struct and Rolodex. Struct is the structure table you just created. It is a temporary table, which Paradox will delete when you exit from the program, or reuse when you create a new table. If you were to exit from the program now, and then restart it, you would see only the name of the Rolodex table when you executed the **View** command.

Figure 3.3: Selecting a table to view.

To view your new table, select it as you would any object on a Paradox menu: by moving the highlight to it and pressing Enter, or by pressing its first letter. If there were more than one table beginning with R, and you had pressed R, you would then see a list of all tables beginning with the letter R. You would then have to select the one you want by using the cursor keys and pressing Enter or typing the second letter of the table name. When you've selected the table, it will appear in your workspace, as shown in Figure 3.4. It has no records in it, because you haven't entered any. As the legend at the top of the screen reminds you,

```
Table is empty
```

You can't see the entire table, only the first few fields, because the table is too wide to fit onto the screen. However, that will change once you begin entering data.

> ▶ You can select tables to view, as well as commands, by typing their first letter. If more than one table begins with the same letter, selecting by letter gives you a shorter list, containing only those tables beginning with the letter you pressed. Type more of the name to narrow the selection.

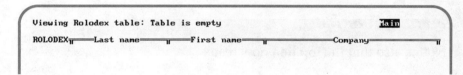

Figure 3.4: An empty table.

43

Viewing Several Tables

You can view more than one table at a time, or several copies of the same table at the same time. To prove this, press

F10	To display the Main menu.
↵	To execute the **View** command, which is selected by default.
↵	To display a list of table names.
↵	To select the first table named. If a table is already selected and on the workspace, it becomes the default item on any menu of table names.

You'll now see two copies of the Rolodex table. They'll be exactly the same. However, the second version appears below the first. Whenever you add a table to the workspace, it appears below the currently selected table. Also, the second table is highlighted with high-intensity text and has the a cursor in it, indicating that this copy of the table is currently selected.

To add another table to the workspace, press

F10	To display the Main menu.
⏎	To execute the **V**iew command.
⏎	To display a list of tables.
S	To select the **S**truct table.

As you can see from the highlighting and the position of the cursor, the STRUCT table is now currently selected.

Finding Your Place

Notice also that the top line now reads

```
Viewing Struct table: Record 1 of 9
```

This may not seem very important at the moment. However, think about what will happen when your Rolodex table has 100 or more entries in it. Most of it won't appear on the screen, because the table will be both too wide and too long. When you're viewing a table, the menu line always tells you the name of the current table and the current record number, even when the first column isn't on the screen.

Moving Within a Table

Let's try moving around within the table. Press the down-arrow key. You'll see the cursor move down in the current column until it reaches the bottom. Then Paradox will honk at you, to let you know it can't go any further. Experiment with the cursor keys, the Home, End, PgUp, and PgDn keys, the Tab and Shift-Tab keys, and the Enter key. You'll find they all move the cursor around in the table. You'll hear the same honk whenever you try to go too far in any direction, or, indeed, whenever you make an error. For reference, Table 3.2 summarizes the effects of the cursor-movement keys while you're viewing a table from the Main menu, creating a table, or editing a table.

Table 3.2: Cursor-movement keys for creating, viewing, or editing a table.

Key	Effect
←, Shift-Tab	Moves the cursor to the left one field; if the cursor is in the first field of a record, moves the cursor to the last field of the previous record.
→, Tab, Enter	Moves the cursor to the right one field; if the cursor is in the last field of a record, moves the cursor to the first field of the next record.
↓	Moves the cursor to the same field in the next record; if creating or editing a table, creates additional blank records when the cursor reaches the end of the table.
↑	Moves the cursor to the same field in the previous record.
Home	Moves the cursor to the current field in the first record.
End	Moves the cursor to the current field in the last record.
Ctrl-Home	Moves the cursor to the first field in the current record.
Ctrl-End	Moves the cursor to the last field in the current record.
PgDn	If the table has fewer than 22 records, moves the cursor to the last record; if the table has 22 or more records, moves the cursor 21 records down, displaying the current record at the top of the workspace.
PgUp	If the table has fewer than 22 records, moves the cursor to the first record; if the table has 22 or more records, moves the cursor 21 records up, displaying the current record at the top of the workspace.
Ctrl-→	If the table is wider than the screen, moves the cursor one screen to the right.
Ctrl-←	If the table is wider than the screen, moves the cursor one screen to the left.
Ctrl-Z	Finds a specific item in the current field.
Alt-Z	Finds the next instance of a given item in the current field.

45

You don't have a field pointer now, because you can't make any changes while viewing a table. You have to enter Edit mode for that. When the field pointer does appear, it will move along with the cursor. Note that as you move the cursor forward or backward a field at a time, it enters the record number column. It didn't do that you were creating the table.

In addition to the cursor keys, a menu command can help you move quickly to any field in your table. Try it now. Press

F10   To display the Main menu.

I   To display the **I**mage menu.

Z   To display the **Z**oom submenu shown in Figure 3.5.

F   To select the **F**ield command.

46

Now enter the name of the field to which you want to move. Highlight

    Field Type

and press Enter. Paradox will quickly move the cursor to the Field Type field of your table. Again, this isn't much help when you have a table of only two columns, but think again of your Rolodex table. Only the first three fields show on the screen. Suppose you wanted to move quickly to the *State* field. This would be the quickest way to get there.

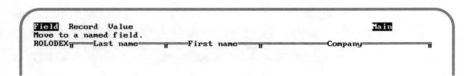

Figure 3.5: The Image/Zoom submenu.

You can also use the **I**mage/**Z**oom command to move to a specific record by number, or to the value found in a particular record in the current field. You'll find these shortcuts useful once you have tables full of data.

You'll learn other ways to get around in a table when you begin entering and editing data. For now, turn your attention to getting around in the workspace.

Moving Among Tables

When several tables are on the workspace, you can make any of them current. Pressing F3, the "Up Image" key, moves the cursor to the table above the one that's now current. (Remember, "image" is Paradox's name for a table as it appears on the workspace. As you'll see, this distinction is important, because you can make changes to the image that affect the way the table appears, without affecting the structure of the table itself.) Pressing F4, the "Down Image" key, moves the cursor to the table below the current one, if there is one. You can use these keys:

▶ When viewing tables in the Main mode, as you are now doing.
▶ When editing the data in tables. (You can edit more than one table at a time.)
▶ When setting up queries involving more than one table.

In fact, these keys will move among tables on the workspace any time more than one table is on display. The only exception is when you enter Create mode. When you execute the **C**reate command, Paradox clears the workspace except for the STRUCTure table.

While you're moving among the images on your workspace, you might try executing the **I**mage/**Z**oom command when one of your Rolodex tables is current.

Clearing the Workspace

To delete the current image from the workspace, press F8, the "Clear Image" key. Again, this merely deletes the visible image from the workspace. It has no effect on a table saved on disk. To use F8, you must be in the Main mode. You cannot delete an image while you are creating or editing it.

47

To clear all images from the workspace at once, press Alt-F8, the "Clear All" key. This, too, affects only the workspace, not the actual tables.

Copying, Renaming, and Deleting Tables

Paradox provides tools for copying, renaming, and deleting tables. All are on the **T**ools menu. For the present, we'll use the **T**ools/**R**ename command.

▶ To save a temporary table, give it a new name.

48

 Renaming a Table

1. Press **T**.	Paradox displays the **T**ools menu, with the **R**ename command selected.
2. Press Enter.	Paradox displays a list of objects that can be renamed with **T**able selected, as Figure 3.6 shows.
3. Press Enter.	Paradox prompts you to type the name of a table, or to press Enter for a list of tables.
4. Press Enter.	Paradox displays a list of all tables in the current directory.
5. Press the key corresponding to the first letter of the name of the table. If there is more than one table beginning with that letter, select the table from the shorter list of tables with the same first letter, and press Enter.	Paradox prompts you to Enter name for new table. Paradox renames the table.

□

To complete this exercise, select the Struct table and enter the new name

```
rolodx_s
```

Paradox routinely deletes only those temporary tables it creates. It recognizes them by name. If you rename a temporary table, it will automatically be saved like any other table when you exit from Paradox.

```
Table  Form  Report  Script  Graph                                    Main
Rename a table and its family of forms, reports, and indexes.
```

Figure 3.6: The Tools/Rename submenu, showing Paradox objects that can be renamed.

The **T**ools menu also includes commands to copy and delete tables. They, too, display a list of the tables in the current directory, and let you choose one. Let's practice with these commands now. You'll copy your Rolodex table, and then delete the copy.

To copy the table, press or type:

T	To display the **T**ools menu.
C	To execute the **C**opy command.
↵	To copy a table, the selected item.
↵	To display a list of tables.
→	To select the Rolodex table.
↵	To confirm your selection.
temp	To name the copy.
↵	To confirm the new name.

Paradox will then create a second table, named Temp, identical to the Rolodex table. If you had already entered data into the table, the data as well as the table structure would be copied. The **T**ools/**C**opy/**T**able command copies all the ancillary files associated with a table, as well as the table itself. Files such as form and report files that go with a specific table are considered part of the table's *family*. You can use the **T**ools/**C**opy/**J**ustFamily command to copy only the members of a table's family to another table, without copying the table itself, if the tables have the same structure.

49

Having created an extraneous table, let's delete it. Press:

T   To display the **T**ools menu.

D   To execute the **D**elete command.

⏎   To delete a table, the selected item.

⏎   To display a list of tables.

T   To select the **T**emp table.

At this point Paradox will display the message

```
If you select OK, Temp and its family will be deleted
```

Press

O   To select OK and confirm that you want to delete the table.

Paradox then deletes the table and its family, and tells you that it's doing so.

Deleting a table automatically deletes all files in its family. However, you can delete any type of Paradox object without deleting the rest of the family, as the **D**elete submenu (illustrated in Figure 3.7) shows.

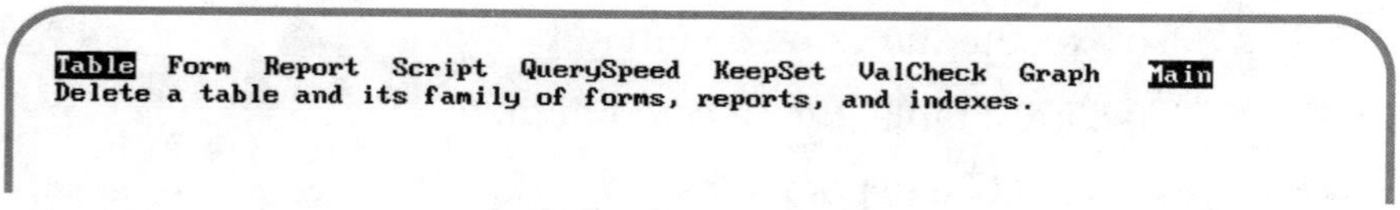

```
Table  Form  Report  Script  QuerySpeed  KeepSet  ValCheck  Graph    Main
Delete a table and its family of forms, reports, and indexes.
```

Figure 3.7: The Tools/Delete submenu.

While you're deleting things, delete the Rolodx_s table. You don't really need it. You may find it useful to be able to refer to the structure table for one table while you're designing another table, but you can always do so with the **Tools/Info/S**tructure command.

More About Data Types

I mentioned the Paradox data types briefly earlier in this chapter. Now it's time to explore them in a little more depth. You'll use them in the next table you create.

To review, Paradox has four data types, each represented by a different letter or symbol: Alphanumeric, Numeric, Currency, and Date. To define a field as being of a certain data type, you enter the letter or symbol for it into the **Field Type** field of the STRUCTure table. In the Rolodex example, you used an **A** to represent the Alphanumeric data type in all the fields. Now for a look at the properties of the various data types.

Your choice of a data type determines:

▶ How the data will appear on your screen.
▶ How the data may be entered.
▶ What kinds of operations can be performed on it.

There are, however, ways you can alter the first two items to some degree, as you'll learn in Chapter 6.

51

Alphanumeric Data

Alphanumeric data is indicated by placing an **A** in the **Field Type** column. Fields defined as Alphanumeric may contain any characters you can type at the keyboard. They are used for data that will be treated as text, and will not be used in numeric operations. You must specify the width of an Alphanumeric field, which may be up to 255 characters.

Numeric Data

Numeric fields are specified by an **N** in the Field Type column. They can contain any type of numeric data, with or without decimal parts. They also can contain parentheses and plus or minus signs. Use the Numeric data type for any data on which you expect to perform arithmetic operations. Do not use the Numeric data type for such items as phone numbers, Zip codes, or Social Security numbers. Data which includes punctuation as well as numbers, and which will not be used in arithmetic operations, should be treated as Alphanumeric.

Currency Data

Currency fields are indicated by a $ in the `Field Type` column. They also contain numeric data. However, fractions are rounded off to two decimal places, and commas are placed between every three digits to the left of the decimal point. Negative numbers are shown in parentheses.

Date Data

Date fields, indicated by **D** in the `Field Type` column, accept only valid date values. Paradox checks all entries to make sure that the entered date is a real date. Dates may be entered in any of the following three formats:

```
mm/dd/[yy]yy
dd.mm.[yy]yy
dd-Mon-[yy]yy
```

where the numbers shown in brackets are optional. (That's so you can specify years not in the twentieth century.) However, they will always appear in tables in the form

```
[m]m/dd/[yy]yy
```

although you'll learn ways to change that in Chapter 6.

You can use eight additional date formats in reports. Valid dates are any dates between January 1, 100 and December 31, 9999, based on the Gregorian (current) calendar. Paradox can do *date arithmetic* on data stored in Date format—that is, it can calculate a date a given number of days before or after a given date, or find the number of days between two dates.

You don't specify the field width for data types other than Alphanumeric. They take their width from the data you enter into them. However, if a numeric or currency value contains more digits than its column in the image (allowing for a decimal point and two decimal places), it may not appear on the screen exactly as you enter it. You'll look at how numeric data appears on the screen in Chapter 4.

There are ways to restrict the values that can be entered into a given field, or restrict them to a given format. You'll see how to create *pictures* to do so in Chapter 6.

Borrowing a Structure

Even though you haven't entered any data in your Rolodex table yet, we'll now borrow its structure for a new table. This will give you an opportunity to try out your knowledge of data types and to use the **B**orrow command. You'll also learn the functions of a few new keys.

You'll use a variation on the structure of the Rolodex table to begin the order-entry application. Execute the **C**reate command and type

```
customer
```

as the name of the table to create. Now press F10, and select the **B**orrow command. Press Enter to display the list of tables, and select the Rolodex table. When you've completed this operation, your screen should now look just about the same as it did in Figure 3.3. However, there is an additional (empty) field at the end of the table, and you're ready to make changes. You can add, delete, or edit field names, types, and sizes anywhere in this structure table.

53

Hints on Borrowing Table Structures

You can borrow the structure of more than one table if you need to create a table that contains fields common to several. You can thus make sure that both tables with the same fields use the same field names and types. Also, you can borrow a table structure at any point while creating a new table. The borrowed structure will appear beginning in the row where the cursor is located. Later, when you've created several linked tables, I'll show you some uses for borrowing from more than one table structure.

To borrow only part of a table structure, delete the field definitions you don't need by moving the cursor to the row in which they appear and pressing the Del or Delete key.

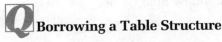
Borrowing a Table Structure

1. Press **C** to execute the Create command.

Paradox asks you to enter the name of a table to create.

2. Type the name of your new table and press Enter.

Paradox creates the blank STRUCTure table in which you'll define your new table.

3. Press F10 to display the Create menu.

Paradox displays the **C**reate menu.

4. Press **B** to execute the **B**orrow command.

Paradox prompts you to enter the name of the table whose structure you want to borrow, or to press Enter for a list of tables.

5. If the table whose structure you want to use is in the current directory, press Enter. Otherwise, type the name of the table, including the path name of the directory where it's located.

If you press Enter, Paradox displays a list of table names. Select the table whose structure you want to borrow, and press Enter. When your table is selected, Paradox displays the field names and field types of the source table in your current STRUCTure table, starting at the position where the cursor was when you invoked the **B**orrow command.   □

54

Editing a STRUCTure Table

In your personal Rolodex, you are free to include or leave out any information in a given record. In a customer database, however, you need complete address information, so you know where to ship the goods you sell. Let's add a department address. Notice that the cursor is in the first column, next to field number 1. Press:

→	To move to the Field Name column.
↓ twice	To move to the Company field name.
Ins or Insert	To make room for a new field name.

Now type

    Department

and then press Tab or Enter to move to the Field Type column, and type

```
A20
```

Let's change the names of the Address fields. Press the Tab, right-arrow, or Enter key until the field pointer appears next to `Address 1`. Now delete the last two characters of the field name with the Backspace key. Press Alt-F5 or Ctrl-F to enter field view, and press Home to move to the beginning of the field. Type

```
Street
```

followed by a space. You have to capitalize the *S*, because this isn't a new field and therefore, Paradox won't automatically do it for you. When you are finished, press Enter to leave field view.

Now move down to the Address 2 field, and press Ctrl-Backspace to delete the field name. Type

```
Suite no. or P.O. box
```

and press Enter. Move on down to the Zip code field name, and go into field view. Use the left-arrow key to move to the *c* in the word `code`. Type

```
or postal
```

followed by a space, and press Enter to leave field view. Move down one more line, press Insert or Ins, and type the following new field information:

```
Country A12
```

(As long as we're setting up a hypothetical business, we might as well make it a big one!)

Now we'll use some new data types. Press End to move to the last line of the STRUCTure table, which should now be record 12. Press left-arrow or Shift-Tab to move to the `Field Name` field and type the following field information:

```
Credit limit  $
Initial order D
```

Remember, you can press Tab, Enter, or the right-arrow key to move from one entry field to the next. If you mistype a field type indicator, you'll hear the familiar honk, and Paradox will tell you

55

Not a Paradox field type

You've now established a Currency-type field and a Date-type field. Your STRUCTure table should look like Figure 3.8. Press F2, the "DO-IT!" key, to save your work.

You're not entirely through with the structure of the Customer table yet. However, leave it for now until you've learned some more advanced concepts. In Chapter 6, we'll modify it using the **M**odify/ **R**estructure command.

Some Points to Ponder

You may have noticed at the bottom of the "FIELD TYPES" help box some information about "key fields." Key fields control many aspects of the way a database functions—most significantly the order in which entries are sorted, the way tables are linked to one another, and the way duplicate entries are handled. You'll learn to use key fields in Chapter 5, after you've entered some data into your tables.

You've done nothing so far that will prevent duplicate entries from being created—one of the functions of key fields.

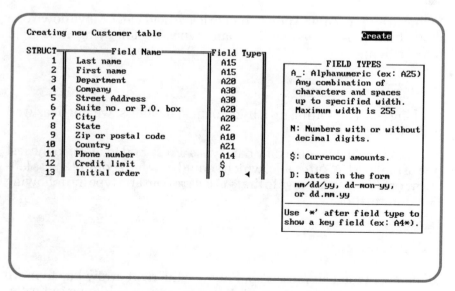

Figure 3.8: The completed Customer table.

The issue of duplicate entries will be different for the Rolodex and Customer databases. You may want to store both home and work addresses and phone numbers for some people in your Rolodex table. How many fields, grouped together, would have to be unique to allow two separate entries for the same person? Which fields would they be? Would this also allow for two entries for different people having the same name?

In the Customer database, would you use the same method for making sure each entry is unique? If not, what method would you use?

Entering and Editing Data

What You Will Learn

▶ Using DataEntry Mode
▶ Using Forms View
▶ Using Edit Mode
▶ Using CoEdit Mode
▶ Entering Numbers and Dates

Now you have created a database table. But there is no data in it. Before you can begin managing data—and extracting useful information from it—you must have some data to work with. You can enter data into your Paradox tables in four quite different ways. In addition, you can transfer data from one table to another. In this chapter, you'll be introduced to three of the methods of entering data, and you'll get your first look at a form.

Entering Data

You reach all the methods of entering data from the **M**odify menu, which appears in Figure 4.1. Press

M To display the **M**odify menu.

D To select the **D**ataEntry command; you will be asked for the name of the table to receive the data.

⏎ To display a list of tables.

⏎ To select the Rolodex table, which is highlighted.

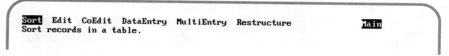

```
Sort  Edit  CoEdit  DataEntry  MultiEntry  Restructure          Main
Sort records in a table.
```

Figure 4.1: The Modify menu.

Your screen should now look like Figure 4.2. It's superficially similar to what you saw when you looked at this table with the **V**iew command. However, there are some significant differences. When you viewed the empty table, all you saw were the field names. Now there's a record number, and a cursor and a field pointer in the first field into which you can enter data.

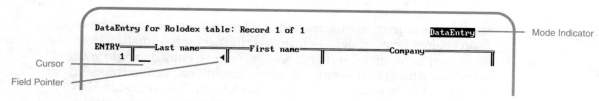

Mode Indicator

Cursor

Field Pointer

Figure 4.2: Preparing to use the DataEntry command.

In addition, the name at the top of the record number column is ENTRY, not Rolodex. When you enter data using the **D**ataEntry method, you enter the data into a separate table—the ENTRY table. Your target table—in this instance, Rolodex—is not affected in any way until you press the "DO-IT!" key, F2. Thus, any data in your target table is protected from stray keystrokes that might alter it unintentionally. In addition, the mode indicator now reads DataEntry.

You enter information the same way you did when you were creating a STRUCTure table. You use the same keys to move through the table. Now, however, you're entering the actual data.

Enter some data into your ENTRY table. The cursor and field pointer are already in the Last name field of record 1. Your first record will contain the following:

```
Frank R. Osterlund
Nationwide Thimsfrabble Co.
7984 Charter Avenue

South China, FL 32378
(904)303-9812
```

Remember, however, that the individual items have to be appropriate to the fields in which you enter them. Thus, you won't type the entire name into the Last name field. While the cursor is in that field, type

```
Osterlund
```

61

(If you make typing mistakes, you can use the Backspace key to delete characters to the left of the cursor, and make the corrections.) When you finish typing the Last name, press Tab, Enter, or right arrow to move to the First name field.

Now type

```
Frank R.
```

and press Tab, Enter, or right-arrow. Remember, we decided not to use a middle name or middle initial field so as to deal flexibly with individuals who use a first initial and a middle name, a first name and a middle initial, two initials, or two names. Therefore, you'll type both the first name and the middle initial into the First name field.

Now press Tab (or one of the other keys—I'll suggest Tab for the rest of this record, but use whichever is most comfortable). The cursor and the field pointer move to the Company field. Type

```
Nationwide Thimsfrabble Co.
```

and press Tab. The table scrolls to the left, leaving the Company field at the left margin of the screen. Type the address

```
7984 Charter Avenue
```

into the Address 1 field. Mr. Osterlund has no Suite or P. O. box number, so press Tab, to skip over the Address 2 field. The table will scroll to the left again.

Now the cursor is in the City field. Type

```
South China
```

Press Tab and type

```
FL
```

into the State field. Press Tab again and type

```
32378
```

into the Zip code field. When you press Tab again, the table will scroll once more. Type the phone number

```
(904)303-9812
```

and you have completed your first record. The right four columns of your screen should now look like Figure 4.3. Press Enter (or Tab or right-arrow) and you'll be ready to enter your second record, as shown in Figure 4.4. You can always enter another record when you complete one, because Paradox creates a blank record when the cursor moves past the end of the current record.

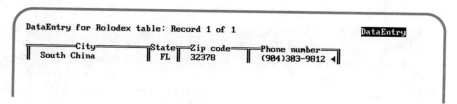

Figure 4.3: A database with one completed record.

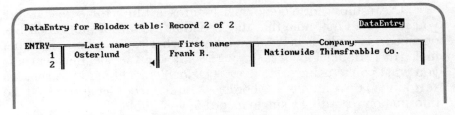

```
DataEntry for Rolodex table: Record 2 of 2                    DataEntry
ENTRY━━━━━Last name━━━━    ━━━First name━━━    ━━━━━━━━━Company━━━━
    1 ┃ Osterlund              Frank R.         Nationwide Thimsfrabble Co.
    2 ┃                     ◀
```

Figure 4.4: Ready to enter the second record.

Now type the second record. See if you can do it without guidance, but remember to skip past empty fields. You'll know a field is empty because there will be a blank line among the items to be entered. In the following record, there is again no second address:

```
Jameson
J. Jonah
Daily Bugle
1 Bugle Plaza

New York
NY
10001
(212)500-9000
```

63

Using Forms View

For the third record, try something different: This time you'll enter the data into a form. Press F7, the "Form Toggle" key. Paradox will briefly display the message

```
Creating standard form F
```

Form F is the default form which Paradox creates automatically for any table. Note that the form is a member of the Rolodex family, not the ENTRY family. ENTRY is a temporary table, and takes its structure from whatever table you are entering data into.

The resulting form is shown in Figure 4.5. Study this screen before you proceed. First, note that the legend at the top of the screen has changed. Not only does Paradox tell you what you're doing, and what table you're doing it to (DataEntry for Rolodex table), but it also tells you what you're using (with form F). Now look at the form itself. It's surrounded by a double-line border. Within the border appears all the information regarding a single record of your table.

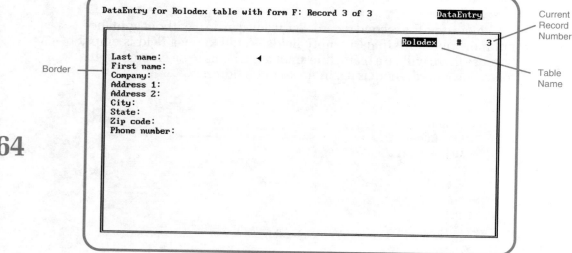

Figure 4.5: *A Paradox default form.*

In the upper-right corner, the name of the table appears in inverse video, followed by the current record number. The field names, instead of being arranged across the top of the table, are now in a column at the left margin of the screen. The entry areas are to the right of the field names, instead of below them. The current field is indicated by the cursor and the field pointer. Try moving down and up through the form with the down-arrow and up-arrow keys. Notice that the cursor moves in a vertical line. (There's an invisible margin one character to the right of the widest field name.) At the same time, the field pointer moves to the right margin of the entry area, just as it does in table view.

Enter the following data in the next record.

```
Khorajian
Corey
Khorajian Plating & Welding Co.
```

```
1923 Chascarillo Avenue
P.O. Box 984
Palomar
CA
90006
(619)906-5432
```

Since the cursor is already in the Last name field, type

```
Khorajian
```

Now press the down-arrow key. Notice that the cursor moves down (as you'd probably expect) to the First name field. This is different from table view, where the up- and down-arrow keys move between records. In this field, type

```
Corey
```

When you move on to the Company field, you'll find that you can't enter the period after Co. The field, as you may remember, was defined as being 30 characters wide. The period is the 31st character. Paradox honks and refuses to accept the period, because you haven't allowed room for it. (Now you know why your name is sometimes spelled funny on bulk-mailed advertisements.) If you wish, you can widen the field when "Changing the Structure of a Table" is discussed in Chapter 6. Or you can simply live with the limitation.

Cursor Movement in Form View

You can still use the Tab, Enter, and right-arrow keys to move to the following field, as in table view. Shift-Tab, up-arrow, and left-arrow all move to the previous field, as before. But there are some differences. In the default form, all fields are in a vertical column. However, in a custom form, you can place fields anywhere on the screen. When the fields are not arranged vertically, the down-arrow key moves the cursor to the first field on the line *below* the current field, even if there are other fields on the same line. You reach other fields on the current line with the left- or right-arrow keys. For reference, the keys that move the cursor through a form and their effects are summarized in Table 4.1. For now, continue to type the data for *Corey Khorajian*. Remember to place the City, State, and Zip code into separate fields.

65

Table 4.1: Cursor movement in form view.

Key	Effect
←, Shift-Tab	Moves the cursor to the previous field; if the cursor is in the first field of a record, moves the cursor to the last field of the previous record.
→, Tab, Enter	Moves the cursor to the next field; if the cursor is in the last field of a record, moves the cursor to the first field of the next record.
↓	Moves the cursor down one field.
↑	Moves the cursor up one field.
Home	Moves the cursor to the current field in the first record.
End	Moves the cursor to the current field in the last record.
Ctrl-Home	Moves the cursor to the first field of the current record.
Ctrl-End	Moves the cursor to the last field of the current record.
PgDn	Moves the cursor to the beginning of the next record; if a record has more than one page (screen), moves the cursor to the beginning of the next page.
PgUp	Moves the cursor to the beginning of the previous record; if a record has more than one page (screen), and the first page is not current, moves the cursor to the previous page.
Ctrl-Z	Finds a specific item in the current field.
Alt-Z	Finds the next instance of a given item in the current field.

When you finish typing the phone number, press PgDn. You should be at the beginning of record 4, as indicated in the upper-left corner of the screen. In forms view, the PgUp and PgDn keys move through a table a page at a time. In this instance, where there are few fields, each page is another record. However, if all the fields won't fit onto a single screen in forms view, Paradox creates a form two or more pages long. When forms are more than a page long, Ctrl-PgUp and Ctrl-PgDn move to the beginning of the previous and the next record, respectively, skipping intervening pages.

Now enter a fourth record, using forms view. Again, try to enter it on your own. Use the following information:

```
Grouch
Oscar T.

123 Sesame Street
Garbage Can
New York
NY
10023
(212)555-0000
```

The "Ditto" Key

For your fifth and sixth records, you'll use a data-entry shortcut: the "Ditto" key. Whether you're in forms view or table view, Ctrl-D automatically copies the information in a given field from the same field in the previous record. Type the following data in forms view:

```
Hernandez
Andrew
Coati del Mundi, Ltd.
1567 E. 83rd Street

New York
NY
10058
(212)112-9009
```

Type the first four fields as usual. Skip the fifth. When you come to the sixth field, City, press Ctrl-D. The text

```
New York
```

appears in the entry field. As usual, press Enter (or Tab, or whatever you like that works) to move to the next field. Press Ctrl-D again. The text

```
NY
```

appears. Move to the next field, and press Ctrl-D again. The Zip code

```
10023
```

appears. This isn't the Zip code you want, but you may find it easier to backspace over the last two characters and correct them than to type the entire Zip code.

Now try entering the phone number with Ctrl-D. It's not the right phone number, but it includes some of the characters you want to use. Edit this field using field view. Press

Ctrl-F or Alt-F5	To enter field view.
Ins or Insert	To enter overtype mode.
Home	To move the cursor to the beginning of the field.
→ (5 times)	To move the cursor to the first digit after the closing parenthesis.
112	To enter the new prefix.
→	To skip over the hyphen.
9	To enter part of the phone number.
→ (2 times)	To keep the two zeros.
9	To complete the phone number.
↵	To leave field view.

Now try the "Ditto" key in table view. Press the "Form Toggle" key (F7) again. Your screen will again display the ENTRY table as a table. (Once you have created a form, you can switch between table view and form view at will by pressing the F7 key.) Press Enter to begin the next record.

```
Schocks
Susan
International Footwear
503 E. 23rd Street

New York
NY
10034
(212)555-1357
```

Once again, use Ctrl-D to enter the City, State, and Zip code. Don't forget to edit the last two digits of the Zip code. You'll see the data appear in the table directly below the equivalent entries in the previous record.

68

This is what actually happened when you used the "Ditto" key, Ctrl-D, in forms view. You'll see three similar entries in these fields, as Figure 4.6 shows.

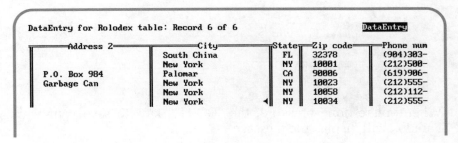

DataEntry for Rolodex table: Record 6 of 6   DataEntry

Address 2	City	State	Zip code	Phone num
	South China	FL	32378	(904)303-
	New York	NY	10001	(212)500-
P.O. Box 984	Palomar	CA	90006	(619)906-
Garbage Can	New York	NY	10023	(212)555-
	New York	NY	10058	(212)112-
	New York	◄ NY	10034	(212)555-

Figure 4.6: The effect of the "Ditto" key.

To complete the table, add four more records, for an even ten. Then you'll try some other ways to enter data into tables. Add the data for the following records, either in table view or in form view. You might even use F7 to switch between them for different records. Be careful to place the information into the correct fields. Remember that if you make mistakes, you can edit a field in field view, or delete the entire contents of a field using Ctrl-Backspace. And be alert for places where you can use Ctrl-D, the "Ditto" key. Here are the entries:

```
Susan Lathom
Sky High Technologies
11200 Dakota Avenue

Fresno, CA 94371
(209)901-6021


Howard K. Franklin
Sky High Technologies
11200 Dakota Avenue

Fresno, CA 94371
(209)901-6027


Anne Joy
Deli Delights
3490 MacArthur Blvd.
```

69

```
Oakland, CA 94602
(415)502-6767


James E. Jones
Empire Sound
3994 Sepulveda Avenue
Suite 901
N. Hollywood, CA 91733
(213)404-4400
```

When you're done press F2, the "DO-IT!" key, to save your work.
Paradox will display the message

```
Adding records from Entry to Rolodex...
```

and the ROLODEX table will appear on your screen, as shown in Figure 4.7. When you use the **Modify/D**ataEntry command, every record you entered into the ENTRY table is copied to the target table when you press F2. However, the ENTRY table doesn't change until you begin the next data entry session, and is erased when you exit from Paradox.

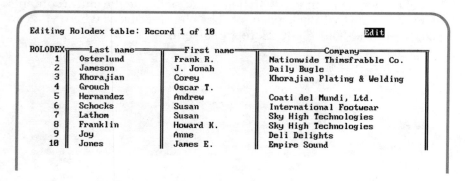

Figure 4.7: Completing a data entry session.

To verify a few of these points, execute the **Modify/D**ata Entry command again, and select the Rolodex table as your target table. You'll see a new ENTRY table, with no records, just as you saw in Figure 4.2. Now enter the data for two more records:

```
James Jones

5110 West End Avenue
```

```
Brooklyn, NY 11267
(718)903-4912


Norma Loquendi
True Recordings
1030 South Street
Suite 10
Alameda, CA 94501
(415)525-0000
```

Press "DO-IT!," F2, when you're done. As you should see on the screen (see Figure 4.8), your two new records are appended to your Rolodex table. However, the ENTRY table isn't emptied until you use it again.

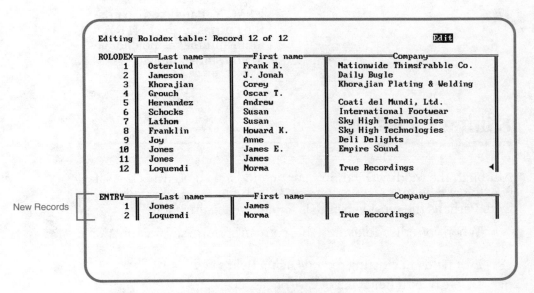

Figure 4.8: Rolodex and ENTRY tables.

DataEntry

1. Press F10.	Paradox displays the Main menu.
2. Press **M**.	Paradox displays the **M**odify submenu.

3. Press **D** to select **D**ataEntry. Paradox asks for the name of a table.

4. Press Enter. Paradox displays a list of tables.

5. Choose the table into which you want to enter new records. Paradox creates a table called ENTRY, with the same structure as the target table.

6. Enter data into the ENTRY table.

7. Press F2 to save your changes, or press F10/**C**/**Y** to discard them. If you press F2, Paradox appends the data you entered into the ENTRY table to your target table, and displays the target table. If you press F10/**C**/**Y**, Paradox discards the entries in the ENTRY table and makes no changes to your target table. □

Editing Tables

Although the **M**odify/**D**ataEntry command is in some ways the safest way to get data into a table, there are other ways you should know as well. Perhaps the most versatile is to edit an existing table.

When you edit an existing table you can perform several functions:

▶ Edit fields in existing records using field view.
▶ Delete or edit fields using Ctrl-Backspace.
▶ Insert new records into the table at any point.
▶ Delete complete records from the table.
▶ Append new records to the end of the table.

Entering Edit Mode

There are two ways to enter Edit mode. If the table you want to edit is on the workspace, the easiest way to enter Edit mode is to make that table the current table and press F9, the "Edit" key. You can also enter Edit mode through the **M**odify/**E**dit command, as you saw in Figure 4.1. With these commands, you select a table, as you did with the **D**ataEntry command, so you may find this more convenient when the table is not already on the workspace.

Since you've already got the Rolodex table on the workspace, try Edit mode on that table. Press

F3   To make the Rolodex table current. (Remember, F3 is
        the "Up Image" key.)
F9   To enter Edit mode.

The mode indicator changes to Edit, and the message at the top of the screen tells you that you are now editing the Rolodex table.

73

Inserting Records into a Table

Your cursor should now be in the record number column. You can't edit this field, as you will find out by pressing any alphanumeric key. So what if you want to change a record number? As a rule, it's best to regard record numbers as arbitrary. If you need to number your records for some purpose of your own (as you will later with the Customer table), it's better to create a field for the purpose.

However, you can create a new record with a given number. To create a new record 3, for example, press

↓ (2 times)   To move to record number 3.
Ins or Insert   To create a new record at this position.

All the other records will move down on the screen, with their numbers increased by 1, as Figure 4.9 shows.

```
┌─────────────────────────────────────────────────────────────────────┐
│  Editing Rolodex table: Record 3 of 13                        Edit    │
│                                                                        │
│  ROLODEX┬───Last name══      ═══First name═          ══════Company═   │
│      1 ║ Osterlund          Frank R.         Nationwide Thimsfrabble Co. │
│      2 ║ Jameson            J. Jonah         Daily Bugle               │
│      3 ║                                                               │
│      4 ║ Khorajian          Corey            Khorajian Plating & Welding │
│      5 ║ Grouch             Oscar T.                                   │
│      6 ║ Hernandez          Andrew           Coati del Mundi, Ltd.     │
│      7 ║ Schocks            Susan            International Footwear     │
│      8 ║ Lathom             Susan            Sky High Technologies      │
│      9 ║ Franklin           Howard K.        Sky High Technologies      │
│     10 ║ Joy                Anne             Deli Delights             │
│     11 ║ Jones              James E.         Empire Sound              │
│     12 ║ Jones              James                                      │
│     13 ║ Loquendi           Norma            True Recordings           │
└─────────────────────────────────────────────────────────────────────┘
```

Figure 4.9: Inserting a record into a table.

How does Paradox handle blank records? Let's find out. Press F2 to end the editing session. You'll find that the new blank record is still in place. However, Paradox doesn't always permit you to leave records blank, as you'll see before the end of this chapter.

Now add the new record. Press F9 to get back into Edit mode. If you haven't pressed any other keys, your cursor should still be in record 3 in the record number column. Press Tab, and type the values for the following entry:

```
O'Neil Spencer
Federated Percussive Effects
900 Harbor Blvd.
Third Floor
Avenel, NJ 07131
(201)555-9332
```

When you press Tab or Enter at the end of the phone number, you'll find that the cursor has moved to the record number column, next to the number 4. If you were to move to the next field (you can't edit the record number) and start typing, new characters would be added to the name

```
Khorajian
```

which already occupies the Last name field in record 4. You must press the Ins or Insert key each time you want to insert a record. (If you inadvertently added some characters, delete them with the Backspace key before proceeding.)

Using the "Zoom" and "Ditto" Keys

You can use the Ins or the Insert key to take advantage of Paradox's ability to copy information from the previous record. Make sure your cursor is in the Last name field, and press Ctrl-Z, the "Zoom" key. You'll be prompted with

```
Value:
Enter value or pattern to search for.
```

Type

```
Jones
```

and press Enter. The cursor will move to record 11, and the highlight will flash in the field. You'll add another James Jones, but the current one has a middle initial, so press Alt-Z. Continuing the Zoom, Paradox moves the cursor to record 12, highlighting *Jones* again.

To use the "Ditto" key, Ctrl-D, the information you want to repeat must be above the current field, just as it would with ditto marks on paper. So you'll now have to move down one more record with the down-arrow key, and press Ins or Insert. A blank record will appear after James Jones. Press Ctrl-D, and

```
Jones
```

appears in the field. Press Tab, and press Ctrl-D a second time. The name

```
James
```

appears in the First name field. Fill out the rest of the record with the following information:

```
Glynphrygh Blivet & Tong Works
91503 Victoria Road

Toronto, ON J1W 7S6
(416)090-4000
```

Appending Records to a Table

Now append some records to the end of the table. Press

End   To move to the last record.

↵   To create a new, blank record.

Add the data for the following record:

```
Walter Bishop
Major Key Works
1420 Sandy Lane

N. Bloomfield, MD 22388
(504)611-2300
```

When you finish that record, press Tab, or Enter. Notice that when you append records in Edit mode, as opposed to inserting them, Paradox creates new records for you to fill in, just as it does in DataEntry mode. If you hold down the down-arrow key, Paradox will append blank records continuously forever. That's okay, because pressing the "DO-IT!" key, F2, automatically deletes any blank records from the end of the table.

Now use the up-arrow key to move back to record 16, and add the following record:

```
Jane Jonas

6701 Colonial Road
Apt. 4H
Philadelphia, PA 30067
(714)502-5891
```

Press the "DO-IT!" key, F2, when you're done, and you'll see all the blank records disappear.

Finding a Value Quickly

You can use Edit mode to modify the data in existing records, as well as to add new ones. Suppose you have just found out the full nine-digit Zip code for *Anne Joy* at *Deli Delights*. You want to change that record to reflect the new information. Use the power of Paradox to find the information for you. Press

F9   To enter Edit mode.
F10   To display the **E**dit menu.
I   To display the **I**mage menu.
Z   To select the **Z**oom submenu.
V   To locate a **V**alue.

Paradox will prompt you to

```
Use ← and → to move to the column you want to search
in...
then press ↵ to select it.
```

Move to the Last name field if the cursor isn't already there, and press Enter. Paradox will prompt you with

```
Value:
Enter value or pattern to search for.
```

Type

```
Joy
```

and press Enter. Paradox will find the item and briefly highlight it, just as it did when you used the "Zoom" key. Now press

F10   To display the **E**dit menu.
I   To display the **I**mage menu.
Z   To select the **Z**oom submenu.
↵   To select **F**ield, which is highlighted.

77

Paradox will display a list of all the fields in the table. As usual with such a list, you can move the cursor to the field name, or press its first letter. If more than one item starts with the same letter, you'll see an abbreviated list. Since you know you want Zip code, press **Z**. Paradox will highlight the item in the Zip code field of the current record.

The techniques you just used to locate a record are available from the **I**mage menu on the Main menu, as well as in the Edit menu. This method of finding an item may seem cumbersome when you're working with a small table such as this one, but when a table is larger than the screen in every direction, it can be a great convenience.

Now just type

```
-1836
```

and your entry is completed.

78   *Special Editing Keys*

While you're still in Edit mode, try a couple of new keys. Press the down-arrow key and add some blank records to the end of the database. Now press the Del or Delete key. You'll see the last blank record disappear. Move up to the first blank record, and press the Del or Delete key again. You'll see the database shrink by a single record. Unless you're in field view, the Del and Delete keys always delete the current record in Edit mode.

It's possible that you might press the Delete key by mistake. However, you needn't worry that you'll lose data as a result. First, nothing becomes permanent until you press the "DO-IT!" key, F2. If you seriously mess up your data, you can always press F10 and use the **C**ancel/**Y**es command. Second, Paradox includes an "Undo" key, Ctrl-U, which undoes the most recent change.

Try the "Undo" key now. Press Home to move to record 1. Now press the Del or Delete key. You'll see the first record disappear, and all the other records move up one position. Press Ctrl-U, and you'll see the message

```
Record 1 reinserted
```

as well as the reappearance of the data for Frank Osterlund.

But the "Undo" key is even smarter than that. Keep pressing the Del or Delete key until you have only one record left. Then press Ctrl-U. The same message appears, because even though Walter Bishop was originally record 17, it was record 1 when you deleted it. Keep pressing Ctrl-U. A record will reappear with each keypress. If you keep it up long enough, the blank records you deleted will reappear. Continue further, and your original table will be restored in its entirety. You'll even lose the addition to Anne Joy's Zip code, and you'll see the message

```
Changes for record 10 undone
```

Press Ctrl-U one more time to restore the addition and press F2 to complete the editing session. For reference, Table 4.2 summarizes the additional command keys used in Edit mode.

Table 4.2: Command keys in Edit mode.

Key	Effect
F9	Enters Edit mode, allowing you to edit any table in the workspace.
F10/**M/E**	Selects a table to edit, and places it in the workspace in Edit mode.
Ins, Insert	Inserts a new record at the current cursor location, moving the following records down one row (and increasing their record numbers by 1).
Del, Delete	Deletes the current record, moving the cursor up to the previous record (and reducing the record numbers of the following records by 1).
Ctrl-U	Undoes the last change you made to your table; successive presses undo previous changes.
F2, F10/**D**	Records your changes permanently.
F10/**C/Y**	Discards changes made in the current editing session.

CoEditing a Table

Another of Paradox's methods for entering data is called *coediting*. This method is specifically designed for use on networks, but it has other uses as well. When used on a single computer, the most important difference between editing and coediting a table is that a record is "posted"—that is, recorded, as soon as you move to another record. On a network this allows several people to update the same table. On a single computer, it means that you don't risk losing any of your entries even if the power goes off before you press "DO-IT!," F2.

In addition, in CoEdit mode Paradox won't let you enter records with duplicate keys. If you do, Paradox will ask you to confirm that you want to change an existing record. In Edit mode, on the other hand, when you enter a new record with the same key value as an existing record, Paradox automatically modifies the existing record.

On the other hand, the Undo command works only on the most recently posted record. Also, as you might expect, there is no Cancel command. Since a record is written to disk as soon as you leave it, there's no way for Paradox to compare the table in memory to its condition before you started editing.

Entering CoEdit Mode

As with Edit mode, there are two ways to enter CoEdit mode. If the table you want to edit is in the workspace, the easiest way to enter CoEdit mode is to make that table the current table and press Alt-F9, the "CoEdit" key. You can also enter CoEdit mode through the **Modify/CoEdit** command, as you saw in Figure 4.1. With these commands, you select a table, as you did with the Edit command, Use the **Modify/CoEdit** command when the table is not already in the workspace.

Enter some records into the Customer database using CoEdit mode. Use the **View** command to bring the Customer table into the workspace, and press "CoEdit," Alt-F9. In the course of this exercise, you'll learn a few new things about Date and Numeric values.

As you'd expect, the mode indicator changes to CoEdit. However, the message at the top of the screen is somewhat different from the one you see in Edit mode. It reads:

```
Coediting Customer table: Record 1 of 1
Entering new record - not yet posted to table
```

This implies—accurately—that when you finish entering the first new record, it will be posted to the table on disk.

Begin entering the following data into the first record:

```
Jack Pollock
Production Dept.
Action Designs
3220 Umbrian Way

Seaside, CA 93732 USA
(408)555-6721
5000
12/12/87
```

(The last two items are the Credit limit and the Initial order date.) You'll see that as soon as you move on to record 2, the message area displays

```
Posted new record 1
```

as shown in Figure 4.10.

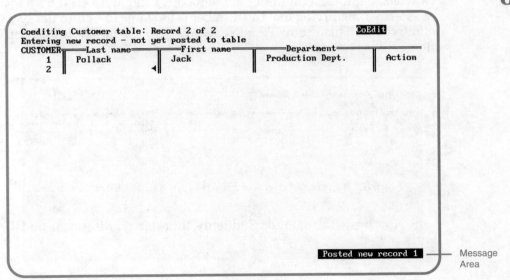

Figure 4.10: Entering a record in CoEdit mode.

How Paradox Displays Large Numbers

Now enter another record. This time we'll have to pay special attention
to how numbers and dates are displayed, so take it a step at a time. Enter
the following values:

```
Jones
Jonathan
Purchasing Dept.
Federated Percussive Effects
900 Harbor Blvd.
Third Floor
Avenel
NJ
07131
USA
(201)555-9332
```

Now, look at the Credit limit field of record 1 in Figure 4.11. It's a row
of asterisks, signifying that the number is too large to fit into the space
allotted to it. This is how Paradox always displays numbers that don't
fit.

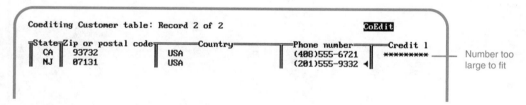

Figure 4.11: How Paradox handles large numbers.

Now press Tab or Enter. Suddenly, the asterisks disappear, and the
entry

```
5,000.00
```

replaces it. Here are two peculiarities. First, the number suddenly fits!
Second, it's formatted with a comma and a decimal point—which you
didn't enter—at the appropriate places. As you'll see in Chapter 6, you
can select any of several formats in which to display numbers. If the
number is entered correctly, it will be displayed in the chosen format.
You can also change the width of the columns on the screen. If you make

columns too small to display the numbers as formatted, you will again see a row of asterisks. You do *not* lose any of the information you enter.

The reappearance of the number reflects the fact that the entire field is now on the screen. Rather than present you with misleading information, Paradox displays asterisks when only part of a field is visible.

The formatting comes from the fact that Credit limit is a *Currency* field, not a *Number* field. In a Currency field, as you may remember, figures are formatted with commas, and rounded off to two decimal places.

How Paradox Displays Dates

Now type, the last two fields:

```
8400
17-jan-85
```

83

After you press Tab or Enter, press Ctrl-right-arrow three times so that your screen looks like Figure 4.12. Notice that the date did not remain in the form in which you typed it. As noted, Paradox accepts date entries in any of three formats. However, in any given field in a table, the program displays dates in only one format. Paradox has converted the date you typed to the default format. As you'll learn in Chapter 6, Paradox lets you choose which of the three formats to use for dates in a table.

Editing Restrictions in CoEdit Mode

Now move the cursor up to the second record. The message area now reads

```
Closed up untouched blank row
```

This is a feature of CoEdit mode. If you inadvertently create a blank row in CoEdit mode (by pressing the Ins or Insert key), Paradox eliminates it. (It assumes that others may be updating the same database, and randomly inserted blank rows would cause confusion.)

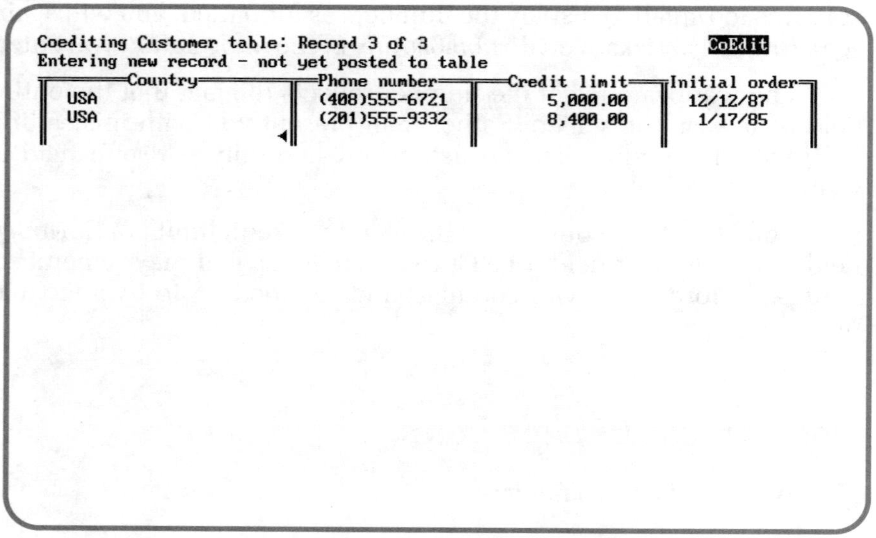

```
Coediting Customer table: Record 3 of 3                        CoEdit
Entering new record - not yet posted to table
       ┌────────Country─────────┬──────Phone number──────┬───Credit limit───┬──Initial order──┐
       │  USA                   │     (408)555-6721       │      5,000.00    │    12/12/87     │
       │  USA                   │     (201)555-9332       │      8,400.00    │     1/17/85     │
       │                    ◄   │                        │                  │                 │
```

84

Figure 4.12: Paradox converts the date you enter into the
default format.

To assure yourself of this feature's functioning, press the Ins or
Insert key. A blank row will appear between records 1 and 2. Now press
the down-arrow key, to return to the record you originally moved to. The
blank record 2 is eliminated, and the same message appears. However,
you'll find the cursor at the beginning of a blank row 3.

Now move your cursor to the field that reads

8,400.00

Press Ctrl-Backspace to clear that field. You'll see the legend

Record is locked

at the top of the screen, signifying that, if you were on a network, no one
else could have access to that record while you were editing it. It has no
effect on the way CoEdit mode works on a single computer, however.

Try typing

84,00

into the field. This is not a legal way of punctuating this value, and
Paradox displays the message

```
Incomplete field
```

because it expects an additional digit. You'll learn about proper number entry in the next section. For now, press Ctrl-U to "Undo" the change you just made, and press F2, "DO-IT!," to end the CoEditing session. You now have a Customer table with two records in it. Press Alt-F8 to clear the workspace.

Restrictions and Shortcuts for Entering Numeric and Date Values

The last exercise suggests that you may need to know more about ways of entering numbers. You don't have a table with a true Numeric field yet, so let's create one just for this exercise. Select **C**reate from the Main menu, and type the table name

```
numbers
```

In the STRUCTure table, type the following information:

```
Number   NBL
Date     D
```

Now save the STRUCTure table with "DO-IT!," F2, and bring the Numbers table to the workspace with the **M**odify/**E**dit command.

Restrictions on Numeric Input

Type the following numbers, pressing the down-arrow key after each. You'll use the Date field later:

```
987654321
9876543.21
12345.6789
345E102
12,345,678
-12
(500)
```

85

When you're done, your screen should look like Figure 4.13.

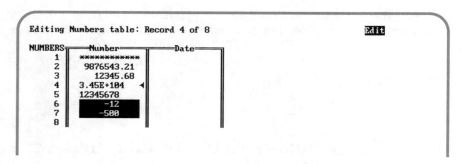

Figure 4.13: Entering data into a numeric field.

The number in the first record, nine digits long, is too long, but the second, which includes an additional character—a decimal point—fits! What's going on? It's simple. By default, Paradox reserves three columns in the field for a decimal point and two decimal places. This does not leave enough room to display nine columns to the left of a decimal point. You'll see this is so by looking at record 3. The value in this record also indicates that Paradox rounds off decimal places beyond two.

You don't actually lose any data, however. If you move the cursor up to record 3, you'll see an asterisk appear next to the field pointer indicating that there are additional decimal places. To see the entire number, press Ctrl-F or Alt-F5 to enter field view. Remember to press Enter when you're through looking at the number.

The fourth record contains an entry in scientific, or exponential, notation. Paradox both accepts and displays scientific notation. However, by default it places only one digit to the left of the decimal point. Therefore, it added two to the exponent, signifying two more decimal places.

Next, note that the commas you entered into record 5 have disappeared. You can enter commas if you place them at the correct points. However, except in a Currency-type field, Paradox won't display them unless you expressly format the field to include them. You'll learn how to format Numeric fields in Chapter 6.

Finally, notice the two negative numbers you entered into records 6 and 7. As you can see, Paradox allows you to enter negative numbers either by preceding them with a minus sign or by enclosing them in parentheses. (It also highlights them if your video display allows it.)

However, it displays them only with a minus sign. Negative Currency values, on the other hand, are always displayed with parentheses.

As a shortcut, you can press the space bar instead of the period key to enter a decimal point into any numeric field.

Shortcuts for Entering Dates

Move your cursor to the Date field of record 1. Press the space bar three times. You'll see the system date appear. (If you see

```
1/1/80
```

you didn't set the date on your computer.) Think of the date as consisting of three sub-fields: the month, the day, and the year. You can use the space bar to enter the current value into any of these sub-fields. Thus, you could enter a month and a day, in any of the three acceptable formats, and press the space bar to enter the current year. However, if you use the hyphenated format, you'll have to press the space bar a second time, because the first time you press it, Paradox will enter only the hyphen.

When you use the hyphenated format, you can also use the space bar to enter the second two characters of the name of the month. Thus, if this were 1991, to enter *29-Apr-91*, you could just type

```
29-A
```

and press the space bar four times. When you move to the next field, however, the display will revert to the form

```
4/29/91
```

87

Sorting and Key Fields

What You Will Learn

▶ Using the Modify/Sort Command
▶ Creating Key Fields
▶ Sorting Using Several Criteria
▶ Dealing with Key Violations

As you undoubtedly noticed when you entered data into your Paradox tables, the records remained in the order in which you entered them. You did some very primitive sorting when you placed one of the Joneses beneath another to take advantage of the "Ditto" key, Ctrl-D.

If you wanted your tables to be in a specific order, you could, in theory, find the appropriate location for each record when you entered it. But, entering data into a large table would become quite tedious.

Paradox provides two very different methods for keeping your databases in order: a Sort command, and a special structural element called a *key*. In this chapter, you'll learn about both of them.

Why Sort Your Database?

In a small table such as Rolodex, it doesn't matter much whether the records are in order. In a full-scale application, however, you might have thousands of records. You'd be hard-pressed to find a given item if the records weren't sorted in some meaningful way. You'd want to sort by Zip code if you were preparing a mass mailing. You'd want to sort by name or company if you were preparing a directory. You might want to sort a table using other criteria for other purposes.

Sorting Using a Sorting Form

In the simplest form of sorting, you just select a single field to be sorted. Paradox quickly rearranges all the records so that the items in the selected field are in ascending—lowest to highest—order. (If the fields are Alphanumeric, they are sorted from A to Z.)

A table needn't be in the workspace for you to sort it, but it's easier to see what's going on if you can see the table. To begin, you'll sort your Rolodex table on a single field. If anything other than the Rolodex table is in the workspace, press Alt-F8, the "Clear All" key, to clear the workspace. Now execute the View command to bring the Rolodex table into the workspace.

To sort a table, you fill out a form in which you specify which field or fields the sort should be based on, and whether the sort should be in ascending order or descending order. Press

F10	To display the Main menu.
M	To display the **M**odify menu.
S	To select the **S**ort command (since it's selected by default, you could press Enter instead).
↵	To display a list of tables.
↵	To select the Rolodex table (because it's already in the workspace, it becomes the default selection).

You'll then be prompted to choose whether to place the results of the sort into the same table, or to create a new table to hold the sorted database. At this point, there's no reason not to use the same table. Since **S**ame is the default, Press Enter. You'll now be in Sort mode, viewing the form itself provides instructions on how to complete the sort.

To sort the file by last name, simply type 1 as shown in Figure 5.2, because the field pointer is already next to the Last name field name.

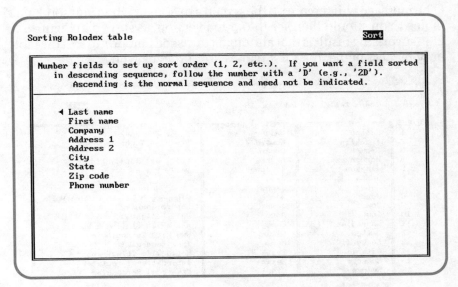

```
Sorting Rolodex table                                              Sort

┌────────────────────────────────────────────────────────────────────┐
│  Number fields to set up sort order (1, 2, etc.).  If you want a field sorted │
│     in descending sequence, follow the number with a 'D' (e.g., '2D'). │
│        Ascending is the normal sequence and need not be indicated.   │
├────────────────────────────────────────────────────────────────────┤
│      ◄ Last name                                                     │
│        First name                                                    │
│        Company                                                       │
│        Address 1                                                     │
│        Address 2                                                     │
│        City                                                          │
│        State                                                         │
│        Zip code                                                      │
│        Phone number                                                  │
│                                                                      │
└────────────────────────────────────────────────────────────────────┘
```

Figure 5.1: The sorting form for the Rolodex table.

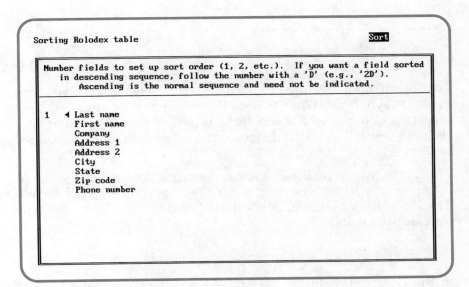

```
Sorting Rolodex table                                              Sort

┌────────────────────────────────────────────────────────────────────┐
│  Number fields to set up sort order (1, 2, etc.).  If you want a field sorted │
│     in descending sequence, follow the number with a 'D' (e.g., '2D'). │
│        Ascending is the normal sequence and need not be indicated.   │
├────────────────────────────────────────────────────────────────────┤
│   1  ◄ Last name                                                     │
│        First name                                                    │
│        Company                                                       │
│        Address 1                                                     │
│        Address 2                                                     │
│        City                                                          │
│        State                                                         │
│        Zip code                                                      │
│        Phone number                                                  │
│                                                                      │
└────────────────────────────────────────────────────────────────────┘
```

Figure 5.2: Selecting a sort field.

As usual, to execute the command, press "DO-IT!", F2. Paradox will display the message

```
Sorting...
```

(The message will remain on the screen a bit longer when you sort larger tables.) You should then see the sorted version, as shown in Figure 5.3. One surprising result is that although you asked Paradox to sort the table only by Last name, the First names are sorted as well.

```
 Viewing Rolodex table: Record 1 of 16                              Main

 ROLODEX┌──────Last name──────┬──────First name──────┬──────Company──────┐
      1 ║ Bishop              │ Walter              │ Major Key Works
      2 ║ Franklin            │ Howard K.           │ Sky High Technologies
      3 ║ Grouch              │ Oscar T.            │
      4 ║ Hernandez           │ Andrew              │ Coati del Mundi, Ltd.
      5 ║ Jameson             │ J. Jonah            │ Daily Bugle
      6 ║ Jonas               │ Jane                │
      7 ║ Jones               │ James               │
      8 ║ Jones               │ James               │ Glynphrygh Blivet & Tong Works
      9 ║ Jones               │ James E.            │ Empire Sound
     10 ║ Joy                 │ Anne                │ Deli Delights
     11 ║ Khorajian           │ Corey               │ Khorajian Plating & Welding
     12 ║ Lathom              │ Susan               │ Sky High Technologies
     13 ║ Loquendi            │ Norma               │ True Recordings
     14 ║ Osterlund           │ Frank R.            │ Nationwide Thimsfrabble Co.
     15 ║ Schocks             │ Susan               │ International Footwear
     16 ║ Spencer             │ O'Neil              │ Federated Percussion Effects
```

Figure 5.3: The sorted table.

To confirm this point, press F9, "Edit", to edit the table, and give *James Jones* of *Glynphrygh Blivet & Tong Works* the middle initial *W*. Now repeat the steps you took to sort the table the first time. You'll see James *W*. Jones now follows James E. Jones. You got more than you bargained for!

In fact, whenever Paradox encounters the same value in a sort field in two records, it makes an effort to find the proper place for each record. Try editing the table again. Delete the *W* from James W. Jones, and type the company name

```
Ocean Products
```

in the Company field for the James Jones (record 7) who had no company affiliation. Repeat the sort. You'll see that the two James Joneses are now sorted by company.

A Descending Sort

Now try another sort. This time you'll sort by Company, in descending order. Execute the **M**odify/**S**ort command as before but type,

```
1D
```

next to the Company field name, as shown in Figure 5.4. When you press F2, "DO-IT!", you'll find that the two employees of Sky High Technologies have been sorted in ascending order, as Figure 5.5 illustrates. (If you think they remained that way because you previously sorted by Last name in *ascending* order, try sorting by Last name in *descending* order, and saving the results, before you sort by Company.)

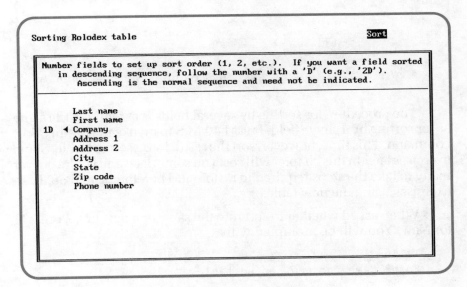

Figure 5.4: Setting up a descending sort.

Sorting by Several Fields

You can force Paradox to sort fields other than the primary one in the order you prefer by specifying more than one field on the sorting form. Try sorting your table in descending order by State, and within that, in ascending order by Zip code. If you have more than one entry for the same State and Zip code (which you do), you can force Paradox to put such entries in ascending order by Last name.

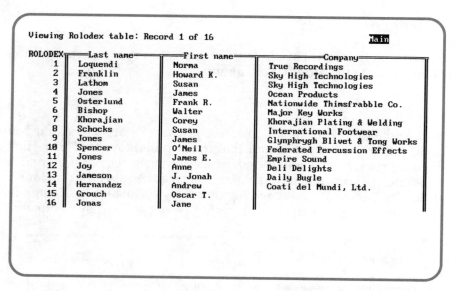

```
Viewing Rolodex table: Record 1 of 16                        Main
ROLODEX┌────Last name────┬────First name────┬──────────Company──────────┐
   1 ║ Loquendi          │ Norma            │ True Recordings
   2 ║ Franklin          │ Howard K.        │ Sky High Technologies
   3 ║ Lathom            │ Susan            │ Sky High Technologies
   4 ║ Jones             │ James            │ Ocean Products
   5 ║ Osterlund         │ Frank R.         │ Nationwide Thimsfrabble Co.
   6 ║ Bishop            │ Walter           │ Major Key Works
   7 ║ Khorajian         │ Corey            │ Khorajian Plating & Welding
   8 ║ Schocks           │ Susan            │ International Footwear
   9 ║ Jones             │ James            │ Glynphrygh Blivet & Tong Works
  10 ║ Spencer           │ O'Neil           │ Federated Percussion Effects
  11 ║ Jones             │ James E.         │ Empire Sound
  12 ║ Joy               │ Anne             │ Deli Delights
  13 ║ Jameson           │ J. Jonah         │ Daily Bugle
  14 ║ Hernandez         │ Andrew           │ Coati del Mundi, Ltd.
  15 ║ Grouch            │ Oscar T.         │
  16 ║ Jonas             │ Jane             │
```

Figure 5.5: The table sorted in descending order by Company.

The procedure for sorting by several fields is essentially the same as for sorting by a single field. Press F10/**M/S** to invoke the **Modify/Sort** command. This time, however, sort the result into a second table. Some exercises later in this chapter will cost you some data, and you're not yet ready to take the steps required to restore it. Therefore, you'll do those exercises using the new table.

When asked whether to sort into the same or a new table, press **N** for **New**. You will be prompted with

```
Table:
Enter name for new sorted table.
```

Type

```
rolotemp
```

The legend at the top of the screen will now read

```
Sorting Rolodex table into new ROLOTEMP table
```

as Figure 5.6 shows, so you don't forget what you're doing.

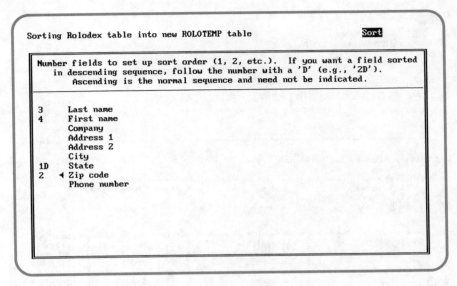

```
Sorting Rolodex table into new ROLOTEMP table                    Sort

 ┌─────────────────────────────────────────────────────────────────────┐
 │ Number fields to set up sort order (1, 2, etc.).  If you want a field sorted │
 │    in descending sequence, follow the number with a 'D' (e.g., '2D'). │
 │       Ascending is the normal sequence and need not be indicated.     │
 ├─────────────────────────────────────────────────────────────────────┤
 │                                                                       │
 │  3      Last name                                                     │
 │  4      First name                                                    │
 │         Company                                                       │
 │         Address 1                                                     │
 │         Address 2                                                     │
 │         City                                                          │
 │  1D     State                                                         │
 │  2   ◄  Zip code                                                      │
 │         Phone number                                                  │
 │                                                                       │
 └─────────────────────────────────────────────────────────────────────┘
```

Figure 5.6: Setting up a sort on several fields.

95

The Sort Submenu

Set up your sorting form as shown in Figure 5.6. Notice that you'll sort on four different fields, three ascending and one descending. Before you complete the task, let's take a detour through the Sort submenu. Press F10 to display the Sort submenu. You'll see it in Figure 5.7. It contains only the ubiquitous **Help**, **DO-IT!** and **C**ancel commands. Thus, as usual, you're not trapped into completing the operation. If you execute the **C**ancel/**Y**es commands, no changes will be made, and you will return to an unchanged workspace.

Now that you've got the Sort menu displayed press **D** to execute the **DO-IT!** command. Paradox will add the ROLOTEMP table to your workspace below the original Rolodex table. You'll see that the two employees of Sky High Technologies—the only ones sharing a Zip code—are in proper alphabetical order. Now press Ctrl-right-arrow twice, to view the State and Zip code fields. Your screen should look like Figure 5.8. Notice that, as expected, the states are in reverse alphabetical order. If you look at the Zip codes for New York and California, you'll see that they are properly sorted into ascending order within each State.

```
Help  DO-IT!  Cancel                                              Sort
Help with sorting a table.
```

Figure 5.7: The Sort submenu.

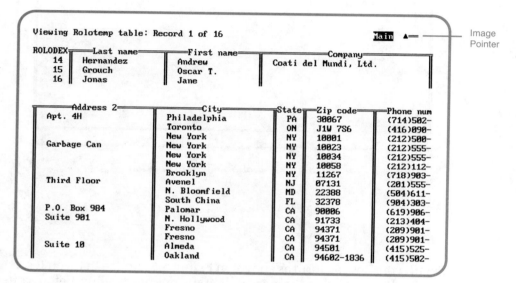

Image Pointer

Figure 5.8: A table sorted by several criteria.

The Image Pointer

While you've got this screen in view, note the symbol next to the mode indicator—a double bar, preceded by an arrow pointing upward. This *image pointer* indicates that there are images on the workspace above the current one. By default, Paradox always shows you as much of the current image as it can, although you can change this with the Image menu, as you'll learn in Chapter 6.

In this instance, all the records from the Rolotemp table are on the screen, leaving room for only three from the Rolodex table, which was on display before you started the latest sort. If you press F3, the "Up Image" key, to make the Rolodex table current, you'll see a downward-pointing pointer appear to the right of the double bar, indicating the presence of records below the last one you can see in the Rolotemp table. This is one of Paradox's many ways of letting you know your place. If an image fills the entire work area, and other images are on the workspace, these pointers will inform you of the fact, and tell you in which direction the additional images can be found.

 Sorting a Table

1. Press F10 to display the Main menu.

2. Press **M** to choose the Modify submenu.

   Paradox displays the **M**odify submenu with the **S**ort command selected.

3. Press Enter or **S** to select the **S**ort command.

   Paradox asks you to select a table to sort.

4. Press Enter to display a list of tables, then select the table to sort.

   Paradox asks whether you want the results placed into the same table or into a new table. If you press **S** or Enter, the results will overwrite the selected table. If you press **N**, a new table with the name you type will be created.

5. Press **S** or **N** and enter a name for the sorted file, if prompted.

   Paradox displays a form on which you select the fields to be sorted, and whether they should be sorted in ascending or descending order.

6. Number the fields to be sorted in their order of priority.

7. Press **D** after the number if you want the field sorted in descending order.

97

8. Press F2, "DO-IT!", to proceed, or press F10/**C**/**Y** to cancel the sort.

If you press F2, Paradox sorts the table according to your specifications, endeavoring to resolve any duplications by finding a criterion by which they can be placed in ascending order, and displays the sorted table on the workspace. If you choose the **C**ancel command, no changes are made.   □

Key Fields

Now you know how to sort a Paradox database table any way you want to. But there's a catch. Suppose you add more records to the table? If you use the DataEntry method, the new records will be appended to the end of the table. Paradox keeps no record of your sorting criteria.

You could repeat your sorting procedure after each data entry session. (It's not too hard to do that with Paradox's automated scripts.) However, there's a better way. Recall that, in Chapter 4, when you created your first tables, you saw a message on the screen telling you how to designate a field as a key field. When you do, the records are always sorted in ascending order according to the values in that field. As soon as you press the "DO-IT!" key, F2, after a data entry session, Paradox places the new records into their proper places. In CoEdit mode, a new or modified record is placed in order as soon as you move to another record.

> ▶ If a field is a key field, the data for that field in each record must be unique in the table. Violations of this rule will be placed in a separate KEYVIOL table. You can correct them later.

But key fields have many other effects. When you designate a field a key field, Paradox requires that each entry in it be unique. (You can see that those Joneses are going to be a problem.) Records with the same value in a key field are automatically eliminated from the table, and placed into a separate table called KEYVIOL (for *Key Violation*). This gives you a chance to edit the offending records and reinsert them. (In CoEdit mode, an offending record is placed into a KEYVIOL table immediately, and you are not permitted to continue until you have resolved the key violation.) In addition, key fields are the means by which you link the information in one table to information in another, as you'll learn in Chapter 10.

There's one more restriction on key fields. All key fields must appear in the STRUCTure table before any non-key fields.

Adding a Key Field to a Table

As you know, you can designate a key field when you create a table by placing an asterisk in the Field Type column of the STRUCTure table. You can also modify existing table structures, and add key fields to them. Try it now. Press

F10	To display the Main menu.
M	To display the **M**odify submenu.
R	To choose the **R**estructure command.
↵	To display a list of tables.
R	To reduce the list to those tables beginning with R.
End	To select Rolotemp (you'll deal with Rolodex in Chapter 6).
↵	To confirm your selection.

Paradox will create a structure table exactly like the one you completed when you created the Rolodex table. The only differences on the screen are the mode indicator, which says `Restructure`, and the legend, which reads

        `Restructuring Rolotemp table`

as you can see in Figure 5.9. Following the directions on the screen, press

Ctrl-End	To move the cursor to the `Field Type` column.
*	To add an asterisk to the Field Type description for the Last name field, making it into a key field.

Your screen should now look like Figure 5.9.

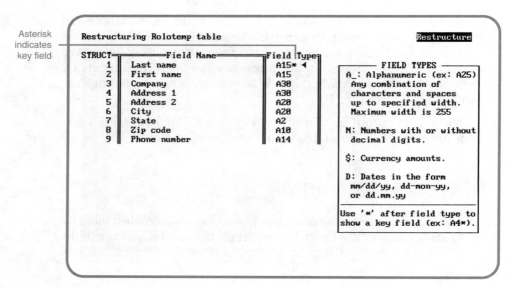

Figure 5.9: Adding a key field to an existing table.

100

Now press F2, "DO-IT!", to restructure the Rolotemp table. The message

```
Restructuring Rolotemp...
```

will appear briefly, followed by the screen you see in Figure 5.10. Notice that both of the James Joneses have been removed from ROLOTEMP, and the KEYVIOL table is current. This gives you a chance to edit the key field in the offending records, and, using the steps described later in this chapter, add the records back into the table.

Notice also that nothing about the table itself tells you that it has key fields. The only ways that you can tell a table has key fields are by their consequences (such as the appearance of a KEYVIOL table) or by looking at the STRUCTure table.

Adding Several Key Fields

> ▶ A table may have more than one key field. Your choice of key fields affects the way the data is sorted, and has other consequences when several tables are linked together.

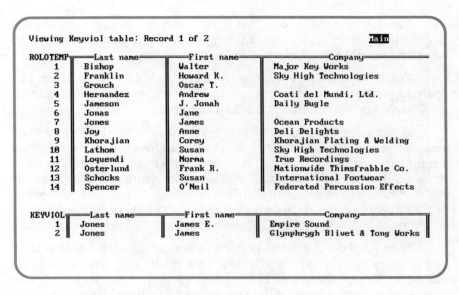

```
Viewing Keyviol table: Record 1 of 2                          Main
ROLOTEMP ┬───Last name───┬───First name───┬──────────Company──────────┐
    1    ║ Bishop        ║ Walter         ║ Major Key Works            
    2    ║ Franklin      ║ Howard K.      ║ Sky High Technologies      
    3    ║ Grouch        ║ Oscar T.       ║                            
    4    ║ Hernandez     ║ Andrew         ║ Coati del Mundi, Ltd.      
    5    ║ Jameson       ║ J. Jonah       ║ Daily Bugle               
    6    ║ Jonas         ║ Jane           ║                            
    7    ║ Jones         ║ James          ║ Ocean Products             
    8    ║ Joy           ║ Anne           ║ Deli Delights              
    9    ║ Khorajian     ║ Corey          ║ Khorajian Plating & Welding
   10    ║ Lathom        ║ Susan          ║ Sky High Technologies      
   11    ║ Loquendi      ║ Norma          ║ True Recordings            
   12    ║ Osterlund     ║ Frank R.       ║ Nationwide Thimsfrabble Co.
   13    ║ Schocks       ║ Susan          ║ International Footwear      
   14    ║ Spencer       ║ O'Neil         ║ Federated Percussion Effects

KEYVIOL ┬───Last name───┬───First name───┬──────────Company──────────┐
    1    ║ Jones         ║ James E.       ║ Empire Sound               
    2    ║ Jones         ║ James          ║ Glymphrygh Blivet & Tong Works
```

Figure 5.10: Changes resulting from adding a key field to a table.

101

A table can have more than one key field. When it does, the value in any one of the key fields may be non-unique, so long as the combined value of all the items in the key fields of a record differs from the combined value in those key fields in all other records in the table.

Think about what this means in your Rolodex table. You have three James Joneses. If you were to make both the Last name and First name fields into key fields, you'd have no problem with James E. Jones. But there's nothing to distinguish between the two remaining James Joneses. Given the limitations regarding key fields, you could make Company into a key field as well. But it's quite possible that there will be several Mary Smiths, say, at a large company. You could make all fields key fields, but that would slow Paradox down somewhat, and it will also create serious trouble when you work with linked tables.

The ideal combination, for this table, would be Last name, First name, and Phone number. Even in a large company, several employees with the same last and first name would be unlikely to have the same phone number. If necessary, you could widen the Phone number field to include an extension number for those companies where all calls go through a central switchboard. However, the Phone number field isn't next to the First name field, so you can't use it. At least, not yet.

Another approach, one that's used very commonly in database applications, is to create an arbitrary field—such as some kind of ID number—and use that as a key field.

You'll see ways to do both of these things in Chapter 6, when you learn more about how to restructure tables. For now, however, make the Last name and First name fields into key fields.

When you restructure a table more than once Paradox empties and reuses the KEYVIOL table. You don't want to lose the Joneses. It's not immediately apparent that you'll have any more key violations, but just to be on the safe side, use the **T**ools/**R**ename command to rename the KEYVIOL table to *Joneses* for the time being. That way, if any more key violations occur, the records now in the KEYVIOL table won't be lost forever.

Proceed with the restructuring. Once again, display the Main menu, execute the **M**odify/**R**estructure command, and select the Rolotemp table. When the STRUCTure table appears, move the cursor to the Field Type column of the First name record, and append another asterisk, as shown in Figure 5.11. Press F2, "DO-IT!", to complete the task. As you'll see in Figure 5.12, no new KEYVIOL table has been created, and the records are sorted by last and first name.

102

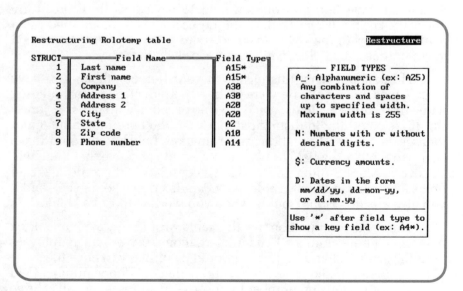

Figure 5.11: Adding a second key field to a table.

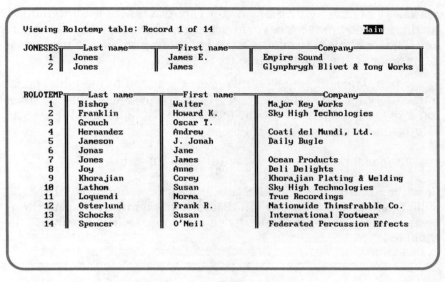

```
Viewing Rolotemp table: Record 1 of 14                        Main
JONESES┬━━Last name━━━━━━┳━━First name━━━┳━━━━━━━━━━Company━━━━━━━━━━━┓
     1 ┃ Jones          ┃ James E.      ┃ Empire Sound               ┃
     2 ┃ Jones          ┃ James         ┃ Glynphrygh Blivet & Tong Works┃


ROLOTEMP┬━━Last name━━━━━┳━━First name━━━┳━━━━━━━━━Company━━━━━━━━━━━┓
     1  ┃ Bishop        ┃ Walter        ┃ Major Key Works            ┃
     2  ┃ Franklin      ┃ Howard K.     ┃ Sky High Technologies      ┃
     3  ┃ Grouch        ┃ Oscar T.      ┃                            ┃
     4  ┃ Hernandez     ┃ Andrew        ┃ Coati del Mundi, Ltd.      ┃
     5  ┃ Jameson       ┃ J. Jonah      ┃ Daily Bugle                ┃
     6  ┃ Jonas         ┃ Jane          ┃                            ┃
     7  ┃ Jones         ┃ James         ┃ Ocean Products             ┃
     8  ┃ Joy           ┃ Anne          ┃ Deli Delights              ┃
     9  ┃ Khorajian     ┃ Corey         ┃ Khorajian Plating & Welding┃
    10  ┃ Lathom        ┃ Susan         ┃ Sky High Technologies      ┃
    11  ┃ Loquendi      ┃ Norma         ┃ True Recordings            ┃
    12  ┃ Osterlund     ┃ Frank R.      ┃ Nationwide Thimsfrabble Co.┃
    13  ┃ Schocks       ┃ Susan         ┃ International Footwear      ┃
    14  ┃ Spencer       ┃ O'Neil        ┃ Federated Percussion Effects┃
```

Figure 5.12: A table with two key fields.

103

Dealing with Key Violations

When two tables have essentially the same structure (that is, except for key fields), it's easy to add records from one to another.

F10	To display the Main menu.
T	To select the **T**ools menu.
M	To select the **M**ore submenu.
A	To execute the **A**dd command.
joneses ↵	To type the name of the source table.
↵	To display a list of tables.
↵	To select Rolotemp, which will be the default because it's in the workspace.

At this point you are given the choice

```
    NewEntries  Update
```

The former choice adds records to the table. The latter choice actually changes the data in existing records. If you choose **U**pdate, Paradox searches for records with the same key values as the records to be added, (in this instance, *James Jones* or *James E. Jones*) and replaces all the non-key fields with fields from the record whose keys match. Since this is a temporary table, go ahead and try it. Press **U**.

Soon, James E. Jones will be properly added to the table. James Jones of Glynphrygh Blivet & Tong Works, however, has replaced James Jones of Ocean Products. As the message at the bottom of Figure 5.13 informs you,

```
Changed records are shown in CHANGED table
```

Press the space bar and the message disappears, revealing the CHANGED table (another temporary table). Paradox thoughtfully doesn't throw away the data, giving you another chance to make it acceptable to the standards you've created.

104

▶ To restore records that have been eliminated from a table, edit them and then execute the **T**ools/**M**ore/**A**dd command.

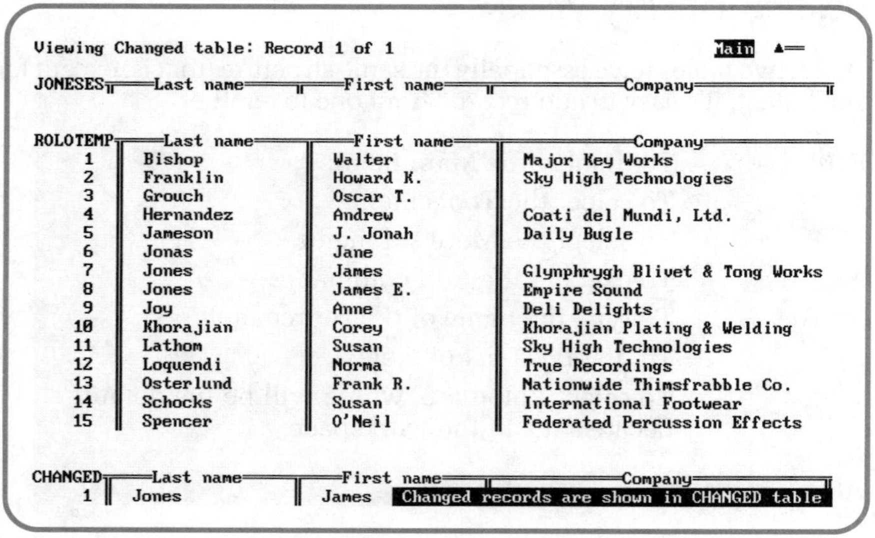

Figure 5.13: Results of the Tools/More/Add command.

To do so, press

F9	To edit the CHANGED table, which is current.
Tab Tab	To move to the First name field.
Space bar W.	To give Mr. Jones the middle initial *W*.
F2	To end the editing session.
F10	To display the Main menu.
T/M/A	To execute the **T**ools/**M**ore/**A**dd command.
↵	To display a list of tables.
C	To select **C**hanged, the current table.
↵	To display a list of tables.
R	To narrow the list.
↵	To select Rolotemp, which is the default.
↵	To confirm your selection.
N	To choose **N**ewEntries.

You'll see the message

```
Adding records from Changed to Rolotemp...
```

and when you're done, the screen should look like Figure 5.14. All your original records are now back in the Rolotemp table, properly sorted.

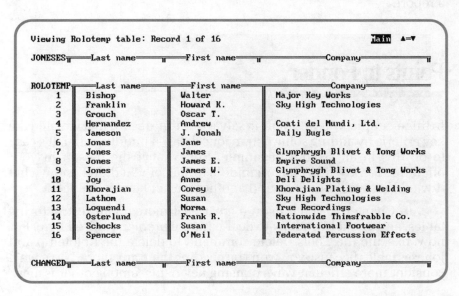

Figure 5.14: Adding changed records back into the source table.

Notice that the image pointer indicates tables with hidden records above and below the current (Rolotemp) table. This means that there are still records in the Joneses and CHANGED tables. The records from these tables have been copied, not moved, to the Rolotemp table. To confirm this, move among the images on the workspace by pressing F3 and F4. As you can see, Paradox gives you every opportunity to recover any data that may be eliminated as the result of changes.

Sorting Tables with Key Fields

You can sort tables that have key fields in the same manner as any other table, with one important restriction: You *must* place the sorted data into a different table. Paradox cannot maintain the integrity of the key fields and at the same time change the order of the records. When you specify a table to hold the data, Paradox creates a table with the same structure as the source table, but without key fields.

106

To maintain the integrity of your data, it's generally a good idea to regard these sorted tables as temporary and delete them when you're finished with them. Otherwise, you'll end up having at least two different versions of the same data on your disk. Updates made to one of the tables will *not* be reflected in the other, and it's too much trouble to keep two versions of the same data current in two separate tables. You'll learn in Chapter 12 how to view data sorted in any order using a report.

Points to Ponder

In this example, you were able to salvage the one record that violated the key criteria by adding some extraneous data—a middle initial. It's easy to do this in an arbitrary example. But what if the person in your offending record didn't have a middle initial, or you didn't know what it was? You would have to find another way of keying the data.

In Chapter 6, you'll learn a great deal more about restructuring tables, and you'll learn how to deal with the problems raised here. For now, execute the **T**ools/**D**elete command to delete the Rolotemp and Joneses tables because you won't be needing them any more. Next, we'll consider more efficient ways of using key fields, among other issues.

Modifying and Fine-Tuning Tables

What You Will Learn

► Restructuring Tables
► Redefining Fields
► Changing the Way a Table Appears in the Workspace
► Formatting Data
► Checking the Validity of Data

In Chapter 5, you used the **M**odify/**R**estructure command to add key fields to a table. But there's more that you can do with this command, and there are other ways to change the appearance of your images. In this chapter, you'll examine these techniques. In the process, you'll learn quite a bit more about key fields.

More About Restructuring

In Chapter 5, you added two key fields to a version of the Rolodex table. As you learned, this resulted in key violations—several records whose key fields contained the same data. I suggested in that chapter that the ideal set of key fields for the Rolodex table would be Last name, First name, and Phone number. However, Paradox requires that all key fields in a table appear in the structure before any non-key fields. At present, the Phone number field is the last field in the STRUCTure table. Fortunately, Paradox also provides an easy way around this problem. But it has consequences.

Moving a Field

108

The first step is to mark your key fields—Last names—First name, and Phone number. Execute the **M**odify/**R**estructure command again, and select the Rolodex table. As you may remember, you mark a key field by placing an asterisk after its description in the `Field Type` column of the STRUCTure table. Place the asterisks in the appropriate records. Press F2, "DO-IT!", to save your work, and you'll see, as you should expect, the message

    Non-consecutive key found for Phone number

What to do? Obviously, you have to move the Phone number field. To do so, move the cursor to the Company field. Press Ins or Insert to create space for a new field. In the `Field Name` column, type

    Phone number

and press Enter. The message

    Moving Phone number field...

appears briefly in the message area, and the Phone number field moves to the required position, after the Last name and First name fields, as shown in Figure 6.1.

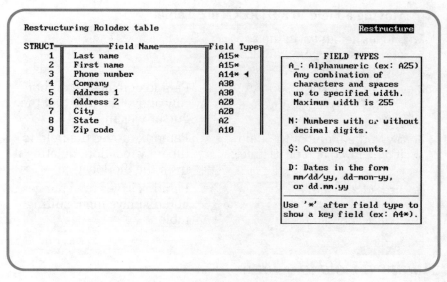

Figure 6.1: Moving a field in a structure table.

Press F2, "DO-IT!", to save your work, and you're done. The Rolodex table will appear in your workspace, with one significant change: the Phone number field now appears next to the First name field, as shown in Figure 6.2, and you don't want it there. Later in this chapter, you'll find out what to do about that.

```
Viewing Rolodex table: Record 1 of 16                          Main
ROLODEX┬────Last name────┬────First name────┬────Phone number────┬────Com
   1   ║ Bishop          ║ Walter           ║ (504)611-2300       ║ Major Key Work
   2   ║ Franklin        ║ Howard K.        ║ (209)901-6027       ║ Sky High Techn
   3   ║ Grouch          ║ Oscar T.         ║ (212)555-0000       ║
   4   ║ Hernandez       ║ Andrew           ║ (212)112-9009       ║ Coati del Mund
   5   ║ Jameson         ║ J. Jonah         ║ (212)500-9000       ║ Daily Bugle
   6   ║ Jonas           ║ Jane             ║ (714)502-5891       ║
   7   ║ Jones           ║ James            ║ (416)090-4000       ║ Glynphrygh Bli
   8   ║ Jones           ║ James            ║ (718)903-4912       ║ Ocean Products
   9   ║ Jones           ║ James E.         ║ (213)404-4400       ║ Empire Sound
  10   ║ Joy             ║ Anne             ║ (415)502-6767       ║ Deli Delights
  11   ║ Khorajian       ║ Corey            ║ (619)906-5432       ║ Khorajian Plat
  12   ║ Lathom          ║ Susan            ║ (209)901-6021       ║ Sky High Techn
  13   ║ Loquendi        ║ Norma            ║ (415)525-0000       ║ True Recording
  14   ║ Osterlund       ║ Frank R.         ║ (904)303-9812       ║ Nationwide Thi
  15   ║ Schocks         ║ Susan            ║ (212)555-1357       ║ International
  16   ║ Spencer         ║ O'Neil           ║ (201)555-9332       ║ Federated Perc
```

Figure 6.2: The result of moving a field.

Q Moving a Field in a STRUCTure Table.

1. Move the cursor to the row
   above which you want to
   move the field.

2. Press the Ins or Insert key.   Paradox creates an empty
                                                row above the row that the
                                                cursor was in.

3. Type the name of the field   Paradox moves the field to
   to be moved and press Enter.   the new location, deleting it
                                                from the old location.

4. Press F2, "DO-IT!"   Paradox saves the changes
                                                and displays the resulting
                                                table.   □

Adding a Field to a Table

In Chapter 5, I suggested that one way to deal with multiple records containing similar information is to create an arbitrary key field. This technique is appropriate for the Customer database, where it's quite likely that you'll have several records with the same names, so we'll add such a field. Press Alt-F8 to clear the workspace. Now execute the **M**odify/**R**estructure command again, and select the Customer table.

You know that key fields must appear before non-key fields. Since you have no key fields yet, and the cursor is in the first record, press the Ins or Insert key to create space for the key field. Type the following data into the new record:

```
Cust. ID    A5*
```

Your screen should now look like Figure 6.3. Press F2, "DO-IT!", to save your work.

> ▶ As with editing a table, you can delete a field from the
> STRUCTure table—and the resulting database—by
> selecting the field and pressing the Del or Delete key. When you
> press the "DO-IT!" key, F2, you'll be asked to confirm that you
> really want to delete the field.

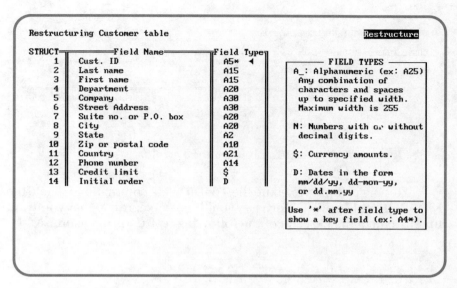

Figure 6.3: Adding a field to a table.

111

Now you have a problem. You've added a key field. The key field is blank in both of your records, so you've got a key violation, as you can see in Figure 6.4. However, as I've suggested, this field should contain an arbitrary value. The simplest way to assign a unique identifier to each field is to use consecutive five-digit numbers. Press F9, "Edit", to edit the KEYVIOL table. Press Tab and type

```
00001
```

in the Cust. ID field.

Now press F3, the "Up Image" key, to edit the Customer table. Press Tab and type

```
00002
```

in the Cust. ID field and press F2, "DO-IT!," to save the changes to both tables. Now execute the **T**ools/**M**ore/**A**dd command to add the record in the KEYVIOL table to the Customer table as explained in Chapter 5. (It won't matter at this point whether you pick **N**ewEntries or **U**pdate.) When you're done, both records will be in the Customer table, sorted by the arbitrary key field.

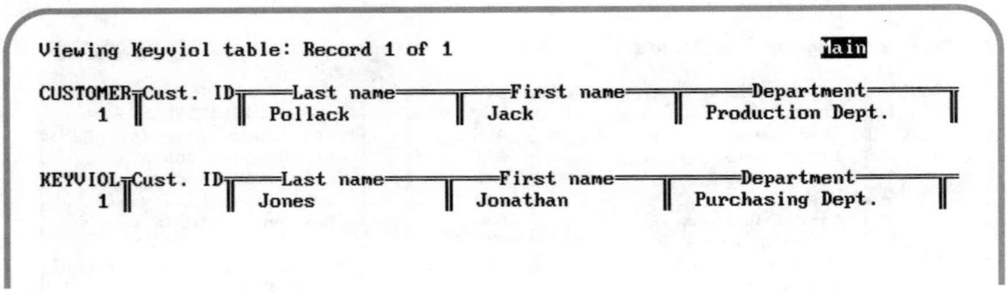

```
Viewing Keyviol table: Record 1 of 1                         Main

CUSTOMER Cust. ID     Last name        First name       Department
         1            Pollack          Jack             Production Dept.


KEYVIOL Cust. ID      Last name        First name       Department
         1            Jones            Jonathan         Purchasing Dept.
```

Figure 6.4: The result of adding a key field.

You may want to execute the **Tools/D**elete command to delete the KEYVIOL table now. Otherwise, you'll have to confirm that you want to reuse the table for each of the following restructuring exercises.

Changing a Field's Characteristics

You can change any field's characteristics by executing the **M**odify/**R**estructure command to display the STRUCTure table, and altering the values in the Field Type column. The most likely reason to do so is that you've made a field too narrow. In the Phone number field, for example (in both tables) you don't have room to enter an extension number. This could become a problem in dealing with companies that use a central switchboard number.

You can widen that field. When you bring the STRUCTure table to the workspace, you'll see that the Phone number field is an Alphanumeric field of 14 characters. This leaves enough for an area code and phone number, with punctuation. You'll need space for an extension of up to four digits, plus something to identify the remaining characters as an extension. The result should look like

(313)555-6009, x.3456

so you'll need room for eight more characters. Move your cursor to the Field Type column of the Phone number record, use the Backspace key to delete the 14, and type

22

Later in this chapter I'll show you how to set up that field so that any phone numbers entered into it conform to the desired format.

(You might want to do something similar to the Rolodex table. You might also want to widen the Company field by a character or two. If you remember, one of the company names was one character too long to fit.)

You can also—sometimes—change a field's data type. Just for practice, change the Credit limit field from a Currency-type field to a Number-type field. Delete the dollar sign from the `Field Type` column of the Credit limit field, and replace it with **N**. Your STRUCTure table should now look like Figure 6.5. When you're done, press F2, "DO-IT!"

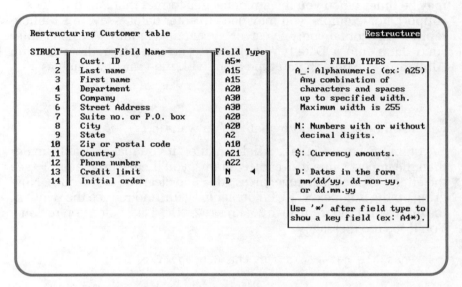

Figure 6.5: Changing field sizes and data types.

113

With this particular change, you will lose no information, because Paradox remembers the complete number you entered regardless of how it's displayed. Later, I'll show you how to display a simple Number field as though it were a Currency field.

For reference, you can successfully make the following type changes:

▶ Number to Currency.
▶ Currency to Number.
▶ Date to Alphanumeric.

▶ Alphanumeric to Date (if the field contains only dates in one of Paradox's approved formats).

▶ Alphanumeric to Numeric, and vice versa (if the field contains only numerals).

Any other type changes will result in an error message.

If you change a Date-type field to Alphanumeric, you'll no longer be able to do date arithmetic, which is a significant loss. However, there may be times when you'll want dates in a format that Paradox doesn't support. For example, you may need to enter dates—say, in a bibliography—that contain only a year, or a year and a month. You can't enter such dates into a Date-type field, but you can enter them into an Alphanumeric field. If you type them with the year first, such as

```
1990/02/25
```

you'll still be able to sort by date if you want to.

114

Finally, you can make a field smaller. If you make a field smaller than the largest value it already contains, you'll have problems. To see the effects of such a change, press Alt-F8 to clear the workspace. Now bring up the Rolodex STRUCTure table again, and reduce the width of the Company field from 30 to 25. Press F2, "DO-IT!," when you're done. You'll see the message

```
Possible data loss for the Company field
```

which lets you know that some of the values already in the field won't fit into the shortened field. However, as the menu at the top of Figure 6.6 shows, you have three options for dealing with the situation:

Trimming	Truncates the values to fit into the new field size.
No-Trimming	Places all the records with fields that don't fit into a separate, temporary table called PROBLEMS. If you choose this option, you can then edit the records in the PROBLEMS table—say, using more abbreviations—and then reinsert them into the source table with the **T**ools/**M**ore/**A**dd command.
Oops!	Returns you to Restructure mode, so you can make further changes or cancel the restructuring.

For now, choose Oops!, and press F10/**C** to cancel the changes.

```
Trimming  No-Trimming  Oops!                              Restructure
Allow trimming Company field values if necessary
```

Figure 6.6: Ways to deal with truncated fields.

 You may have seen the message

`Updating form F-modified fields will be deleted from form`

when you restructured the Rolodex table, for which you have
created a default form. This doesn't matter much with the
default form, because the next time you create a default form,
Paradox will automatically replace all the fields that were
deleted. However, when you have created custom forms,
altered fields are deleted from those forms as well. You will
then have to use the **F**orms menu to place those fields back
onto the form.

115

Changing a Table's Image

Whether or not you change the structure of a table, you can adjust the
way it appears on the workspace—that is, adjust its image. You might
want two particular fields next to each other, so you can see the values
in both of them at once. Or you may wish that your field displays were
narrower so you could see more of a table at one time.

Reordering the Display of Fields

Now you'll learn to move fields in an image without affecting the
corresponding table. Start with what you have in front of you—the
Rolodex table. The Phone number field is in the wrong place, as you saw
in Figure 6.2. It belongs at the end of the table, but because you made

it into a key field, it is now in the third column. The easiest way to move it is with the "Rotate" key, Ctrl-R. Move the cursor to the Phone number field and press Ctrl-R. Immediately, the third field changes to Company—just as it was in the original table. If you move past right edge of the screen, you'll see that it's still followed by the Address 1 field, as it should be.

Where has the Phone number field gone? Press Ctrl-End to move to the last column in the table. You'll see that it's now the Phone number field. When you rotate fields, you move the current field to end of the table, and move all the intervening fields one column to the left. If you return the cursor to the third column and press Ctrl-R six more times, the Phone number field will appear in its old position, because you're rotating six columns. Press Ctrl-R a seventh time, and the Phone number field moves back to end of the image.

Now that you've seen that the view of a table on the workspace need not match its structure, you might contemplate other changes. Consider the effects of key fields on sorting order. When a table has key fields, Paradox sorts it according to the key fields. If it has more than one key field, Paradox sorts the database using the values in all the key fields, taken together. The order in which the key fields appear in the STRUCTure table determines their order of precedence in sorting. Thus, two people with the same last name will be sorted by their first names. Two people with the same first and last names will now be sorted by phone number (not by address as they were before you added key fields). But that's not necessarily the most comfortable order in which to view the table or to enter data into it.

You might, for example, prefer to have the First name field shown first, followed by the Last name field. You could make this change with the "Rotate" key, Ctrl-R, but it would require a lot of fancy fingerwork. After all, if you began by rotating the First name field, it would end up at the far end of the table. Then you'd have to move to the second column, and rotate that column until the Last name field reappeared.

There's a better way. Press

F10	To display the Main menu.
I	To display the **I**mage menu, shown in Figure 6.7.
M	To select the **M**ove command.

You are prompted with

```
Name of field to move:
```

and shown a list of field names. Since Last name is selected, press Enter. You are then prompted to

```
Use → and ← to show the new position for the field...
then press ↵ to move it.
```

Move the cursor to the First name field and press Enter. Mission accomplished!

```
TableSize ColumnSize Format Zoom Move PickForm KeepSet Graph Main
Change the number of records to show in the current image.
```

Figure 6.7: The Image menu.

The changes you've made apply only to the image as it appears on the workspace. Moreover, they are not permanent. They will disappear when you exit from Paradox unless you save them. To save changes made to an image, press

117

F10	To display the Main menu.
I	To display the **I**mage menu.
K	To execute the **K**eepSet command.

The last command tells Paradox to make the changes you have made permanent (keep the settings). Remember, the changes affect only the display of your table, not its structure.

 Rearranging the Columns in an Image

1. Use the cursor keys to select the column in which you want a different field to appear.
2. Press Ctrl-R, the "Rotate" key, until the desired field appears in the selected column.
3. Alternatively, press F10.　　　　Paradox displays the Main menu.

<table>
<tr><td>4. Press **I**.</td><td>Paradox displays the **Image** menu.</td></tr>
<tr><td>5. Press **M** to select the **Move** command.</td><td>Paradox displays a list of field names.</td></tr>
<tr><td>6. Select the field to move.</td><td></td></tr>
<tr><td>7. Select the field now occupying the position to which you want to move the field, and press Enter.</td><td>Paradox moves the field to the new location.</td></tr>
<tr><td>8. Optionally, to make your changes permanent, press **F10/I/K** to execute the **Image/KeepSet** command.</td><td>Paradox saves the changes you made, so that the image will always appear as it does now. The table itself is not affected. □</td></tr>
</table>

Changing Column Width

Suppose you want a full view of the addresses in your Rolodex table. You press Ctrl-right-arrow to move a screen to the right, displaying the Address and City columns. But you can't see the State and Zip code columns. To remedy that, display the Image menu, and select the ColumnSize command. You will be prompted to

```
Use → and ← to move to the column you want to
resize...
then press ↵ to select it.
```

Since there's a lot of extra space in the Address 1 column, and it's already selected, press Enter. The screen appears as shown in Figure 6.8, and you're prompted to

```
Now use → to increase column width, ← to decrease ...
press ↵ when finished.
```

Press the left-arrow key seven times, then press Enter. Move to the Address 2 column and repeat the procedure. Now do the same to the City column, reducing its width by five characters. As Figure 6.9 shows, you can now see all five address columns. (If you want to keep these widths, execute the **Image/KeepSet** command again.)

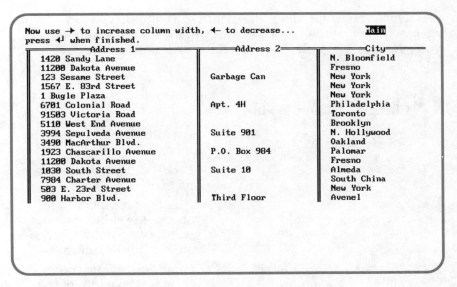

Figure 6.8: Viewing the Address and City fields.

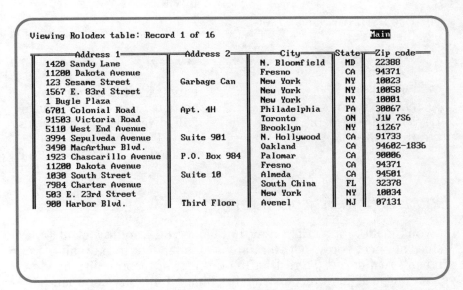

Figure 6.9: The Address fields reduced to fit on the screen.

Once you have reduced the width of a column, you can expand it again with the right-arrow key. However, if it's an Alphanumeric field, you can expand it only up to its width as defined in the STRUCTure table.

Q Changing Column Width

1. Press F10.	Paradox displays the Main menu.
2. Press **I**.	Paradox displays the **Image** menu.
3. Press **C**.	Paradox prompts you to choose the column whose width you want to change by moving the cursor to it.
4. Move the cursor into the column you want to size and press Enter.	Paradox prompts you to increase the width of the column with →, or decrease it with ←.
5. Use the arrow keys to set the width.	
6. Press Enter when the column is the desired width.	
7. Optionally, to make your changes permanent, press F10/**I/K** to execute the **Image/KeepSet** command.	Paradox saves the changes you made, so that the image will always appear as it does now. The table itself is not affected. ☐

Changing the Size of an Image

It won't matter much right now, but when you want to look at several tables at once, you won't want any single table to take up all of your screen's real estate. To restrict the number of records displayed in a given image at any time, execute the **Image/TableSize** command. You can then decrease the height of the table with the up-arrow key. Press Enter when the table is the desired size. As with narrowing a column, you can again increase the height of your table up to the number of records it contains, or to full-screen size, whichever is less, by executing the **Image/TableSize** command and using the down-arrow key.

Once you have reduced the height of a table, you scroll through it the same way you would if it were too large to fit onto the screen. Figure 6.10 shows the Rolodex table reduced to a height of 10 records, with a group of records from the middle of the table on display.

Changing the Size of an Image

1. Press F10.   Paradox displays the Main menu.

2. Press **I**.   Paradox displays the **I**mage menu.

3. Press **T**.   Paradox prompts you to increase the size of the image with ↓ or decrease it with ↑.

4. Press ↑ or ↓ to set the height.

5. Press Enter when the image is the desired height.

6. Optionally, to make your changes permanent, press F10 **I/K** to execute the **I**mage/**K**eepSet command.   Paradox saves the changes you made so that the image will always appear as it does now. The table is not affected.   ☐

121

> ▶ The Rotate, ColumnSize, and TableSize commands are all available from the Image menu in Edit mode as well as in Main mode.

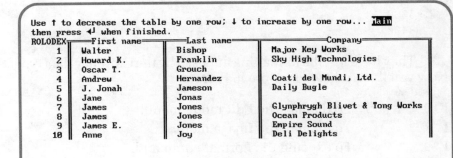

Figure 6.10: Reducing the height of a table.

Controlling What Appears in a Field

I've noted several circumstances under which you'd want to control the appearance of a field. You lost your number formatting when you changed your Credit limit field from Currency-type to Numeric-type, for example, and it would be nice to impose uniformity on the display of phone numbers. When you set up controls of this type, there's another—possibly greater—advantage: you ensure that any new data entered into the field conforms to the format you establish.

Two different commands impose such controls: the Image/Format command allows you to impose certain formats on Numeric, Currency, and Date fields, while the ValCheck command lets you impose validity checks on a field. A validity check may restrict entries to a certain range, supply a default value, or assign a picture to a field. A picture—sometimes called an "edit mask"—defines exactly what types of characters can appear in a field, and automatically fills in any required characters. You'll explore both of these types of controls now, and look further at validity checks when you learn ways to use multi-table databases.

Formatting Numbers

You can execute the Image/Format command either in Main or Edit mode, but the ValCheck command is available only in Edit mode. Begin by bringing up the Customer table and entering Edit mode by pressing F9, "Edit". Move to the Credit limit field. You'll see that the numbers in the column read

```
5000
8400
```

They have lost the formatting imposed by the Currency data type. Now you'll learn how to restore it. Press

F10	To display the Edit mode menu.
I	To display the Image menu.
F	To execute the Format command.

You'll be prompted to select the field to reformat with the cursor keys. Select the Credit limit field and press Enter. You'll see the menu shown in Figure 6.11, giving you the following four options:

General	The default format. Numbers are aligned on the decimal point; up to two decimal places are shown.
Fixed	The same as General, but you can choose the number of decimal places to appear.
Comma	Numbers larger than 999 are displayed with commas between each group of three digits; two decimal places are always displayed.
Scientific	Numbers are displayed with one integer place and two decimal places followed by a positive or negative exponent, indicated by an E.

For this field, select **C**omma. You'll be asked how many decimal places to use; a default of 2 is supplied. Press Enter to accept it. The field should now look exactly as it did when it was defined as a Currency field.

 There is no difference between a Numeric field in comma format with two decimal places and a Currency field.

123

```
General  Fixed  Comma  Scientific                              Edit
Separators inserted; negatives in parentheses (x,xxx.xx) or (x.xxx,xx).
```

Figure 6.11: The Number Format menu.

To try out the other number formats, bring the Numbers table to the workspace, and try using the other formats from the **I**mage/**F**ormat menu.

Formatting Dates

Now go back to the Customer table, move to the Initial order field, and see what date formats the **I**mage/**F**ormat command allow. Figure 6.12 shows you the available formats. As you can see, you have the choice of the same three formats in which you can enter dates. If you select one of these formats other than the default, you can still enter dates in any of the three formats. Only the display is affected.

```
MM/DD/YY  DD-Mon-YY  DD.MM.YY                                    Edit
All numeric month, day, year: e.g. 9/23/85.
```

Figure 6.12: The Date Format menu.

Pictures: Formatting Alphanumeric Fields

As usual, you control the appearance of Alphanumeric and sometimes Numeric fields by supplying *pictures* for them. Pictures contain three types of elements:

▶ Constant characters, which are displayed literally.
▶ Variables, which restrict entries to any character of a given type.
▶ Command characters, which tell Paradox how to treat the other characters.

Look at a couple of examples first, and then I'll explain the rules.

We'll begin with the Phone number field. You'll recall that we wanted phone numbers to appear in the format

```
(313)555-6009, x.3456
```

Press

F10	To display the Edit mode menu.
V	To choose the **V**alCheck submenu.
D	To Define a validity check, rather than Clear (remove one).
← (twice)	To select the Phone number field.
↵	To confirm your selection.
P	To enter a **P**icture.

You are then prompted with

```
Picture:
Enter a PAL picture format (e.g. ###-##-####).
```

124

You may recognize the example as the format for a Social Security number. In pictures, the pound sign (#) stands for any Numeric character. Type the following value, and press Enter when you're through:

```
(###)###-####[;, x.####]
```

When you press Enter, you'll see the message

```
Picture specification recorded
```

Now create a new record with the down-arrow key. Move to the Phone number field, and type

```
(313
```

You'll see the close parenthesis appear. Type

```
555
```

and you'll see the hyphen appear. Now type

```
6009
```

and press Enter. Your entry is accepted.

Now move back to the Phone number field and press the space bar. The characters

```
, x.
```

appear, just as you entered them into the picture. You can now enter a four-digit extension. However, the picture isn't perfect yet. If you type, say, a two-digit extension and then press Enter, Paradox displays the message

```
Incomplete field
```

and refuses to let you continue. For now, type the full four-digit extension, **3456**, and press Enter. You can fix the picture later.

The PAL programming language includes five command characters and five variable characters for pictures; they are summarized in Table 6.1. Any characters in a picture other than those into the table are placed into the field automatically.

Table 6.1: Picture command and variable characters.

Command Characters

[]	Items in brackets are optional elements.
,	Separates groups of acceptable alternatives.
*n	Allows entry of up to n characters of the specified type; if n is not specified, the number of characters may vary from none to the maximum the field will hold.
;	Indicates that the following character is to be entered literally if it would otherwise be a command character or a variable.
{}	Groups sets of characters to be separated by a comma.

Variable Characters

#	Only numeric characters are accepted.
?	Only alphabetic characters are accepted.
&	Only alphabetic characters are accepted; the entered character is converted to uppercase.
@	Any character is accepted.
!	Any character is accepted; if alphabetic, the entered character is converted to uppercase.

As you can see, the picture you created includes two of the command characters: the brackets for the optional extension, and the semicolon to let Paradox know that the comma, a command character, is to be entered literally. The problem is that the optional extension contains its prefix (the comma, space, etc.), and exactly four Numeric characters.

The variable has to be a bit more complex. Repeat the keystrokes you used to enter the picture. The current picture will be displayed for editing. Press Ctrl-F or Alt-F5 to enter field view, and change the picture so that it reads

```
(###)###-####[;, x.##[#][#]]
```

Granted, it's ugly, but here's how it works.

Paradox treats everything enclosed with in a set of brackets as a unit. Within the brackets defining the optional extension, each of two numeric character place-holders is enclosed in an extra set of brackets. This means that if you enter an extension, Paradox will supply the characters.

```
, x.
```

and expect two digits. You can now optionally enter three or four, instead of two. If you had enclosed the two optional characters in only one extra set of brackets, such as

```
[;, x.##[##]]
```

you could enter just two characters, but if you entered a third, Paradox would insist on a fourth.

Here's an easier example. Select the State field. Select the `Picture` command, and type the picture

```
&&
```

Now, when you enter a State abbreviation in lowercase, it will automatically appear in uppercase. If you enter anything other than a letter, Paradox will honk and refuse to accept it.

You can also provide alternatives. Select the Zip code field. The picture you'll create will accept either an American Zip code of either five or nine digits, or a British Commonwealth postal code. If you review Table 6.1, you'll see that you can provide alternatives by separating them with a comma. Type this picture:

```
#####[-####],&#& #&#
```

The first part of this picture, before the comma, is the American Zip code. Note that the last four digits are optional because of the brackets, but the hyphen is supplied automatically if you go past the first five digits. If you start your entry with a number, Paradox will expect a Zip code, because the only alternative starts with a letter. Conversely, if you start with a letter, you will be forced to enter a British Commonwealth postal code. Try out a few entries, and you'll see that this is true. Remember, you can clear a field with Ctrl-Backspace.

> One limitation of pictures is that they have no effect on data already entered into the table. Indeed, all validity checks occur only when you press a key that moves the cursor out of the field to which the validity checks apply. To make old entries conform, you must delete and reenter them. Deleting them and pressing the "Undo" key (Ctrl-U) unfortunately doesn't work. For this reason, you should always set up your validity checks *before* you enter data into a table.

Other Types of Validity Checks

The ValCheck menu, shown in Figure 6.13, includes several other types of validity checks. As you might guess from their command names, you can set a minimum value for a field with LowValue, a maximum with HighValue, or a default entry with Default. If your company never extends more than $25,000 of credit to any customer, for example, you might enter 25000 as the maximum acceptable value for the Credit limit field with the HighValue command. Paradox would then refuse to accept any entries greater than that amount.

```
LowValue  HighValue  Default  TableLookup  Picture  Required        Edit
Specify the lowest acceptable value for the field.
```

Figure 6.13: The ValCheck menu.

Another useful validity check is the **R**equired command. If you assign this validity check to a field, the field may not be left blank. You can use **R**equired in combination with other validity checks. Thus, you might use the picture

#####

along with the **R**equired status in the Cust. ID field. You might want to make all fields **R**equired except some parts of the address. Think carefully, however, before selecting **R**equired fields. If there were **R**equired fields for which some customers could offer no appropriate values, such as Department or Suite no., your clerks would be unable to process those orders.

The remaining command on the **Val**Check menu, **T**ableLookup, is appropriate only in applications using several related tables.

Chapter 7

Getting Information from Your Database

What You Will Learn

▶ Selecting Data to Display
▶ Manipulating the ANSWER Table
▶ Fine-Tuning the Results of a Query

Now that you know how to create databases, fine-tune their structure, and enter data into them, you may be curious why you're doing it. Obviously, you create databases in order to get information from the data you've stored in them.

You get information from a database by viewing selected groups of items sharing some common characteristics. For example, you might have a database of sales made by your sales staff, and want to see a list of all salespeople who sold at least $25,000 worth of goods in any month. Or you might want to compare January's sales with July's sales. You might want to find out from which states the most orders came, or which states generated the largest orders.

These examples all suggest ways of selecting a group of *records* from your database. But you might also want to select *fields*. You might, for example, want a list of the names and phone numbers of all your customers, or a list of companies and their states and Zip codes for planning a mass mailing.

Further, you might want to limit your selections by both field and record. Having found that, say, your largest orders came from Texas, you might want a list of the names and companies representing all your orders from that state.

In essence, then, you get information from your database by *searching* for various items, or by *querying* your data as it's called. In this chapter you'll learn many ways to query your databases. In Chapter 8, you'll learn ways of using Paradox's sophisticated querying techniques to make changes to the data stored in your databases.

Creating a Query Table

The method of querying databases in Paradox is called *query by example* (QBE), and it's extremely easy to use. You simply fill out a form telling Paradox the information that you want to look at, and Paradox finds it for you.

All queries start with the **A**sk command. You begin by selecting a table from which you want information. When you press F10/**A**sk, Paradox prompts you with

```
Table:
Enter name of table to ask about, or press ⏎ to see a
list of tables.
```

You respond to a request for a table here as you normally do: type the name of the table, or press Enter and select the table by first letter. When you do, you see what looks like an empty version of the table itself. This is a *query table*. You use this table to select fields and values to display. When you have made your selections and processed the query, everything matching the criteria you have established appears in a separate, temporary table called ANSWER. If you don't delete the ANSWER table from the work space after each exercise, you'll see its contents replaced by the result of each successive query.

Selecting Fields to Include

The methods for selecting fields to include in the ANSWER table are different from those for selecting the values—or the records—to include. We'll start with fields.

Use your Rolodex table since it has enough information in it to make queries interesting. The following exercise will display just the two name fields in the ANSWER table. Press

F10	To display the Main menu (if it's not already visible).
A	To execute the **A**sk command.
↵	To display a list of tables.
R	To select the Rolodex table.

Paradox places what appears to be an empty copy of the Rolodex table on the workspace, as you see in Figure 7.1. Note the legend at the top of the screen:

✓ [F6] to include a field in the ANSWER; [F5] to give an Example

133

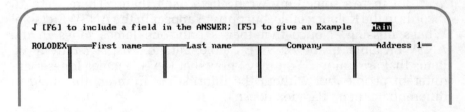

Figure 7.1: A query form.

This is just a reminder of the first step to selecting both fields and values to display. To include a field, you place a checkmark in it with the "Check" key, F6. Move the cursor to the First name field and press F6. You'll see a highlighted checkmark appear at the left border of the column. Now do the same in the Last name field. You should see another checkmark appear. Your query table should look like the upper image in Figure 7.2. You have now selected two fields to include in your ANSWER table. Press F2, the "DO-IT!" key, to process the query. The message

```
Processing query...
```

will appear briefly. The result should look like Figure 7.2.

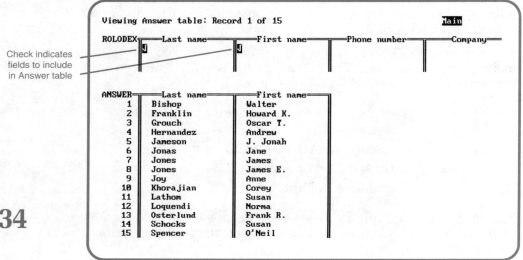

Check indicates fields to include in Answer table

```
Viewing Answer table: Record 1 of 15                        Main

ROLODEX    Last name       First name      Phone number       Company
           √               √


ANSWER     Last name       First name
     1     Bishop          Walter
     2     Franklin        Howard K.
     3     Grouch          Oscar T.
     4     Hernandez       Andrew
     5     Jameson         J. Jonah
     6     Jonas           Jane
     7     Jones           James
     8     Jones           James E.
     9     Joy             Anne
    10     Khorajian       Corey
    11     Lathom          Susan
    12     Loquendi        Norma
    13     Osterlund       Frank R.
    14     Schocks         Susan
    15     Spencer         O'Neil
```

Figure 7.2: Displaying selected fields.

But there's something wrong here, isn't there? There were 16 records in the Rolodex table, but only 15 appear in the ANSWER table! What's missing? Notice that there's only one James Jones in the ANSWER table. In the ANSWER table, Paradox displays only those items that are unique. You may know that the two James Joneses are different people, but without the information from another field to differentiate them, Paradox doesn't.

Including All Records

Paradox is smart enough to realize that you may want to see all the records, regardless of whether or not they are unique. So it gives you a tool for doing so. Press F3, the "Up Image" key, to move back to the query table. Choose one of the fields you selected with a Checkmark, and press F6 again. The Checkmark disappears.

> ▶ The "Check" key is a toggle. It places a checkmark in a field if none is present, and removes the checkmark when there is one.

Now press Alt-F6, the "Check Plus" key. You'll see a plus sign appear in the highlighted area next to the checkmark. This tells Paradox to include all records, even duplicates, in that field. Press F2, "DO-IT!," and you should now see all your records as illustrated in Figure 7.3.

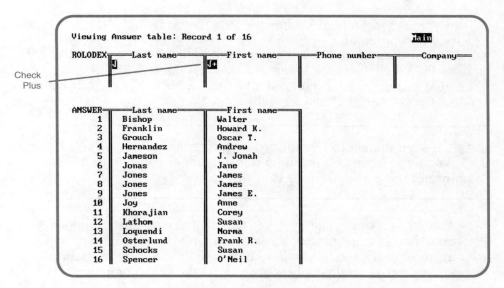

Figure 7.3: *The effect of the "Check Plus" key.*

135

Sorting the ANSWER Table

Notice that in the ANSWER table, Last name comes before First name, which is not true in the query table. By default, the order of fields in an ANSWER table reflects the STRUCTure table, not the image.

As you may remember, if you sort a table with a sort form, and don't specify any sort fields, the table is sorted from left to right. ANSWER tables are sorted the same way. (Even though the source table may be keyed, ANSWER tables have no key fields.) You can, of course, use the **M**odify/**S**ort command with ANSWER tables, as you can with any other tables.

You can change this by running the Custom script. (Using the Custom script was explained at the end of Chapter 2.) Select **S**cripts/**P**lay, and then enter

```
\PDOX35\CUSTOM
```

at the `Script:` prompt. Execute the command **D**efaults/**D**efaults/**Q**ueryOrder/**I**mageOrder to change the default. Press **R** for **R**eturn, press F2, and then specify whether you want changes saved to hard disk or network. You'll then have to restart Paradox. When ANSWER tables are sorted in image order, you can affect the order of the records by rotating the columns in the query table.

> ▶ If you change the default to image order, you may have some difficulty executing certain advanced commands. I'll point out these situations as they arise.

Assume that you've changed your default to image order. Suppose you want a list of the people in your database sorted by the company for which they work. Of course you'll want the people sorted by last name, in case you have several people who work for the same company.

Place a Checkmark, F6, in the First name, Last name, and Company fields. Now place the cursor in the first field in the image. Press Ctrl-R, the "Rotate" key, twice, to make Company the first field. Move to the second column, and press Ctrl-R until the second column is the Last name field. You can repeat the procedure to place the First name field in the third column, but it's not necessary. Because only one other field has a Checkmark, it will necessarily be third in the ANSWER table. Now press F2, "DO-IT!" You see the result in Figure 7.4. Later in this chapter I'll show you how to exclude the records that don't contain a company name.

136

Sorting in Reverse Order

If your query order is set to image order, you can sort your records in reverse order if you wish. To do so, use the "Check Descending" key, Ctrl-F6.

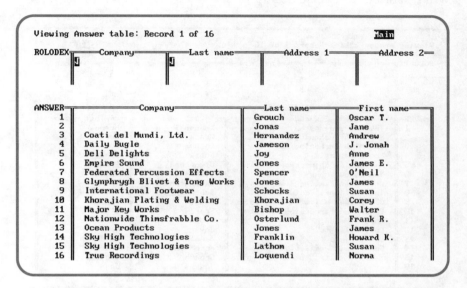

```
Viewing Answer table: Record 1 of 16                        Main

ROLODEX┬──────Company──────┬──────Last name──────┬─────Address 1──────┬──────Address 2═══
       │ⓊⓊ                 │ⓊⓊ                   │                    │
       │                    │                     │                    │
       │                    │                     │                    │


ANSWER┬────────────Company────────────┬─────────Last name──────┬──────First name═══
   1  │                                │ Grouch                 │ Oscar T.
   2  │                                │ Jonas                  │ Jane
   3  │ Coati del Mundi, Ltd.          │ Hernandez              │ Andrew
   4  │ Daily Bugle                    │ Jameson                │ J. Jonah
   5  │ Deli Delights                  │ Joy                    │ Anne
   6  │ Empire Sound                   │ Jones                  │ James E.
   7  │ Federated Percussion Effects   │ Spencer                │ O'Neil
   8  │ Glynphrygh Blivet & Tong Works │ Jones                  │ James
   9  │ International Footwear         │ Schocks                │ Susan
  10  │ Khorajian Plating & Welding    │ Khorajian              │ Corey
  11  │ Major Key Works                │ Bishop                 │ Walter
  12  │ Nationwide Thimsfrabble Co.    │ Osterlund              │ Frank R.
  13  │ Ocean Products                 │ Jones                  │ James
  14  │ Sky High Technologies          │ Franklin               │ Howard K.
  15  │ Sky High Technologies          │ Lathom                 │ Susan
  16  │ True Recordings                │ Loquendi               │ Norma
```

Figure 7.4: Using image order to choose the sorting order of your ANSWER table.

The following steps will produce an ANSWER table with the companies sorted in reverse order. Press F3, "Up Image", to go back to the query table, select the Company field, and press Ctrl-F6 twice. Now the Checkmark is followed by a pointer pointing downward, as Figure 7.5 shows. This figure also displays the result of this query. As you can see, the company names are now in reverse alphabetical order. (Computer software is written by programmers instead of by normal people, so Z-to-A is considered "descending" order because the code number by which Z is represented to the computer is higher than the code number for A.)

▶ All four Checkmark keys—F6, Ctrl-F6, Shift-F6, and Alt-F6—are toggles, and will clear any type of Checkmark from a field in the query table.

137

Note that if your query order is table order, or if you use the "Check Descending" key, Ctrl-F6, in a field other than the first, it has a different effect. The table will be sorted from left to right, as usual, *except for the field with the "Check Descending" mark*. In that field, only records that are the same as each other in all fields to the left of the descending field will be sorted in reverse order.

Check
descending
order

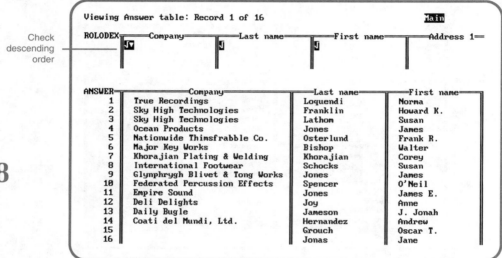

Figure 7.5: Sorting in reverse order.

Saving the Results

There are two ways to save the results of a query. If you want to reuse the information in the ANSWER table *in its present form*, you can execute the **T**ools/**R**ename command to rename the table, making it permanent. Bear in mind, however, that the renamed table has no intrinsic connection to the table from which the information was drawn. Changes made to the source table will not be reflected in the renamed table.

If you want a paper record of the result of a query, just select the ANSWER table (by default, it will already be selected) and press Alt-F7, the "Instant Report" key. Paradox will produce a report on your printer, listing the items in the ANSWER table in columns headed by the field names.

Setting Search Conditions

Most commonly, when you want to get information from your database, you're interested in looking at the records that meet certain criteria you have in mind—not necessarily all the records in a particular field or set of fields. As the term "query by example" suggests, you tell Paradox what to look for by giving it an example. These examples can be a specific value, a range of values, something similar to a given value, or even several different values.

Before proceeding, add a field to the Rolodex table, so that you have a bit more to work with. Execute the **M**odify/**R**estructure command. Add a field number 10 called *Last contact*, and make it a Date-type field. Press F2 to save the change.

Imagine that this file is a list of clients that you contact monthly. Each time you complete a call to a client, you record the date in the new field. You'll use a query to find out which clients are due for a call. (Unfortunately, when you restructure a table, you lose the settings you saved with the **I**mage/**K**eepSet command in Chapter 6. You might want to rotate the fields again, so that the first two are First name and Last name, and the Phone number field is now next to last.)

Press F9, "Edit", to edit the table, and type dates within the last two months into the new field. (If you leave out the year, Paradox automatically supplies the current year when you move to the next field with the down-arrow key.) The last part of your table should look something like Figure 7.6.

Matching Specific Values

To match a specific value, select the field in which it's located, press F5, "Example," and type the value you want Paradox to search for. Let's start with the Joneses again because there are so many of them. Press Alt-F8 to clear the workspace, and get a query form for the Rolodex table.

You already know that unless directed otherwise, Paradox shows only one instance of any given value. Thus, if you were to place a Checkmark in the Last name field and ask for *Jones*, you'd see just a single instance of the last name *Jones*. So check both the Last name and First name fields with F6.

139

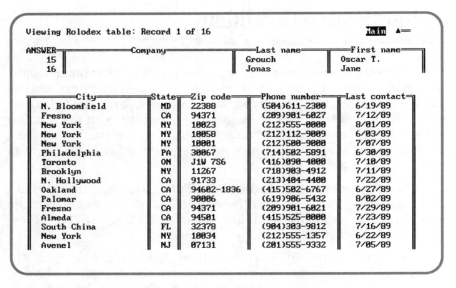

```
Viewing Rolodex table: Record 1 of 16                          Main  ▲═

ANSWER┬───────────Company───────────┬──────Last name──────┬────First name────┐
    15 ║                             ║ Grouch              ║ Oscar T.         ║
    16 ║                             ║ Jonas               ║ Jane             ║


┌────────City────────┬─State┬─Zip code─┬────Phone number────┬─Last contact─┐
  N. Bloomfield        MD     22388        (504)611-2300       6/19/89
  Fresno               CA     94371        (209)901-6027       7/12/89
  New York             NY     10023        (212)555-0000       8/01/89
  New York             NY     10058        (212)112-9009       6/03/89
  New York             NY     10001        (212)500-9000       7/07/89
  Philadelphia         PA     30067        (714)502-5891       6/30/89
  Toronto              ON     J1W 7S6      (416)090-4000       7/10/89
  Brooklyn             NY     11267        (718)903-4912       7/11/89
  N. Hollywood         CA     91733        (213)404-4400       7/22/89
  Oakland              CA     94602-1836   (415)502-6767       6/27/89
  Palomar              CA     90006        (619)906-5432       8/02/89
  Fresno               CA     94371        (209)901-6021       7/29/89
  Almeda               CA     94501        (415)525-0000       7/23/89
  South China          FL     32378        (904)303-9812       7/16/89
  New York             NY     10034        (212)555-1357       6/22/89
  Avenel               NJ     07131        (201)555-9332       7/05/89
```

Figure 7.6: The Date field filled in.

Now you need to provide an example. Move the cursor to the Last name field. Contrary to what you might expect, you do *not* press F5 to tell Paradox what to search for. Just type

```
jones
```

in the Last name field. Now place Checkmarks (F6) in the Last name and First name fields, and press F2, "DO-IT!", to process the query. Surprise! You get an empty ANSWER table!

Why? Because unless you tell it otherwise, Paradox searches for an *exact* match of what you enter. All of your Joneses begin with an uppercase *J*. So press

F3	To go back to the query table.
Tab	To select the Last name field.
Ctrl-F or Alt-F5	To enter field view.
Home	To move to the beginning of the field.
Del or Delete	To delete the lowercase j.
J	To replace it with an uppercase J.
Enter	To leave field view.

While you're at it, go back to the First name field, and replace your Checkmark with "Check Plus" (Alt-F6). Remember, Paradox otherwise will show you only unique values, and you have more than one James Jones. Now when you press F2, "DO-IT!", you should see an ANSWER table showing all three of your James Joneses, as Figure 7.7 illustrates.

 If your ANSWER table is empty, either there are no values that match your query, or your query has an error in it.

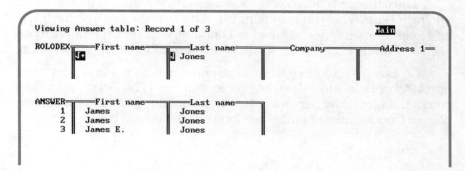

```
Viewing Answer table: Record 1 of 3                           Main
ROLODEX    First name        Last name        Company        Address 1
           J+                J  Jones



ANSWER     First name        Last name
    1      James             Jones
    2      James             Jones
    3      James E.          Jones
```

Figure 7.7: A properly constructed exact-match query.

141

Finding Inexact Matches

To help you with situations of this type, Paradox has two quite different ways of finding *inexact* matches:

▶ The wild-card characters you used with the **Zoom** command.
▶ The *like* operator.

Try the *like* operator first. Go back to the query table, and replace Jones with

```
like jones
```

This tells Paradox to search for all values that resemble "jones." The *like* operator always matches the first character of the value you give it to search for, and finds anything reasonably close. Your ANSWER table should now display:

```
ANSWER      First name      Last name
1           J. Jonah        Jameson
2           Jane            Jonas
3           James           Jones
4           James           Jones
5           James E.        Jones
```

It's a bit less precise than the exact match, but of course, that's what you asked for. And it's quite useful when you're not exactly sure of the spelling of the item you're looking for.

The wild-card characters @ and .. can also simplify searches when you're not sure what you're looking for. What was the name of that blivet and tong company? Something like Glenfree, wasn't it? But how do you spell it? Paradox can find it if you give it a reasonable approximation.

Go back to the query table, and, with your cursor in the top row, press Del or Delete to delete the previous query. (The Del or Delete key works the same way here as it does in an actual database table.) Now place a Checkmark (F6) into the Company field, and type

```
Gl@n..
```

Remember, the @ symbol replaces any character, and the double period (..) stands for any group of characters. Press F2, "DO-IT!," to process this query, and sure enough, your ANSWER table shows only the Company field, with the single entry

```
Glynphrygh Blivet & Tong Works
```

(What would you see if you searched the Last name field for *..an..?*)

Finding Non-Matches

Suppose you want to find only records that *don't* match a certain value? To do so, use the *not* operator. The following steps will display everybody *except* the Joneses. Again, use the Del or Delete key to clear the previous query. The query will resemble some of the earlier ones. Place a "Check Plus" mark (Alt-F6) in the First name field and a Checkmark (F6) in the Last name field. Now type

```
not Jones
```

into the Last name field and press "DO-IT!," F2. Your ANSWER table should show everything but the Joneses, as Figure 7.8 illustrates. (What do you think would have happened if you typed

```
not like jones
```

instead of *not Jones*?)

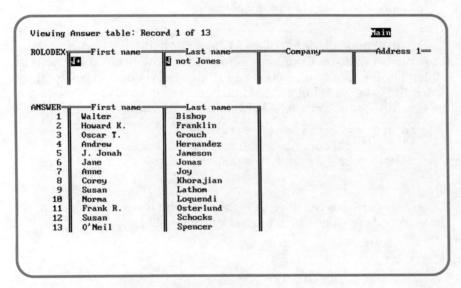

Figure 7.8: Using the not *operator.*

Searching for Empty Fields

Why would you want to exclude certain values? You'll see why in the next example. Remember when you got a list of records sorted by Company? There were three blank records at the top of the list. If you wanted to show just those records, you could use the *blank* operator. Rotate your query table as you did in that exercise, and place a Checkmark (F6) into the Last name and First name fields, as shown in Figure 7.9. In the Company field, type the word

```
blank
```

143

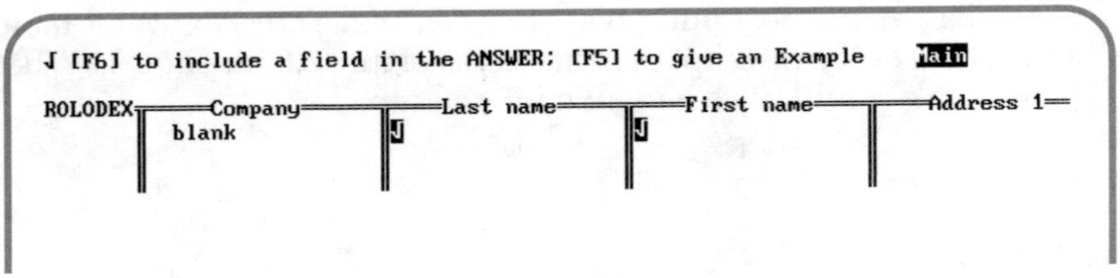

```
J [F6] to include a field in the ANSWER; [F5] to give an Example    Main

ROLODEX┬─────Company──────────────┬─Last name───────┬──First name──────┬───Address 1──
       │     blank                │N                │N                 │
       │                          │                 │                  │
```

Figure 7.9: Using the blank *operator.*

Notice that you *didn't* place a Checkmark into the Company field. This means that the Company field won't show up in the ANSWER table. (The field containing your selection criteria need not be displayed.) Since the Company field *should* be blank, why look at it? When you process the query, your ANSWER table should show:

```
ANSWER    Last name     First name
1         Grouch        Oscar T.
2         Jonas         Jane
3         Jones         James
```

If you compare this result with Figure 7.4, you'll see that these are the three records with no entry in the Company field.

Combining Operations

You're by no means restricted to a single operation per query. In the examples that follow in this chapter, you'll often use more than one criterion to select the information to display. The next exercise re-creates the ANSWER table shown in Figure 7.3, but without the blank records. You'll use both the *not* and *blank* operators.

Go back to the query table, place a Checkmark (F6) into the Company field, and change the text in that field to read

```
not blank
```

In other words, you've asked Paradox to include in the ANSWER table only those records whose Company field is not blank. You'll see, in Figure 7.10, the table you wanted to see in Figure 7.3.

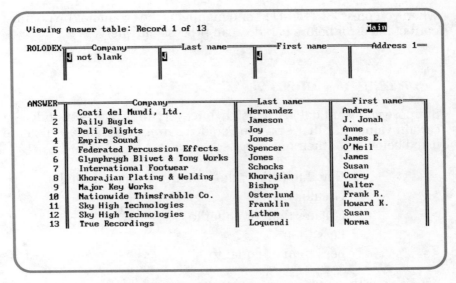

```
Viewing Answer table: Record 1 of 13                                    Main
ROLODEX      Company         Last name       First name        Address 1
          not blank

ANSWER            Company                 Last name          First name
    1     Coati del Mundi, Ltd.          Hernandez         Andrew
    2     Daily Bugle                    Jameson           J. Jonah
    3     Deli Delights                  Joy               Anne
    4     Empire Sound                   Jones             James E.
    5     Federated Percussion Effects   Spencer           O'Neil
    6     Glynphrygh Blivet & Tong Works Jones             James
    7     International Footwear          Schocks           Susan
    8     Khorajian Plating & Welding    Khorajian         Corey
    9     Major Key Works                Bishop            Walter
   10     Nationwide Thimsfrabble Co.    Osterlund         Frank R.
   11     Sky High Technologies          Franklin          Howard K.
   12     Sky High Technologies          Lathom            Susan
   13     True Recordings                Loquendi          Norma
```

Figure 7.10: Excluding blank fields.

145

Changing Field Names

The names of the fields in the ANSWER table don't have to be the same as those in the query table. You might want to change them in order to use the changed names in reports based on your ANSWER table. To change field names, use the *as* operator. As an example, change the query now on the workspace so that the text in the Company field reads

```
not blank, as Firm
```

Notice, as you add the new words, that the field widens to accommodate them. A field will accept queries of up to 255 characters, and adjust its size to fit the query. When you process the new query, the only change should be that the heading at the top of the first column now reads `Firm` instead of `Company`.

Notice also the comma in your new query. The comma separates several operations pertaining to a single field. If you leave out the comma, Paradox displays the warning

```
Missing comma
```

when you press F2, "DO-IT!," and highlights the errant field. You must correct the error before Paradox can process the query.

Searching for Ranges of Values

Suppose you want not just a match, but everything over—or under—a certain value? For that, you use Paradox's *range operators*, which are listed below with their meanings.

=	Equal to (this is the default, and is optional)
>	Greater than
>=	Greater than or equal to
<	Less than
<=	Less than or equal to

You can use the range operators in any type of field. For example, you could search for only those companies whose names are not blank and are in the first part of the alphabet by typing `<M.` into the Company field. The ANSWER table would then include only

```
Coati del Mundi, Ltd.
Daily Bugle
Deli Delights
Empire Sound
Federated Percussive Effects
Glynphrygh Blivet & Tong Works
International Footwear
Khorajian Plating & Welding Co
```

You could restrict the selection further by specifying both ends of the range. If you typed the search condition

```
<M, >G
```

into the Company field, your ANSWER table would include only the last three of the records in the previous table.

In the hypothetical example at the beginning of this chapter, you wanted a list of salespeople who had sold at least $25,000 worth of goods in any month. Assume that you have a table with each of your salesperson's sales figures for each month. You would put Checkmarks (F6) in the Last name and First name fields, and type the formula

```
>=25000
```

into the Sales figures field. The resulting ANSWER table would display only the names of those of your sales staff who had met or exceeded the specified goal. If you wanted to see in which month they did so, you'd have to include that field as well. (Note: This isn't the best way to structure such a table.)

> ▶ When entering values in Numeric and Currency fields, you can enter only digits and decimal points—commas and currency symbols are not allowed.

Try searching for a range of dates. Presumably, the dates you entered into your Rolodex table aren't the same as those in mine, but let's use mine for the example. Suppose you wanted to find out which people you had last called in July. You'd set up the query as shown in Figure 7.11. (I've rotated the fields so that you can see all the pertinent columns). Note that both the beginning and the end of the range of dates have been specified, separated by commas. The search criteria could just as easily have been specified as

147

```
6/30/89, <8/1/89
```

but it would be a bit more confusing. The result, as you can see in the same figure, is an ANSWER table showing the names, phone numbers, and dates of last contact of those people you last called in July.

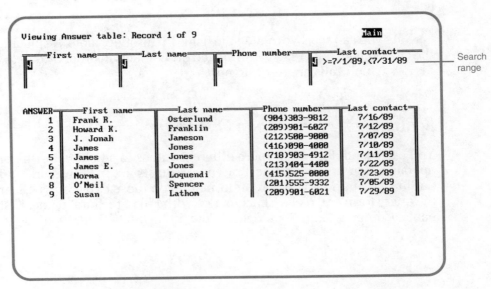

Figure 7.11: Searching for a range of dates.

Using the Current Date

Paradox has a special operator for the current date: *today*. If you type `today` into a Date-type field, all records with today's date will appear in the ANSWER table. If a field of your order-processing database, contains scheduled dates for various items, for example, you could use this feature to find the records to be processed on any given day.

But the real value of the today operator lies in *date arithmetic*. Remember why you added the Date field to the Rolodex table? It was to keep track of the last time you called each person listed. Your goal was to call each one monthly. To find out who's actually due for a call, you need a list of the names and phone numbers of everyone you last called more than a month ago. To get those records, you need to find the ones with dates that are 30 days or more before today. The way to express this value in a date field is

```
< today - 31
```

(The actual number at the end of this expression will depend on the number of days in the previous month.) In other words, you ask Paradox to display any date that is before (less than) 31 days before today's date. Figure 7.12 shows the query and the result.

 You can leave out the spaces in expressions involving range operators. *<today-31* would work equally well.

As you can see, I've rotated the fields in the query table. By placing the Last contact field first, I've arranged my contacts in order by date, so I know which calls are most urgent.

Searching for More Than One Value

You can search for two or more different values in a field using the *or* operator. You know that most of your contacts are in New York and California. Suppose you want information on those two groups. Clear the query form and place Checkmarks (with F6) in the First name, Last name, Company, and State fields. Now, in the State field, type

```
CA or NY
```

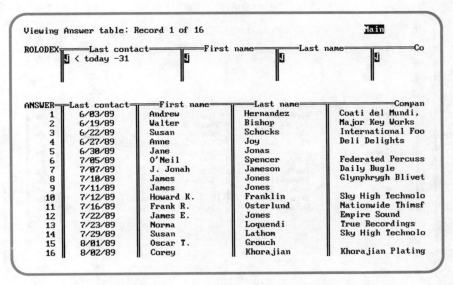

Figure 7.12: Date arithmetic using the today *operator.*

149

The result, shown in Figure 7.13, includes the records of people in either of the selected states, but no others. When you use *or*, any value that matches either of the conditions you specify appears in the ANSWER table.

Similarly, you can use the comma to specify values in a single field that meet two different criteria. To see only the records for states *other* than New York and California, type

```
not CA, not NY
```

into the State field. You'll see the expected result in Figure 7.14.

Another, quite different, technique allows you to search for several different values even if the values are not in the same field. To do so, set up several queries in the same query table, one for each item. Just make sure that you have Checkmarks (F6) in all the columns to appear the ANSWER table in *each* row of the query table.

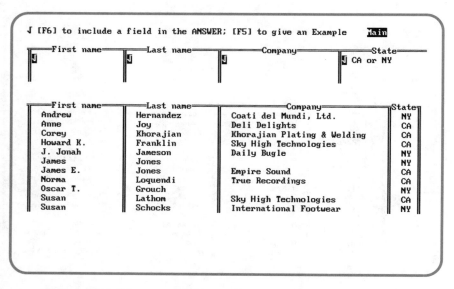

Figure 7.13: The or operator.

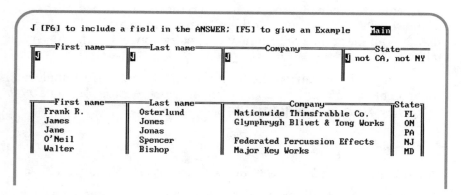

Figure 7.14: Combining two search conditions.

Here's an example. Suppose you want to see all the records of people named *Susan*, all the records from *Florida*, and all the records of *Joneses* in *California*. You'll need the Last name, First name, and Company fields, so place Checkmarks (F6) in those fields.

Now, you can't specify the search criteria as *Susan* in the First name column, *Jones* in the Last name column and *FL* or *CA* in the State column, because that would pull up only records for people named *Susan Jones* from Florida or California. That's not what you're looking for.

Instead, construct the query table in three rows, as shown in Figure 7.15. Notice that each row specifies a different set of conditions. In the ANSWER table, also in Figure 7.15, the first condition (everyone whose first name is *Susan*) accounts for records 3 and 4; the second condition (everyone from *Florida*) accounts for record 1; and the third condition (*Joneses* from *California*) accounts for record 2. The records are sorted by first name, since the First name column appears first in the query table.

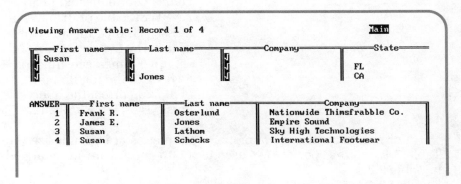

Figure 7.15: Using multiple rows in a query statement.

Executing a Query

1. If it's not already displayed, press F10 to display the Main menu.

2. Select **A**sk from the Main menu.

   Paradox asks you for the name of the table about which you want to ask.

3. Enter a table name, or press Enter to select a table name from the list.

   Paradox displays a query table, which looks just like the table you selected, except that it's empty.

4. Use the Checkmark keys (F6, Alt-F6, and Ctrl-F6) to place Checkmarks into the fields you want to see in your ANSWER table.

   If you use F6, Paradox displays all unique values in the field. If you use Alt-F6, Paradox displays all matching values in the field. If you use Ctrl-F6, Paradox displays the matching values in reverse order.

151

5. Enter the values for which you wish to search into the appropriate fields. You may use any of the query operators, or wild-card characters, to specify the type of match you want.

6. Press F2, "DO-IT!"

Paradox either displays the values you requested in an ANSWER table or displays a message indicating an error in the way the query table is set up. If a message appears, go back to the highlighted field and correct the query. Press "DO-IT!", F2, again. □

For reference, the operators used in queries are summarized in Table 7.1, and the special keys used to set up queries are summarized in Table 7.2.

Table 7.1: Query operators.

Operator	Effect
like	Finds all values similar to the search criterion.
not	Finds all values that do not match the search criterion.
blank	Finds all records with no value entered in the field.
today	Finds all records with today's date entered in the field; allows date arithmetic based on today's date.
or	Finds all values that match either of the conditions specified.
,	Finds all values that match both of the conditions specified.
as	Changes the name of the field in the ANSWER table.
+	Adds Numeric values or concatenates Alphanumeric values.
–	Subtracts the value following the sign.
*	Multiplies values.
/	Divides by the value following the / sign.
()	Groups values for arithmetic operations.
>	Specifies all values greater than the given value.

Operator	Effect
>=	Specifies all values greater than or equal to the given value.
<	Specifies all values less than the given value.
<=	Specifies all values less than or equal to the given value.
=	Specifies all values that are the same as the given value (the default).
..	When placed before or after a group of characters, finds a value with any characters preceding or following the specified characters.
@	Finds a value with any character in the position of the @ symbol.
sum	Finds the sum of the values in a field.
average	Finds the average of the values in a field.
count	Displays the number of values in the field.
min	Finds the lowest value in a field.
max	Finds the highest value in a field.
all	Modifies the sum or average operator to include all values in the field, whether or not they are unique.
unique	Modifies the sum or average operator to include only one instance of any non-unique values.

153

Table 7.2: Special keys used in query tables.

Key	Effect
F6	Places a Checkmark in a field, telling Paradox to display all unique values in that field which match the search criterion.
Alt-F6	Places a "Check Plus" mark in a field, telling Paradox to display all values, regardless of uniqueness, in the field which match the search criterion.
Ctrl-F6	Places a "Check Descending" mark in a field, telling Paradox to display, in reverse order, all unique values in that field which match the search criterion.
Shift-F6	Places a "Group By" mark in a field, indicating that the values in the field should be used to group the records for summary calculations, but does not include the field in the ANSWER table.

(continued)

Table 7.2: (continued)

Key	Effect
F5	Allows you to enter an example element, standing for all values in a field, which you can then use to perform calculations on the values in the field or to link a field in one table to a field in another table.
"	Allows you to search for characters or groups of characters which would otherwise be interpreted as operators.

154

Chapter 8

Queries Using Calculations and Example Elements

What You Will Learn

- ▶ Using Queries to Create New Values
- ▶ Entering Example Elements in a Query
- ▶ Calculating Values Based on Several Fields
- ▶ Concatenating Alphanumeric Values
- ▶ Creating Scripts

Up to now, you've searched your database for values that are actually present. In this chapter, you'll learn how to use those values to derive new values that don't appear in your database. You'll also get your first introduction to scripts.

The techniques you learn here will not change any of the values in your source database, only in your ANSWER table. In Chapter 9, you'll learn some query techniques to change the values in your database.

Calculating New Values

Paradox gives you many ways to create ANSWER tables that have new values not found in the source table. One of the most powerful is the *calc* operator. This operator tells Paradox to perform some type of calculation. It has two uses:

▶ To perform arithmetic operations on Number, Date, or Currency fields.

▶ To combine the values found in Alphanumeric fields.

You'll learn both uses of this operator.

Entering Example Elements

In order to use the *calc* operator on more than one field, you have to use an *example element*. An example element is a dummy value that stands for any value in the field. To enter an example element, you select the field where it is to appear and press F5, the "Example" key. An inverse video highlight will flash briefly. This is your cue to type a dummy value. The value will appear in inverse video, to distinguish it from the search conditions you've been entering up to now.

Example elements have two purposes:

▶ To tell Paradox to do something to any value in the field in which it appears.

▶ To link fields in one table to those in another in a query involving two or more tables.

You'll learn the latter use of example elements in Chapter 10. For now, we'll use example elements in calculations.

Without example elements in a calculated expression, you're simply doing arithmetic. If you used an expression such as

```
calc 25000 + 100
```

all records in the ANSWER table would have the value

```
25100
```

in the field where the expression appears. If you replace the value *25000* with a dummy value, on the other hand, Paradox will add 100 to every value in the field.

> ▶ If you make a mistake entering an example element, you can delete it with Ctrl-Backspace. Once you delete an example element, however, you have to press F5, the "Example" key, again to enter a new one.

Example elements with calculations are invaluable in an application such as preparing invoices. You could use two example elements, one for the number of items ordered and another for the unit price, to calculate the total cost. Then you could use a fractional value such as 1.065 to calculate the price with sales tax of 6.5% added. In the course of this section, you'll see how to place such information into new fields, which don't exist in your source table.

157

Performing Arithmetic Operations

In the next exercise, you'll extend the previous example by adding a calculated value with an example element. Move to the Last contact field of the query table. Press

Ctrl-Backspace	To clear the current search condition.
F6	To remove the Checkmark.
F5	To enter an example element.
a	To use the letter *a* as an example element.
, calc	To separate the example element from an expression, and tell Paradox to calculate a new value.
F5	To enter an example element on which to perform the calculation.
a	To use the element you just entered.

```
+ 30 as Next Call
```
To define the calculation and rename the
Last contact field to Next Call.

The entry fields should appear as shown in Figure 8.1.

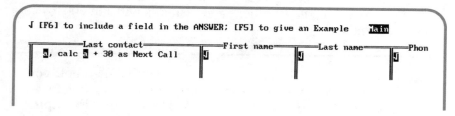

```
J [F6] to include a field in the ANSWER; [F5] to give an Example    Main
========Last contact========           ======First name======    =====Last name=====        ======Phon
a, calc a + 30 as Next Call         J                       J                      J
```

Figure 8.1: Setting up a calculation.

In this strange formula, you've told Paradox to take all the values
in the Last contact field, add 30 to them, and place them into a new field
called *Next Call*. If you didn't give the field a new name, it would be
called, quite logically,

```
Last contact + 30
```

Press F2. As you can see in Figure 8.2, the ANSWER table now includes
a field called *Next Call*. All the records from the Rolodex table are
present, with new dates in the new field. The new dates are a month
later than the dates in the Rolodex table. Press Alt-F7, "Instant Report,"
to print a report of the ANSWER table, and you can copy the new dates
into your calendar.

Note that *you have not changed the original Rolodex table in any
way.* You can, in fact, change the data in a table using queries, but that's
the subject of the next chapter.

Introducing Scripts

I've mentioned that Paradox can record your actions as they occur so
that you can repeat them at a later time. This not only saves keystrokes,
but can help prevent errors. For example, you might want to create the
ANSWER table with the Next Call field every week. But it's a bit of a

nuisance to set up, and you might forget a step, or make a mistake the next time you tried to create it. Fortunately, once you've got a query that works, you can save it.

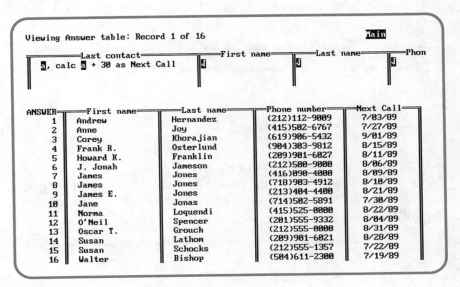

Figure 8.2: The result of a calculation.

Query Scripts

Now that you have a working query, here's how to save it. Press

F10	To display the Main menu.
S	To display the **S**cripts menu shown in Figure 8.3.
Q	To execute the **Q**uerySave command.

You will be prompted with:

```
Query script name:
Enter name to be given to new query script.
```

Type

```
calls
```

159

and press Enter. Now you can repeat this query any time by executing the **S**cripts/**P**lay command, pressing Enter, and selecting Calls. This command will bring the query form you just used to the workspace. Then you'll have to press F2, the "DO-IT!" key, to complete the calculation.

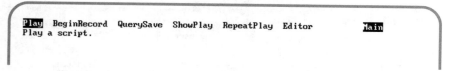

Figure 8.3: The Scripts menu.

Figure 8.4 shows what your query script looks like in the Script Editor or in a text editor. As you can see, it's just a mock-up of your query table. When you save a query script, you don't actually save anything more than the query table itself.

160

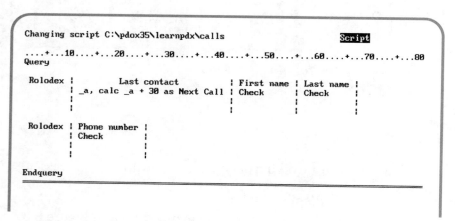

Figure 8.4: A query script.

Saving a Query Script

1. Press F10.	Paradox displays the Main menu.
2. Press **S**.	Paradox displays the **S**cripts menu.
3. Press **Q**.	Paradox asks for the name for your query script.

4. Type the name of your
   script, and press Enter.   □

Instant Scripts

We can simplify the procedure of generating the ANSWER table with
the Next Call field even further. Paradox has an "Instant Script" key,
Alt-F3. It records the keystrokes you enter, as you enter them. Try it out.
Clear the workspace with Alt-F8. Now press

Alt-F3	To begin recording your keystrokes.
S	To display the **S**cripts menu shown in Figure 8.5.
P	To select the **P**lay command; you'll be prompted for a script name.
calls	Type the name of the script.
↵	To confirm your choice.
F2	To execute the query script.
Alt-F7	To print the ANSWER table.
Alt-F8	To clear the workspace.
Alt-F3	To finish recording the script.

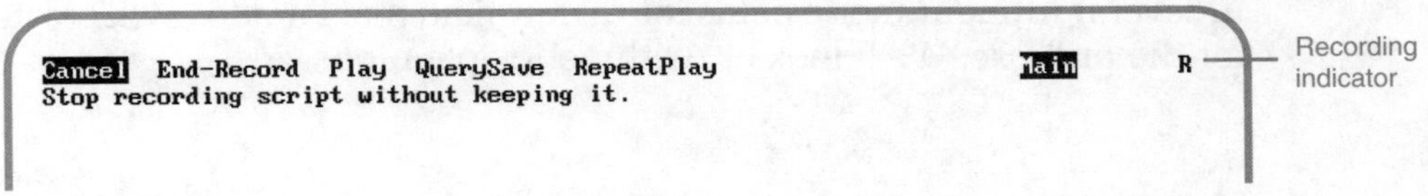

```
Cancel End-Record Play QuerySave RepeatPlay                    Main      R
Stop recording script without keeping it.
```
Recording indicator

Figure 8.5: The Scripts menu while recording an Instant script.

Notice that the Scripts menu that appeared while you were
recording the Instant script was different from the one you used to
save your query. The R in the upper-right corner of the screen indicates
that you're now recording. The additional commands—Cancel and
RepeatPlay—apply to the script you're currently recording. If you
make a mistake during a script, and decide not to record it, execute the
Scripts/**C**ancel command to interrupt the recording and keep the script
from being saved on disk.

When you press the Alt-F3 key, Paradox informs you that it's starting or ending the Instant script. If you look at the **S**cripts/**P**lay submenu again, you'll see a script called `Instant` when you request a list of scripts. Although the script is permanently recorded on disk, *Instant* is a temporary name, just like the names of temporary tables. The next time you record an Instant script, the current one will be discarded. To make the script you recorded permanent, use the **T**ools/**R**ename/ **S**cripts command to rename it. Give it the name

```
nextcall
```

You'll learn more about scripts later in the book. You might note, however, that there's an "Instant Script Play" key, Alt-F4, that always plays whichever script is currently called *Instant*.

162 Calculations on Several Fields

You can use example elements to refer to the values in more than one field in a calculation expression. In doing so, you can derive new values based on the values in several fields—sums, averages, and so on. You can also use the technique described below to combine the text found in several Alphanumeric fields into a new field that Paradox will create for the purpose. We'll look at Arithmetic operations first.

Arithmetic Operations Combining Several Fields

Suppose, for example, you had a table of sales records structured like the example shown in Figure 8.6, listing the sales figures for six consecutive months. You have sales figures for each salesperson for each month in the appropriate field. You'd like to find out the average monthly sales of each member of your sales staff.

You'd create a query table based on this table, place Checkmarks in the name fields, and enter **a**, **b**, **c**, **d**, **e**, and **f** into each of the six monthly fields as example elements. That is, you'd press F5 in each field before pressing the letter. Then, with the formula shown in Figure 8.7, you would get a table showing each salesperson's average. This formula simply adds the values represented by the six example elements and divides the sum by 6. The parentheses ensure that the division is performed on the sum, not simply on the last value.

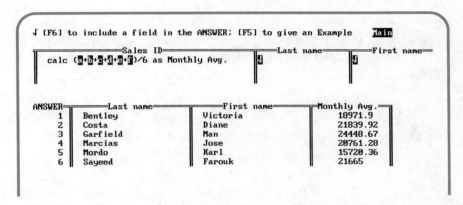

```
Viewing Salesper table: Record 6 of 6                          Main

SALESPER┬─Sales ID──┬──Last name─┬─First name─┬──────Jan──────┬──────Feb──────┐
   1    ║           │  Garfield  │  Man       │    26690.63   │    21180.44   │
   2    ║           │  Marcias   │  Jose      │    29430.85   │    12808.81   │
   3    ║           │  Costa     │  Diane     │    19940.31   │    20280.62   │
   4    ║           │  Sayeed    │  Farouk    │    18890.82   │    20280.62   │
   5    ║           │  Bentley   │  Victoria  │    13780.85   │    10541.65   │
   6    ║           │  Mordo     │  Karl      │     6995.9    │     8301.1    │
```

Figure 8.6: The structure of a table of sales records.

```
J [F6] to include a field in the ANSWER; [F5] to give an Example    Main
═══════════════Sales ID═══════════════╤═══════Last name═══════╤═══════First name═══
  calc (a+b+c+d+e+f)/6 as Monthly Avg. │ J                     │ J

ANSWER┬─────────Last name─────────┬─────────First name─────────┬──Monthly Avg.──┐
   1  ║  Bentley                  │  Victoria                  │    18971.9     │
   2  ║  Costa                    │  Diane                     │    21839.92    │
   3  ║  Garfield                 │  Man                       │    24448.67    │
   4  ║  Marcias                  │  Jose                      │    20761.28    │
   5  ║  Mordo                    │  Karl                      │    15720.36    │
   6  ║  Sayeed                   │  Farouk                    │    21665       │
```

Figure 8.7: Calculating the average of several fields.

163

Concatenating Alphanumeric Fields

Suppose you want to print a series of mailing labels, or create a file to use in a mail-merge with a form letter in your word processor. The data in the Rolodex table can be used to create four-line, name-and-address labels. Press Alt-F8 to clear the workspace, and get a new Rolodex query table. (By now, the old one is so out of kilter that you need a fresh start.)

You'll need five example elements. Remember, to distinguish an example element from a search criterion, you press F5 before entering the example element. Enter the following example elements in the specified fields:

First name	a
Last name	b
City	c
State	s
Zip code	z

Remember, the actual content of the example element can be completely arbitrary. I've used *c*, *s*, and *z* simply for mnemonic purposes.

Place Checkmarks (F6) in the Address 1 and Address 2 fields. Now you're ready for the hard part.

 When a calculation produces a new field, you can place the calculation in any field in the query table.

In the Company field, type

calc (space)	To ask Paradox to calculate a new value.
F5	To enter an example element.
a	To refer to the First name field.
+ " "+	To add the space character (represented by a space between two quotation marks) to the First name.
F5	To enter another example element.
b	To refer to the Last name field.
as Name	To give the new field a new name.

This tells Paradox to create a new field called "Name," containing the value from the First name field, followed by a space, followed by the value from the Last name field.

Now, in the Company field, you're going to create a single field for the City, State, and Zip code. It's a bit hard to describe all the steps, but if you remember that the inverse video represents example elements entered with F5, you can copy the entry from Figure 8.8. Notice that the comma to separate City and State appears *within* the quotation marks. Otherwise it would be interpreted as a separator between two search conditions.

> ▶ Use quotation marks to surround a value entered in a
> search condition whenever the value you're searching for
> contains a character or command that would otherwise be
> interpreted as a command by Paradox. To search for someone
> with the last name of *Blank*, for example, you could type **"Blank"**
> into the Last name field, so Paradox won't search for blank
> records. Similarly, to search the Rolodex table for *Coati del
> Mundi, Ltd.*, you'd have to enclose the search criterion in
> quotation marks in order to include the comma.

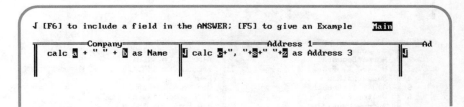

Figure 8.8: Concatenating Alphanumeric fields.

When you press F2, the "DO-IT!" key, Paradox combines the
values as you requested, placing them into the fields you named, as
shown in Figure 8.9. You'll have to rotate the fields to get them into the
right order for printing labels, but you already know how to do that.
Again, the values in your original table are not affected by this procedure.

Additional Calculation Operators

Paradox includes several additional calculation operators that are
beyond the scope of this book. The calculation operators are summarized below:

+	Add or concatenate the values on each side
–	Subtract
*	Multiply
/	Divide
( )	Group items in an expression
count	Display the number of values in a field

sum	Display a total of the values in a field
average	Display an average of values in a field
max	Display the highest value in a field
min	Display the lowest value in a field
all	Include all values in the result
unique	Include only unique values in the result

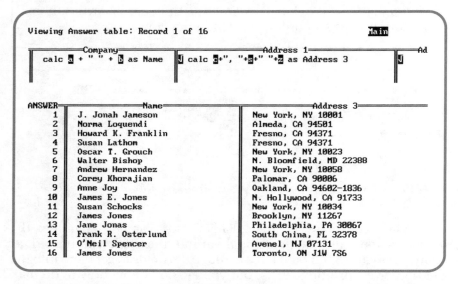

Figure 8.9: The result of concatenating Alphanumeric fields.

Changing Data Using Queries

What You Will Learn

▶ Finding Specific Records
▶ Deleting Groups of Records
▶ Adding Groups of Records
▶ Changing Values in Groups of Records

You now know how to use queries to find information in your databases, and how to calculate new values based on those contained in the databases. However, you can also use queries to add, change, and delete records—three of the most fundamental processes of database management. In this chapter, you'll learn how to use the editing operators to accomplish these tasks.

Several of the techniques you'll learn in this chapter use a different method of constructing queries: placing commands in the leftmost column. As you become more familiar with Paradox, you'll find that many advanced operations—queries involving *groups* or *sets* of records, for example, use a similar technique. (Operations of this type are beyond the scope of this book.)

Finding Specific Values

The simplest of these operations is finding a specific record. You've already seen how to find a value in a field with the "Zoom key," or with the Image/Zoom command. The *find* operator is a somewhat more sophisticated version of the same thing. To display a query form, type the word

```
find
```

in the leftmost column, beneath the table name, and type the values to find in any fields you wish to specify.

The *find* operator differs from a normal query in that, instead of placing the matches into an ANSWER table, it brings the source table to the workspace, and highlights the record number of the first matching record. This is the easiest way to find a record you want to edit in a large table.

The advantage of this method over using the "Zoom" key is that you can specify a value in more than one field at a time. For example, you know that you have more than one Susan, and more than one entry for Sky High Technologies. To find the record containing both values, set up the query as shown in Figure 9.1 and press F2, the "DO-IT!" key. Paradox displays the Rolodex table, briefly highlights record number 12 (Susan Lathom, of Sky High Technologies), and leaves you in View mode. You can now press F7, "Form Toggle," to view the record in a form, and press F9, "Edit," to make any needed changes.

Deleting Records with a Query

Now that you've tried out one editing operator, let's try something just a little more dangerous. Don't worry—there's a way to back out. You can delete records matching any criteria you can specify by entering the criteria, and placing the *delete* operator in the leftmost column. You specify the search criteria exactly the same way you would when you want to *find* information.

168

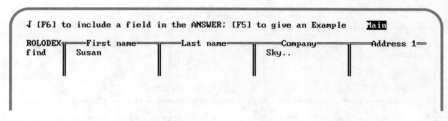

Figure 9.1: A find query.

This technique is especially useful for deleting records with dates earlier than a certain date. For example, you may want to drop customers from your mailing list who haven't placed an order in two years. To delete their records, create a query form for the appropriate database, type the word

```
delete
```

in the leftmost column, and type the value

```
<= today - 730
```

in the Last order column. (The number *730* represents two 365-day years.)

To see the effects of the *delete* command, delete all the records of people from New York from the Rolodex table. Get a query form, and type

```
delete
```

in the leftmost column. Now type

```
NY
```

in the State column, and press F2, the "DO-IT!" key. As you can see in Figure 9.2, the deleted records are not spirited off into limbo, but are stored in a new temporary table called DELETED. If you look at the Rolodex table now, you'll see that it has only 11 entries, instead of 16. The records in the DELETED table are truly gone from the source table.

169

```
√ [F6] to include a field in the ANSWER; [F5] to give an Example      Main

ROLODEX════════╤══════Last name═══════╤═══════First name═══════╤════════State═══════╤═══════Zip c
delete         │                      │                        │    NY              │
               │                      │                        │                    │
               │                      │                        │                    │
               │                      │                        │                    │


DELETED══╤══════Last name══════╤══════First name══════╤══Phone number══╤═State═╤═Zip code
      1  ║  Grouch             ║  Oscar T.           ║  (212)555-0000  ║  NY   ║  10023
      2  ║  Hernandez          ║  Andrew             ║  (212)112-9009  ║  NY   ║  10058
      3  ║  Jameson            ║  J. Jonah           ║  (212)500-9000  ║  NY   ║  10001
      4  ║  Jones              ║  James              ║  (718)903-4912  ║  NY   ║  11267
      5  ║  Schocks            ║  Susan              ║  (212)555-1357  ║  NY   ║  10034
```

Figure 9.2: A delete query.

You can save the table of deleted records by giving it a new name with the **T**ools/**R**ename/**T**able command. You might want to do that with your hypothetical old customers, so you could get them back again if they placed a new order. Or, more significantly, when processing a day's orders or shipments, this is a step you could take toward storing the day's records in a history file. Chapter 10 demonstrates such a procedure.

Undoing a Delete Query

For now, let's get the deleted records back. Remember, you can add records from one table to another if their structures are the same. Since the DELETED table is taken directly from the Rolodex table, it has the same structure. As you may remember, the command to use is **T**ools/**M**ore/**A**dd. The source table is DELETED, and the target table is Rolodex. Add the records as **N**ewEntries rather than **U**pdates. (When you're replacing deleted records, you don't want to make changes to the existing records. With **N**ewEntries, the worst that can happen is that you'll have some key violations in a KEYVIOL table. With **U**pdates, you might actually replace some records in the target table.)

After you enter the name of the target table, it appears in the workspace. As you can see, you now have all 16 records again, and in their original order. As with most temporary tables, however, the DELETED table is not emptied by this procedure. If you wanted to do some further work with the deleted records, you could. It's safer, however, to edit your records in place than to delete them and reinsert them. If for some reason you have to exit from Paradox, or if the power goes off, your deleted records will be gone forever.

Adding Records with a Query

You've just reviewed how to add records from one table to another when their structures are the same. Paradox also allows you to add records from one table to another when their structures differ. The restriction, obviously, is that the table to which records are to be added must have appropriate fields for at least some of the data in the source table.

This is our first example of a multi-table query. To set up an *insert* query, you need *two* query forms—one for the source of the records to be inserted and one for the table in which you want them to appear. You have a perfect opportunity already on disk: You can add the people from the Rolodex table to the Customer database. Below is a comparison of the fields in the two tables.

Rolodex	**Customer**
	Cust.ID
Last name	Last name
First name	First name
Company	Company
	Department
Address 1	Street address
Address 2	Suite no. or P.O. box
City	City
State	State
Zip code	Zip or Postal code
	Country
Phone number	Phone number
Last contact	Initial order
	Credit limit

As you may recall, all the fields in the Rolodex table are Alphanumeric except Last contact, which is a Date. All the fields in the Customer table are also Alphanumeric, except for the Date field, Initial order; and the Numeric (formerly Currency) field, Credit limit. The Customer table has a few more fields than the Rolodex table, but there is an equivalent field in the Customer table for every field in the Rolodex table. (Last contact and Initial order aren't really equivalent logically, but they are both Date-type fields. Thus, for this exercise you can pretend that they are equivalent.)

Filling Out the Query Forms

To complete this procedure, you need to create a relationship between the fields in your source table and the fields in the target table into which the data should be placed. To do so, use example elements. Remember, example elements merely indicate the data in a field generically—they do not stand for any particular values. Also, they can be completely arbitrary, although they need not be.

Start by getting a query form for the Rolodex table. Place the following example elements into the following fields (press F5 before typing each example element):

Field	Example Element
First name	a
Last name	b
Company	c
Address 1	d
Address 2	e
City	f
State	s
Zip code	z
Phone number	p
Last contact	date

Now get a query form for the Customer table. Type

```
insert
```

in the leftmost column.

 The *insert* command goes into the leftmost column of the *target* table.

Place the following example elements into the following fields. Leave the fields that have no example elements blank.

Field	Example Element
Cust. ID	
Last name	b
First name	a
Company	c
Department	
Street address	d
Suite no. or P.O. box	e
City	f
State	s
Zip or Postal code	z
Country	
Phone number	p
Initial order	date
Credit limit	

I can't show you the complete query tables, but the leftmost screen columns appear in Figure 9.3. If your example elements are not in inverse video, they *aren't* example elements. Paradox will try to treat them as search criteria and get very confused.

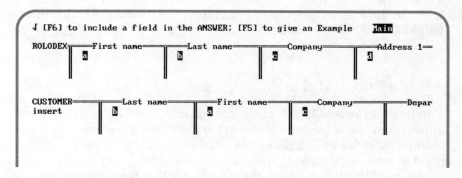

Figure 9.3: Setting up an insert query.

Notice the relationship of the example elements in the two tables. First name is the first field in the Rolodex table, and the second field in the Customer table. Both are indicated by the example element *a*. Similarly, both Last name fields are marked by the example element *b*. If you go down the list of example elements, you'll see that each one in the Rolodex table has an equivalent in the Customer table. This congruence tells Paradox into which fields to insert the data from the source table.

> ► When a given example element appears in fields in different tables, it creates a link between those tables, telling Paradox to treat the fields with the same example element as equivalent fields.

All set? Press F2, the "DO-IT!" key, and when Paradox finishes processing the query, you'll see a table called INSERTED, showing all the records you added, and their placement in the fields of the target table. A portion of the INSERTED table appears in Figure 9.4. However, if you now view the Customer table, you'll see that only one record has actually been added to that table. Why? Remember that the Cust. ID field is a key field. That means that every record must have a unique value in that field. Since the Rolodex table doesn't have an equivalent field, all the records to be inserted have a blank in that field. The Customer table can have only one such record. Thus it rejects all but one of the records.

In this instance, the INSERTED table is more or less equivalent to a KEYVIOL table. The only difference is that the one record that was actually inserted into the target table would not appear in a KEYVIOL table. In the following section, you'll treat the INSERTED table as you would treat a KEVIOL table.

Completing the Procedure

You'll need the additional customer records to set up the multi-table application you'll be developing in Chapter 10, so you have to get the records from the INSERTED table into the Customer table. It would be good to have department affiliations for everyone, and they'll have to have Credit limits. However, the only factor that *prevents* your adding the records is the fact that they don't have proper keys.

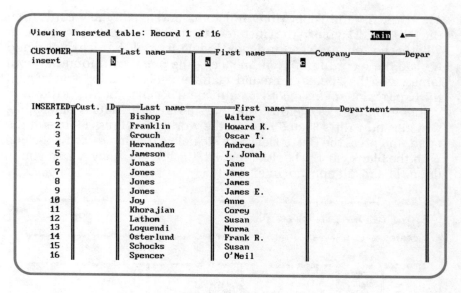

Figure 9.4: The results of an insert query.

To solve this problem, select the INSERTED table, and press F9 to edit it. Move to the Cust. ID field, and type

    00003

pressing the down-arrow key when you finish. You'll move down to the second record in the table. Type

    00004

Continue down the column, increasing the number by 1, until you reach record 16. The value in that record should be

    00018

Press, F2, the "DO-IT!" key when you're finished.

Now use the **Tools/More/Add** command to add the records from the INSERTED table to the Customer table. This time it doesn't matter whether you choose **NewEntries** or **Update**. It would be nice if you could update the record for O'Neil Spencer—the one record found in both tables, with the **Update** command. Unfortunately, Paradox won't regard the two versions of his record as equivalent because they have different values in the only key field. So the final step is to edit the Customer table, which is now the selected table in the workspace. Press F9 to edit the table, and press the Del or Delete key to delete the first record—the one with the blank Cust. ID field. Press F2, the "DO-IT!" key, when you're done. The result appears in Figure 9.5.

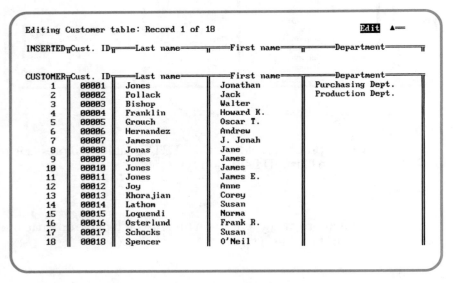

Figure 9.5: Adding the updated records.

Altering Values with a Query

The newly-expanded Customer table now has 18 records. (Granted, the Last call dates have been miraculously transformed into the dates of the new customers' first orders.) But the customers all need Credit limits as well. The *changeto* operator makes global changes in a field, so you can use it for the purpose.

Unlike the other editing operators, *changeto* is not placed in the leftmost column. In fact, *changeto* queries resemble normal search queries. However, in common with the other editing operators, *changeto* requires no checked fields. You'll perform several *changeto* operations before you're through, so you can taste the power of the *changeto* operator.

Making Global Changes

Let's assume that $2,000.00 is the company's minimum credit limit, and assign it to all the new customers. First, bring the Customer table to the workspace, so you can watch the changes as they occur. Next, get a query form for the Customer table. In the Credit limit field, type

```
blank, changeto 2000
```

This tells Paradox to place the value 2,000 into any record in which this field is blank. When the entry is correct, press F2, the "DO-IT!" key.

```
Use ↑ to decrease the table by one row; ↓ to increase by one row... ▓Main▓  ▲=▼
then press ↵ when finished.
CUSTOMER╥Cust. ID╥═══Last name═══╥═══First name═══╥═Credit limit═╥═Initial
   1 ║ 00001 ║ Jones      ║ Jonathan    ║    8400    ║  1/17/
   2 ║ 00002 ║ Pollack    ║ Jack        ║    2000    ║ 12/12/
   3 ║ 00003 ║ Bishop     ║ Walter      ║    2000    ║  6/19/
   4 ║ 00004 ║ Franklin   ║ Howard K.   ║    2000    ║  7/12/
   5 ║ 00005 ║ Grouch     ║ Oscar T.    ║    2000    ║  8/01/
   6 ║ 00006 ║ Hernandez  ║ Andrew      ║    2000    ║  6/03/
   7 ║ 00007 ║ Jameson    ║ J. Jonah    ║    2000    ║  7/07/
   8 ║ 00008 ║ Jonas      ║ Jane        ║    2000    ║  6/30/
   9 ║ 00009 ║ Jones      ║ James       ║    2000    ║  7/10/
  10 ║ 00010 ║ Jones      ║ James       ║    2000    ║  7/11/


CHANGED╥Cust. ID╥═══Last name═══╥═══First name═══╥═Credit limit═╥═Initial o
   1 ║ 00002 ║ Pollack    ║ Jack        ║            ║ 12/12/8
   2 ║ 00003 ║ Bishop     ║ Walter      ║            ║  6/19/8
   3 ║ 00004 ║ Franklin   ║ Howard K.   ║            ║  7/12/8
   4 ║ 00005 ║ Grouch     ║ Oscar T.    ║            ║  8/01/8
   5 ║ 00006 ║ Hernandez  ║ Andrew      ║            ║  6/03/8
   6 ║ 00007 ║ Jameson    ║ J. Jonah    ║            ║  7/07/8
   7 ║ 00008 ║ Jonas      ║ Jane        ║            ║  6/30/8
   8 ║ 00009 ║ Jones      ║ James       ║            ║  7/10/8
   9 ║ 00010 ║ Jones      ║ James       ║            ║  7/11/8
```

Figure 9.6: Globally changing the Credit limit.

A new, temporary table called CHANGED will appear with all the records that were originally in the Rolodex file. In Figure 9.6, I've displayed the Customer and CHANGED tables, with the table size changed with the **I**mage/**T**ableSize command and the fields rotated, so you can compare the two. As you can see, the records in the Customer table now have a Credit limit of $2,000.00. In the CHANGED table, the Credit limit field is still blank. When Paradox changes a value in a record, it saves the old version of the record in the CHANGED table. As with inserted and deleted records, this gives you a chance to edit the results, or to undo the change if you made a mistake.

Changing Values Based on Values in Another Field

The *changeto* operator can perform even more complex tasks. You know you have one record from Canada. But the Country field is blank for all the records you inserted. The form of a Canadian postal code is different from a Zip code. You can use that information to give the Canadian record its proper Country designation.

Delete the previous query from the query form. Now move to the Zip or Postal code field. Type the text

```
@@@ @@@
```

This is a wild-card pattern of any three characters, followed by a space, followed by any three characters. A postal code will match that pattern, but not a Zip code. Now, in the Country field, type

```
changeto Canada
```

You see the results in Figure 9.7.

You might want to use the command

```
USA, changeto blank
```

in the Country field as well to delete the two USA entries. Presumably, this business is in the United States, and you don't need to enter a value into this field for domestic orders. Repeat this command often to keep your records consistent if some of your order clerks generally fill in the country and others leave it blank.

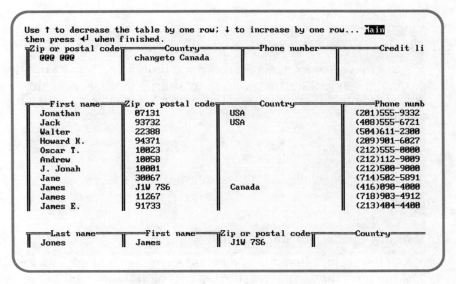

Figure 9.7: Changing values in a different field.

Processing Several Changes at Once

You can process several changes at once, using separate lines in your query form. Let's arbitrarily assume that customers who have been with the company for three months deserve a credit increase of 40 percent, and those who have been customers for two months deserve an increase of 20 percent. Select the customers by the values in their Initial order field. You'll have to set ranges of dates to look for, and use example elements to change the Credit limit. (Since you know the actual values, you could do a simple change such as

```
changeto 2800
```

but the following method will show you how to use example elements in a *changeto* query.)

On the first line in the Initial order field, type

```
< today - 30, > today - 60
```

This sets the range of dates for which you'll grant a 20 percent increase. Now on the next line in the same field, type

```
< today - 60, > today - 90
```

This formula selects the group for the 40 percent increase.

Now move to the first line of the Credit limit field. Press F5 to enter an example element. It can be anything (I used *limit*). Follow the example element with a comma and the *changeto* operator, so your entry looks like

```
limit, changeto
```

Type the example element again followed by * 1.20

```
limit * 1.20
```

to multiply the current value by 1.20.

On the second line, use a *different* example element (curr) and repeat the procedure, changing the last part of the command to * 1.40 so your entry looks like

```
curr, changeto curr * 1.40
```

(If you use the same example element on both lines, the query would affect the same values twice.) You can see both the proper form for the query and the result in Figure 9.8.

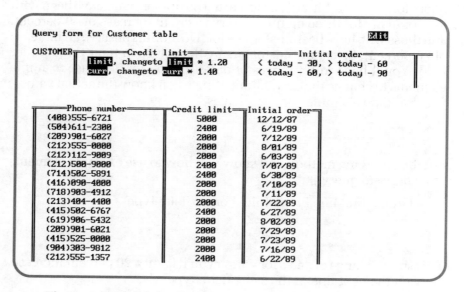

Figure 9.8: Multiple changes with example elements.

In these exercises, you've barely begun to tap the power of the Paradox editing commands. As your mastery of these commands increases, you will find many more ways to use them.

181

Chapter 10

Creating Relationships Between Tables

What You Will Learn

▶ Planning Applications Using Multiple Tables
▶ Dealing with Redundancy
▶ The Limits of Hierarchy
▶ Linking Related Tables

Up to now, you've been working with records in a single file. But the true power of Paradox lies in the ease with which it handles data organized into a group of related files. As you may remember from Chapter 1, Paradox is a *relational* database. Its remarkable quality is the ease with which it lets you link data in several related tables.

You've already gotten a small taste of working with several tables in completing an *insert* query. In this chapter, I'll present a multi-table order entry application. In ensuing chapters you'll see how Paradox's power makes this application work.

It takes both planning and experimentation to set up a multi-table application. Don't be surprised if it doesn't immediately work the way you want it to. However, the procedures, at least in the first stages, are the same as those for setting up a single-table application. Only the logic is different.

You have to approach your data from a different point of view. Ideally, you want as little redundancy as possible.

Therefore, the most important design principle is a simple one: *don't store an item of information in more than one place*. There's one very important exception to this principle, as you'll see. Also, the limitations of Paradox (yes, there are a few) sometimes make it impossible to follow this rule to the letter. You'll learn why, and what to do about it, later in this chapter.

In the following pages, I'll present the details of the application first, so you can see what's to be accomplished. After that, I'll explain how to set it up. Then I'll explain the theory behind the setup, and how Paradox handles an application of this type.

Why Use Multiple Tables?

First let's consider the practical situation. The goal is to have an automated, on-line, order-entry system which updates your inventory files and your billing files. It would also be helpful if your order clerks could check the inventory while ordering, to ensure that items are in stock, and that the item numbers are accurate.

The Application

We'll set up this application for a hypothetical mail-order office and computer supply company called SuperService Supply Co. We'll assume that all your customers use the same address for billing and shipping, and that all orders are on credit. These assumptions will simplify the application by reducing the number of variables you have to deal with.

Keeping separate files for billing and shipping addresses would be relatively little trouble. Both files would have the same structure. But it's easier to maintain one file than two.

Assuming that all orders are credit orders eliminates the problem of adding new customers to the database while taking a first order. However, once you understand how a multi-table application works, you can probably add the steps necessary to add these features.

What Information Do You Need?

Think about the items of information that should appear on the order form. Obviously, you'll want to have your company name and address, but that will be the same for all orders so you needn't worry about it. You'll want the customer's complete name and address for billing and shipping purposes. The header of your order should include:

► The order number
► The date
► Some way of identifying the salesperson
► The method of shipping requested by the customer

You'll need a series of detail lines, each of which shows:

► The catalog number of the item ordered
► A description of the item ordered
► The quantity of items ordered
► The unit price of the item
► The extension, or unit price multiplied by the quantity

In addition, you'll want some summary fields which would be calculated at the time of the order:

► Total cost of the items ordered
► Shipping charge
► Sales tax, if any
► Grand total

Assume that the shipping charge is included automatically so you don't have to think about it. The resulting order form might look like Figure 10.1.

What Database Fields Do You Need?

Now this information must be translated into database fields. The primary table will be called Orders. One might consider including all of the following fields. (I've grouped the fields conceptually, to make it easier to see the relationships among them.)

185

| ORDER NO: | DATE: | SOLD BY: | SHIP VIA: |

SuperService Supply Co.

1990 Avian Way
Bldg. 4
Palomar, CA 90006
(619) 906-5000   (800) 040-2143

Cust ID No.

SHIP TO: _____

Item No.	Quantity	Description	Price	Total
			Sub Total	
			Sales Tax	
			Total	

Figure 10.1: An order form.

Customer Information	Customer ID
	First name
	Last name
	Department
	Company
	Street address
	Suite no. or P.O. box
	City
	State
	Zip code
	Phone number (for informational purposes, in case of an error)
Order Information	Order Number
	Sold by
	Date
	Ship via

Detail Items	Item number
	Description
	Unit price
	Quantity sold
	Extension
Summary Items	Subtotal
	Sales tax
	Total

(You may recognize the customer information from the Customer table you've been working with.)

Now think about what this will do to your order table. If you had a table with all these fields, you'd have to include the complete customer information in *each* record, along with the detail items for every item ordered. There are several things wrong with that picture:

▶ It violates the first principle: data for each customer appears many times in the same table.

▶ The resulting file will be very large.

▶ You won't be able to calculate the summary items, because each record will include the information on only one item purchased.

187

The solution is a series of linked tables. One, which you already have, contains the customer information. Another contains the items unique to each order: the combination of order number, date, salesperson, and shipping method. A third holds all the detail items.

Now where do you put the summary information? It might go into the order file. However, Paradox can calculate these items for you whenever you need them. Moreover, your data is more likely to be current if you calculate these items as needed.

So how do you get the information from the Customer table into the order? And how do you look up items in the inventory? More to the point, how will anyone know which detail lines belong to which order? The ideal solution appears in Figure 10.2. Unfortunately, as you'll learn, you can't implement this ideal solution, and must modify it somewhat.

In the figure, the links are indicated by lines connecting a field in one table to a field in another. You'll notice that each table has one field in common with a table to which it's linked. (Shaded fields are key fields.)

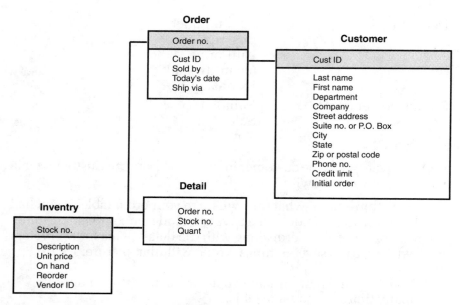

Figure 10.2: Four linked tables for an order-entry application.

Limiting Redundancy

Think for a moment about the logic of this arrangement. The Orders table is your master table. It contains a duplicate of the Cust. ID field from the Customer table. Remember, you set up the Customer table so that this field was unique (which it must be if it's a key field) and arbitrary. Thus, the unique Cust. ID number can appear in only one customer's record in the Customer table. By having access to this single item, Paradox can pull in all the information you need about a given customer, because Paradox will know which record to look for.

Similarly, the Detail table is linked to the Inventry table by means of the Stock no. field. Again, this is a unique and arbitrary item. As you can see, it's a key field in the Inventry table. Once you have the stock number, you can quickly find out the correct description, the price, and the number of items on hand, because Paradox uses that item to find the correct record.

Finally, records in the Detail table are linked to the order to which they refer by the Order no. field. Notice that this is a key field in the master table, but not in the Detail table.

A record in the Detail table contains only three items. In fact, the only unique item in the Detail table is the quantity ordered. Thus, the Detail table serves as a link between the Orders table and the Inventry table.

But won't you run into a problem because you've stored the Order no., Stock no., and Cust. ID in two places each? No, because you've repeated only enough information to find all the items you need. These are the fields that link the tables.

Setting Up the Tables

Now that you know what you're trying to accomplish, it's time to set up the tables. You already have the Customer table, so you needn't concern yourself about it. The next major table is the inventory table, which we'll call Inventry. It should have the following structure:

Field Name	Field Type
Stock no.	A8*
Vendor ID	A5
Description	A40
Unit price	$
On hand	N
Reorder	N

When you're done, press F2.

Press F10, select the **M**odify/**E**dit command, and select the Inventry table, so you can enter information for the table. Figure 10.3 shows a set of sample records to enter into this table.

In these records, the Stock no. field contains a five-digit number preceded by a two-letter department code. You can simplify entering the stock numbers by placing this picture into the Stock no. field with the **V**al**C**heck/**D**efine/**P**icture command:

```
&&-#####
```

Then you won't have to capitalize the letters. Format the On hand and Reorder fields with the **I**mage/**F**ormat command to eliminate the decimal places since you won't need them.

190

3/12/91	Standard Inventory Report		Page	1	
Stock no.	Vendor ID	Description	Unit price	On hand	Reorder
CF-10023	10234	Printer stand 14" w. fan	489.95	37	12
CF-10024	10234	Printer stand 12" w. fan	439.95	16	10
CF-10025	10234	Printer stand 14"	439.95	12	8
CF-10026	10234	Printer stand 12"	389.95	9	8
CF-12874	10234	Printer acousitic cover 14" tractor	329.95	28	12
CF-12875	10234	Printer acoustic cover 12" tractor	299.95	11	12
CF-12876	10234	Printer acoustic cover 12" short	279.95	18	12
CF-12877	10234	Printer acoustic cover 14" short	299.95	19	12
CO-25437	10005	NoName 286-12 base unit	679.95	106	50
CO-25442	10005	NoName 286-16 w. cache base unit	799.95	26	12
CO-25443	10005	NoName 386SX-16 base unit	949.95	34	36
CO-25444	10005	NoName 386-25 w. cache base unit	1,399.95	11	24
CO-25445	10005	NoName 386-33 w. cache base unit	1,399.95	39	24
CO-29812	10005	EZPort 286SX notebook w. 40mb H.D. VGA	2,699.95	37	24
CO-29813	10005	EZPort 286-12 notebook w. 20mb H.D. VGA	2,299.95	42	23
CP-30893	10005	Perfect Printer 24-pin DM wide carriage	469.95	15	8
CP-30894	10005	Perfect Printer 9-pin DM wide carriage	299.95	17	11
CP-30897	10005	Perfect Printer 9-pin DM std carriage	249.95	28	12
CS-10211	10005	5 1/4" DSDD Diskettes Premium (10)	10.50	880	800
CS-10212	10005	5 1/4" DSHD Diskettes Standard (10)	12.50	446	500
CS-10213	10005	5 1/4" DSHD Diskettes Premium (10)	15.89	963	300
CS-10214	10005	3 1/2" DSDD Diskettes Standard (10)	10.50	1820	800
CS-10215	10005	3 1/2" DSDD Diskettes Premium (10)	12.50	619	500
CS-10216	10005	3 1/2" DSHD Diskettes Standard (10)	14.98	576	300
CS-10217	10005	3 1/2" DSHD Diskettes Premium (10)	17.98	724	290
CS-23101	10005	5 1/4" diskette labels (100)	1.39	826	194
CS-23102	10005	3 1/2" diskette labels (100)	2.49	647	200
PP-79863	10222	Roller Pens Fine Red	.89	18974	14400
PP-79864	10222	Roller Pens Fine Blue	.89	16713	14400
PP-79865	10222	Roller Pens Fine Green	.89	9072	7194
PP-79866	10222	Roller Pens Fine Brown	.89	9078	7200
PP-79867	10222	Roller Pens Fine Turquoise	.89	12339	7194
PP-79868	10222	Roller Pens Fine Black (12)	9.49	1124	1188
PP-79869	10222	Roller Pens Fine Red (12)	9.49	1543	1200
PP-79870	10222	Roller Pens Fine Blue (12)	9.49	1298	1200
PP-79871	10222	Roller Pens Fine Green (12)	9.49	1233	600
ST-20381	10222	Legal pads yellow 14"	1.69	6902	7200
ST-20382	10222	Legal pads yellow 11"	1.39	7881	7190
ST-21919	10222	Fine folders 1/3 cut letter gross	21.99	420	143
ST-21920	10222	Fine folders 1/3 cut legal gross	24.99	385	144
ST-23121	10222	Mailing envelopes tyvec 9x12 (12)	6.29	235	144
ST-23122	10222	Mailing envelopes tyvec 10x12 (12)	6.59	299	132
ST-23123	10222	Mailing envelopes tyvec 12x14 (12)	6.99	120	144
ST-38274	10222	Binder 8.5" x 11" x 2"	4.39	1918	1434
ST-38275	10222	Binder 8.5" x 11" x 1.5"	3.39	1870	1440
ST-38276	10222	Binder 8.5" x 11" x 1"	2.39	1683	1440

Figure 10.3: A sample inventory database.

Note that Stock no. is a key field, and that, following the principles established earlier in this book, the values are arbitrary and unique. The only nonarbitrary part of the stock number is the department code. The five-digit numbers are assigned sequentially within each department.

You may wonder about the Vendor ID field. We'll actually be creating one more table—a table of wholesalers and distributors from whom you get your equipment. We'll use this table to demonstrate some important principles of report design in Chapter 12.

The Orders table is also relatively simple to set up. However, it violates a rule you learned earlier. I'll explain the reasons for this in a moment. Create this table with the following structure:

Field Name	Field Type
Order no.	N*
Cust. ID	A5
Sold by	A3
Today's date	D
Ship via	A9

191

Press F2 to save the structure. Notice that the key field is a Numeric, not an Alphanumeric field. Earlier, I suggested that you use numbers *only* when arithmetic operations would be performed on the values in a field. Since the key value is arbitrary and fixed, why use a number? In Chapter 13, I'll show you a simple script that will increment the value automatically each time you fill out an order. In Chapter 11, you'll add validity checks to this field to ensure that the numbers conform to a standard format.

For now, select the **M**odify/**D**ataEntry command for the new Orders table. Enter information for at least three orders in the following form:

Order no.	Cust. ID	Sold by	Today's date	Ship via
100002	00002	104	8/13/89	Ground
100003	00005	118	8/13/89	Air
100004	00006	103	8/14/89	Express

Press F2 when you're done.

How Paradox Handles Hierarchy

Now you've reached the point where you must violate the cardinal rule. As noted, ideally, the Detail table should have only three fields, and would provide the link to the Inventry table. Unfortunately, Paradox permits only one level of hierarchy. That is, you can link one table to another, but you can't link a third to the second. Therefore, you need some other way of getting the information from the Inventry table into your order form.

The solution is to add fields to a Detail table. This table will contain a list of inventory items included in every order. To create the Detail table, select the **Create** command, type

```
detail
```

and press Enter. Now press:

F10	To display the **Create** menu.
B ↵	To choose the **Borrow** command and display the list of tables.
O	To select the Orders table.
↓	To move to the second line.
Del or Delete (4 times)	To delete all fields except Order no.
F10	To display the **Create** menu.
B ↵	To choose the **Borrow** command and display the list of tables.
I	To select the Inventry table.
↓ (2 times)	To move to the third field.
Del or Delete (once)	To delete the Vendor ID field.
↓ (2 times)	To move down two fields.
Del or Delete (2 times)	To delete extraneous fields.

Now, you need to insert a field that's unique to the Detail table: the Quant field. Move up to the Description field, and press Ins or the Insert key to create a field. Type Quant for the field name and N for the field type. When you're done, press F2 to save the Detail table. The Detail table should now have the following structure:

Field Name	Field Type
Order no.	N*
Stock no.	A8*

```
Quant          N
Description     A40
Unit price      $
```

Note that, unlike an ideal Detail table, which has no key fields, the real one has two key fields. This is another aspect of how Paradox handles hierarchy. When you link tables, one table is always the master table, and the others are subordinate tables. If you've planned your application correctly, the relationship will be such that you may have many records in the subordinate tables linked to a single record in the master table. (This, in database parlance, is a *one-to-many* relationship.) In order to establish such a relationship, Paradox *requires* that the linking fields in the subordinate tables be key fields. Since the link is established on Order no., this must be a key field. However, if it were the *only* key field, you could have only one detail line for each master record in the Orders table—other records with the same order number would be key violations. Therefore, the Stock no. field is a second key, allowing all detail records to be linked to the single master form.

Now that you have a Detail table in place, press F10, select the **M**odify/**D**ataEntry command, and select the Detail table, so you can type a few entries in the table. Type the following entries, so you'll have something to work with later. Make sure the order numbers match the order numbers you entered in the Orders table:

Order no.	Stock no.	Quant	Description	Unit price
100002	CS-10211	10	5 1/4" DSDD Diskettes	10.50
100002	CS-10217	10	3 1/2" DSHD Diskettes	17.98
100003	PP-79863	5	Roller Pens Fine Red	.89
100004	ST-23122	12	Mailing envelopes tyvec	6.59

Press F2 when you're done. You'll learn an easier way to enter this inventory information later.

You have one more table to create—The Vendors table. You won't need to fill this one in completely. Use the **C**reate command to get a STRUCTure table. Press F10 and use the **B**orrow command to borrow the structure of the Customer table. Change the name of the Cust. ID field to Vendor ID, and delete the Last name and First name fields. Move to the bottom and delete the Credit limit and Initial order fields. Your new table will have the following structure:

Field Name	Field Type
Vendor ID	A5*
Department	A20
Company	A30
Street address	A30
Suite no. or P.O. box	A20
City	A20
State	A2
Zip or postal code	A10
Country	A21
Phone number	A22

Press F2, the **DO-IT!** key, to create this table. Now bring the Vendors table back to the workspace with the **M**odify/**R**estructure command. Move down to the second row, and press the Ins or Insert key. Type

```
Company
```

in the blank line. Paradox will reverse the positions of the Company and Department fields. (This doesn't work when you're creating a table, only when you're restructuring one.) Press F2 again, to save the change.

We won't need most of the information that should go into this table, so we'll just create parts of a few records. Bring the table to the workspace, press F9, and enter the following data in the Vendor ID and Company fields, pressing the ↓ key after you type each company name:

```
10005     Micro Services Plus
10222     Sams Stationery Supplies
10234     Great Office Furniture
```

Press F2 when you're finished, and forget about this table until Chapter 12.

Establishing the Links

How does Paradox know that the tables are supposed to be linked? It doesn't. In fact, you establish the links either through forms, through reports, or through queries.

Linking with a Query

As you might guess from Chapter 9, one way you can link the tables is to set up a query with example elements linking the tables. For example, set up a query such as the one shown in Figure 10.4. This query will generate a table containing all the information that makes up an order.

Use the **S**cripts/**Q**uerySave command to save the query as Mastordr.

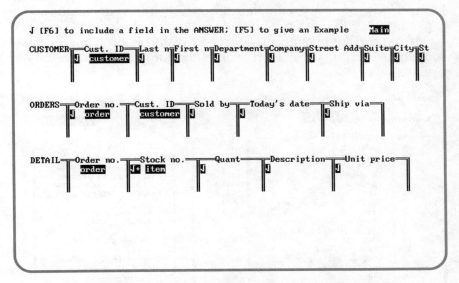

Figure 10.4: A query to bring order information together.

Study this query carefully. (Assume that all fields in the Customer table except the Credit limit and Initial order fields have a Checkmark.) Notice that the linking fields each have an example element. The example element *customer* links the Cust. ID field in the Customer table with the same field in the Orders table. Notice also that only one of the two Cust. ID fields has a Checkmark. If they both had Checkmarks, there would be two Cust. ID fields in the ANSWER table. Similarly, the two Order no. fields are linked by the example element *order*. Again, only one is checked. The "Check Plus" in the Stock no. field of the Detail table ensures that every detail line for a given order will appear in the final table.

In Figure 10.5, you'll see that the ANSWER table has fields for all the items in the order form except for the summaries. Keep in mind that the ANSWER table is temporary. To save your work, execute the **T**ools/**R**ename/**T**able command to rename the ANSWER table (call it Mastordr).

The next time you need to generate an invoice for an order, use the Mastordr query to generate the appropriate ANSWER table. Next, execute the **T**ools/**C**opy/**R**eport command to copy the report to the ANSWER table. Finally, execute the **R**eport/**O**utput/**P**rinter command to print the report. That way, you always have a copy of the report available.

However, there's still a problem. In fact, it's the same problem you started with. *Every record would have complete customer information.* Moreover, you'd have to complete the order by filling in records in two separate tables, the Orders table and the Detail table. In addition, you'd have to repeat the Order no. in each record of the Detail table. Obviously something's wrong here! Aren't computers supposed to *increase* our productivity?

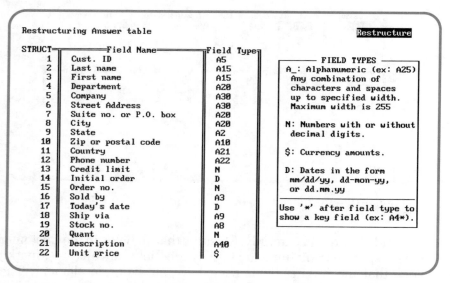

Figure 10.5: The structure of the ANSWER table.

Linking with Forms and Reports

The proper procedure is to create forms and reports which link the various tables. Paradox can embed one table within another in a custom-designed form. In Chapter 11, you'll learn the techniques for creating a custom form. In addition, if the two tables are linked via a common field, you can use a form to enter information into both tables at once. You'll see in Chapter 11 how to create a form that will function as an order-entry tool.

The printed version of the invoice will be produced as a report, which you'll learn about in Chapter 12. In Chapter 12, you'll learn how to create a custom report, and you'll see what such a report looks like. You'll use the report to link the tables for preparing the invoice.

In Chapter 13, you'll create a script to take an order using a multi-table form, update the tables which actually store the information, and print an invoice that includes the summary information.

Before we proceed, however, consider the larger business situation into which this little four-table application fits. Obviously, the final orders must go to the Accounts Receivable Department for billing. The items ordered must be subtracted from the inventory. In turn, the Purchasing Department needs the latest inventory figures to maintain the stock. The Accounts Payable Department will need the information from the purchase orders generated by the Purchasing Department. The Shipping Department will need copies of the completed orders—minus pricing information—to pack and ship the orders.

Figure 10.6 shows how the information needed for all these functions can be stored nonredundantly in a relatively small number of tables. (The Shipping Department isn't shown because the information it receives duplicates information found throughout the system.)

Each box represents a single database table. The three fields indicated by arrows are actually calculated fields, which are derived from the items in the detail tables. I've included them in the diagram so you can see where the information comes from.

The diagram is still not complete. Presumably, the data in the Orders, order detail (Detail), purchase orders (PO), and purchase order detail (PODetl) tables are moved periodically to history files, to prevent updating the inventory with the same information more than once. The last two fields in the Customer database—Credit limit and Initial order—no longer appear in the Customer file. That information is now stored in a file accessible only to the Accounting Department. (Assume that if customers order more than their credit limit allows, the Credit Department will cancel the order. It might be better if the order clerks could do so, but it complicates the picture.)

If you study the diagram carefully, you'll see how it embodies the cardinal rule. Moreover, if you follow the connecting lines, you'll see how all the information needed for any function is available through linking fields.

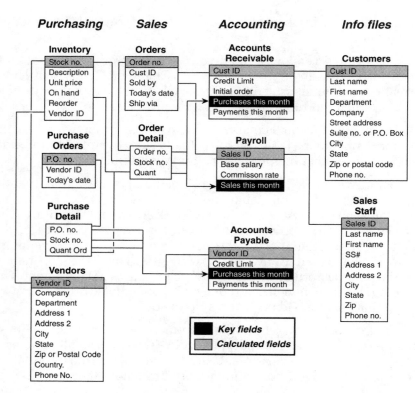

Purchasing   **Sales**   **Accounting**   **Info files**

198

Figure 10.6: The flow of information through a database application.

Creating and Using Forms

What You Will Learn

▶ Designing and Changing Forms
▶ Linking Tables Using Forms
▶ Looking Up Values in Related Tables

You've already been introduced to forms. As you may remember, you can create a default form for any table by pressing F7, the "Form Toggle" key. A form gives you another view of your data. It allows you to view a record at a time, and to see all the fields in a given record at once (if they all fit on one screen).

However, with proper planning, forms can do a great deal more. If they are set up effectively, forms are especially helpful for both viewing and entering data. In addition, as you just learned, properly structured forms can allow you to enter data into several tables at once—or to view data in linked tables. In this chapter, you'll learn the basics of creating custom forms. Then you'll create and use multitable forms to link the tables in the order-entry application you began in Chapter 10.

Designing A New Form

The procedure for creating a form is fairly simple. At each stage, the legend at the top of the screen guides you through the necessary steps.

When you select the Forms command, you are given two options:

▶ Design a new form
▶ Change an existing form

Since you don't have any forms yet, press **D** to design a new form. You'll be asked to select a table with which the form should be associated. Select a table in the usual manner. We'll begin with a simple form for viewing the Rolodex table.

Having selected the table, you'll see a peculiar-looking menu such as the one shown in Figure 11.1. As you may remember, you can have up to 15 different forms for each table. By default, Form F is the standard form created by the "Form Toggle" key, F7. Each of the numbers represents a potential form. Choose 1 and press Enter. You'll then be prompted with

```
Form description:
Enter description for the new form.
```

Type

```
Rolodex viewing form
```

and press Enter. You'll then be presented with a nearly blank screen, as Figure 11.2 shows. The numbers shown as

```
<1, 1>
```

show the current cursor position—at the upper-left corner of the workspace. The first figure represents the row, and the second figure represents the column. The numbers shown as

```
1/1
```

at the upper-right corner indicate that you're on the first page of a form that so far includes only one page. Press F10, and you'll see the Form mode menu, shown in Figure 11.3.

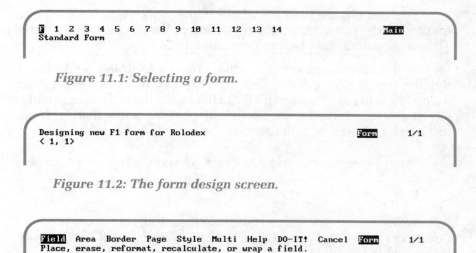

Figure 11.1: Selecting a form.

Figure 11.2: The form design screen.

Figure 11.3: The Form mode menu.

201

Placing the Fields

As you can see from the legend, you use the `Field` command to place fields on the form, to move them around, or to change their characteristics. You can place a field anywhere on the screen. Since the `Field` command is highlighted, press Enter. Press Enter again to `Place` a field. You will then be asked to choose the type of field:

`Regular`	A field that you can alter when you're in any editing or data-entry mode.
`DisplayOnly`	A field that you can look at but not alter.
`Calculated`	A field that shows the results of a calculation, similar to the calculations used with the *calc* operator in a query.
`Record`	A field that displays the number of the current record.

Every form *must* have at least one `Regular` field. Since this form is primarily for *viewing* records, make all the fields `DisplayOnly` except the Last call field. This is a form you can use when making your calls. You'll use a separate form to add new records or make changes to existing records.

You can place a field anywhere in the workspace. You can also move a field—or any rectangular portion of the screen—at any time. Therefore, you needn't be too fussy initially.

In the following example, you'll create a form that looks like a Rolodex card. When you select `DisplayOnly` from the **F**ield/**P**lace **S**ubmenu, you are then shown a list of fields, similar to the lists of tables you've already worked with. Begin with the First name field (you can just press **F**). You'll be prompted to

```
Use ↑ ↓ ← → to move to where you want the field to
begin...
then press ↵ to place it...
```

Move the cursor to somewhere near the middle of the screen about three rows down, and press Enter. A series of dashes will appear—one for each character in the field—with a block cursor at the end. You are then prompted to

```
Now use → and ← to adjust the width of the field...
then press ↵ when finished.
```

This implies that the actual display field on the form can be smaller than the field width as defined in the STRUCTure table. When you're using a form with such fields, you can scroll with the cursor keys through fields whose contents appear to be truncated. You don't actually lose any data. For this form, there's no reason not to use the complete field, so just press Enter. The row of dashes changes to an underscore line.

If you think about it, this isn't very informative. There's nothing on the screen to tell you what that line is for. You can, however, type any text you want on your form. You might, for example, enter the name of each field, followed by the field marker.

This form, however, merely displays information, and most of it is self-explanatory. But, it would be nice if you could keep track of what you're doing. In fact, if you move the cursor to somewhere on the underscore line, you'll see the legend

```
DisplayOnly, First name
```

in the upper-right corner of your screen.

Take the following steps to place this information on your screen so that it will remain there until you finish designing the form. Press

F10	To display the **F**orm mode menu.
S	To select the **S**tyle submenu.
F	To select the **F**ieldnames command.
S	To **S**how the field names.

Now each field on the screen will have its name in the area designated for the field. These names will *not* appear in the actual form when you use it. They are only for your information while designing the form.

Keep placing the fields until your form looks like Figure 11.4. Remember, the Last contact field is a **R**egular, not a **D**isplayOnly field.

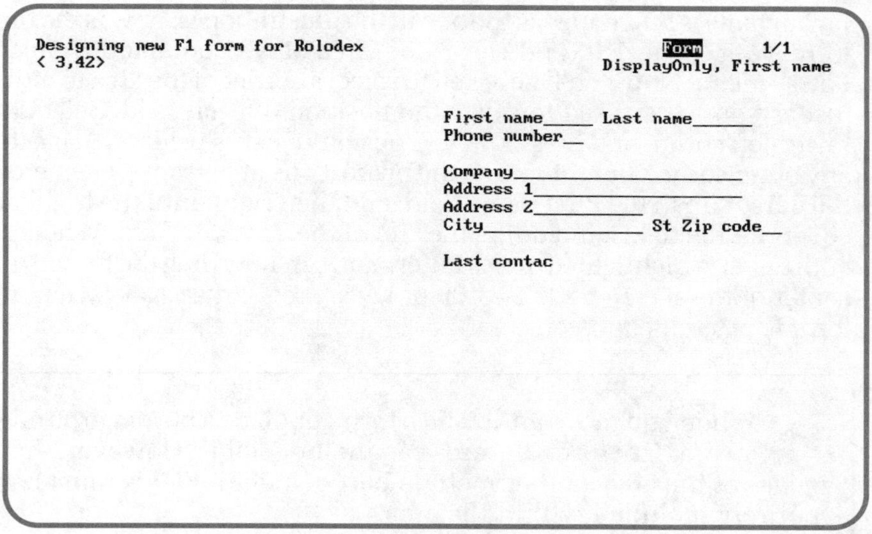

```
Designing new F1 form for Rolodex                        Form      1/1
< 3,42>                                              DisplayOnly, First name


                                     First name_____ Last name_____
                                     Phone number__

                                     Company_____
                                     Address 1_____
                                     Address 2_____
                                     City_____ St Zip code__

                                     Last contac
```

Figure 11.4: All the fields placed.

203

Placing a Field in a Form

1.	Move the cursor where you want the field to begin.	
2.	In the Forms Editor, press F10.	Paradox displays the Forms menu.
3.	Press **F**.	Paradox displays the **Fields** submenu.
4.	Press **P**.	Paradox gives you a choice of field types: Regular, DisplayOnly Calculated, and #Record.

5. Press the key corresponding to the first letter of the type of field you want to display. If you choose Calculated, type a calculation and press Enter.

Paradox displays a list of the fields in the table.

6. Select the field you want to place.

Paradox places the field in the form, beginning at the cursor location. ☐

Adding Refinements

If your table is off-center, as the one in the illustration is, now is the time to move it. Press F10 and select the **A**rea/**M**ove command from the **F**orms menu. Now you'll be asked to select a corner of the area to move, just as you were asked to select the position of each field. Select the lower-left corner and press Enter. (You could just as well have selected any other corner, but this one is the nearest one at present.) Then move the cursor up to the First name field, and then right until the highlight covers all the fields, including the end of the Zip code field. When the entire area is highlighted, press Enter. You can now drag the form to the center of the screen with the cursor keys. Press Enter again when the form is positioned to your liking.

> ▶ When you move an area in a form, or place a border around an area in a form, the area can include fields. However, the edges of the area cannot include part of a field. Fields must be entirely included within the area.

Now let's add a border. Press F10 and select the **B**order/**P**lace command from the Form menu. You can choose a **S**ingle-line, a **D**ouble-line, or **O**ther type of border. If you choose **O**ther, you'll be asked what character to use. Choose **S**ingle-line. You select the position of the border the same way you selected the area to move. Since the cursor is already at the upper-right corner of the form, just move it up and to the right one space, and press Enter. Now move the cursor left, and you'll see a line form above the form. Move the cursor down and the line will become a box. Keep moving the cursor until the box surrounds all the fields. Press Enter when you're done. The screen should look like Figure 11.5. Press F2, "DO-IT!," to save the completed form.

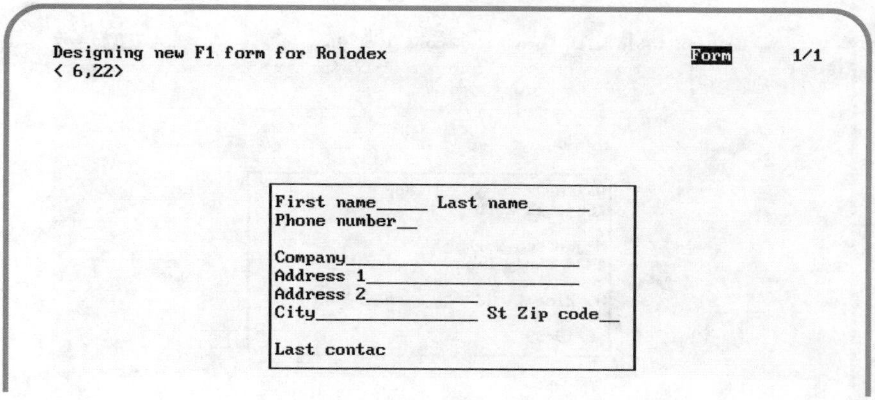

```
Designing new F1 form for Rolodex                    Form      1/1
< 6,22>



               First name_____  Last name_____
               Phone number__

               Company_____
               Address 1_____
               Address 2_____
               City_____  St Zip code__

               Last contac
```

Figure 11.5: A completed form.

Testing the Results

205

To try out the form, bring the Rolodex table to the workspace. As usual, it will appear in table view. Now press the "Form Toggle" key, F7. You should see the default form. Execute the **I**mage/**P**ickForm command to choose your new form. You should then see a list of forms consisting of

    F 1

When you move the cursor to 1, the legend

    Rolodex viewing form

which you typed as the description of your form, appears. Press Enter to select this form, and your screen should now look like Figure 11.6. Each time you press PgDn, another record appears. You can now browse through your on-screen Rolodex just as you would the paper version!

To make this the default form, execute the **I**mage/**K**eepSet command. Now, your Rolodex viewing form will be the default form the next time you use the Rolodex table.

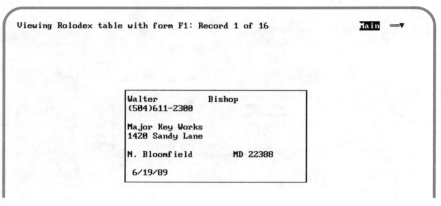

Figure 11.6: Viewing the table with the form.

Choosing a Default Form

1. If the menu is not visible, press F10 to display it.

2. Press **V** and then Enter.

   Paradox asks you for the name of a table to view.

3. Select the table for which you want to choose a form.

   Paradox places the table in the workspace.

4. Press F10 and then **I/P**.

   Paradox displays a list of form numbers.

5. Press → to move the cursor through the form numbers.

   As each form number is selected, Paradox displays the form title on the legend line.

6. When you see the title of the form you want to make the default, press Enter.

7. Press F10, and then **I/K**.

   Paradox records your selection. The form you selected will be the one you see when you press F7, the "Form Toggle" key, until you change the default again. □

But you could make the form better. That date at the bottom may not be entirely meaningful. And remember, you need the date for your *next* call, as well as for your last call. Make a couple of improvements.

Begin by executing the **F**orms/**C**hange command, and select the same table and form. As you'll see, the effects of the **S**tyle/**F**ieldnames/**S**how command were temporary. The field names no longer appear, so you'll have to re-enter that command to see what you're doing.

You'll need more room, so erase the border by executing the **B**order/**E**rase command. You erase the border the same way you placed it—move the cursor to a corner, press Enter, and then move the cursor to the opposite corner. Press Enter when you're done. Now use the **F**ield/**E**rase command to delete the Last contact field. In its place, type

```
Last contact:
```

Now one space after that, place the Last contact field as a `Regular` field again.

A Calculated Field

207

Next, you'll have Paradox tell you when to make your next call. Directly under what you just typed, type

```
Next call:
```

Move the cursor directly beneath the beginning of the Last contact field. Execute the **F**ield/**P**lace/**C**alculated command, and type the expression

```
[Last contact] + 30
```

and press Enter three times. In forms and reports, you perform calculations on the contents of a field by placing the field name in brackets, rather than by using example elements.

Thinking a bit further about what you've done, might it not be a good idea to change Phone number to a **R**egular field? If it were a **R**egular field, you could go into Edit mode and change the number if you suddenly found that the phone number of one of your contacts had changed. Make that change now, by executing the **F**ield/**E**rase command and then the **F**ield/**P**lace/**R**egular command. You'll find that once you remove a field, your cursor will be where the erased field began, so you'll be in position to enter it again.

Finally, redraw the border and press F2, "DO-IT!". The next time you use the "Form Toggle" key, F7, with the Rolodex form, your screen should look like Figure 11.7. The cursor will appear in the Phone number field or Last contact field, which are the two fields you can actually edit using this form.

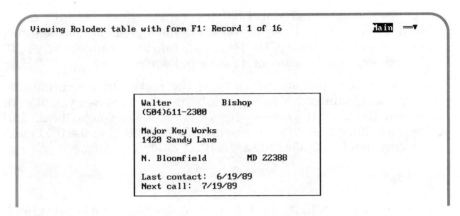

```
Viewing Rolodex table with form F1: Record 1 of 16          Main  ═▼

                        ┌──────────────────────────────┐
                        │ Walter        Bishop          │
                        │ (504)611-2300                 │
                        │                               │
                        │ Major Key Works               │
                        │ 1420 Sandy Lane               │
                        │                               │
                        │ N. Bloomfield      MD 22388   │
                        │                               │
                        │ Last contact:  6/19/89        │
                        │ Next call:  7/19/89           │
                        └──────────────────────────────┘
```

Figure 11.7: Viewing the table with the revised form.

208

Some Principles and Techniques of Form Design

You've just designed and modified a relatively simple form. You've tried at least one command on most of the submenus. But there are a few more things you should know about the Forms menu, and the way Paradox treats the form design screen, before you design more complex forms.

First, if you want someone to enter data into a form you created, you should give them explicit directions. You can add help information at the bottom of a screen, to direct the user, just by typing it on the form design screen.

Second, be aware of the way the Ins or Insert and Del or Delete keys work. In overtype mode (the default), the space bar moves the cursor, and deletes any text it passes over. (To delete fields, you must use either the Field/Erase or the Area/Erase commands.) If you press the Ins or Insert key, however, the space bar inserts space characters, moving anything on the line in front of the cursor—including fields—to the right. If you push text or fields to the right border, Paradox will honk and refuse to let you go further. The Del or Delete key deletes the character to the right of the cursor. (It, too, will move, but not delete, fields.) Thus, in insert mode, you can use the Ins or Insert and Del or Delete keys to adjust the position of both text and fields.

If there's not enough room for a field to the right of the cursor, Paradox will truncate it to fit. However, move the leftmost character of the field to the left with the Del or Delete key, and you can execute the **Field/R**eformat command to expand the field up to its defined width, provided there's room.

The cursor wraps around the edges of the screen. If you're at the right border, the right-arrow key takes you to the left border, and at the left border, the left-arrow key takes you to the right border. Similarly, at the top of the screen, the up-arrow key takes you to the bottom, and at the bottom of the border, the down-arrow takes you to the top of the screen. This is especially helpful when placing or moving areas or borders.

When you're editing—that is, not executing any of the menu commands—the Enter key simply moves the cursor to the beginning of the next line. It never has any other effect.

When a form has more than one page, at least one **R**egular field must appear on each page. **R**egular fields can appear only once in a form, but **D**isplayOnly fields can appear any number of times.

For reference, the cursor-movement keys in Form mode are summarized in Table 11.1.

Now that you know the basics of the Forms Editor, set up the form shown in Figure 11.8. Remember, in an entry form, all fields must be Regular fields. When you finish placing the text and the fields, we'll add some styling and help information to the form.

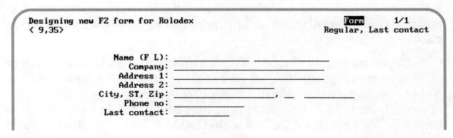

Figure 11.8: Setting up an entry form.

Adding Styling to a Form

As you may have noticed, the actual fields are not set off from the screen background in any way unless there is data in the field. We're going to add some styling to the form, so you can see exactly where to enter the data.

How you proceed depends in part on the type of monitor you have. The steps are slightly different for monochrome and color monitors. When you use a monochrome monitor, you can set up any part of the Forms screen so that it displays text using one of the following *attributes*:

▶ Normal
▶ High-intensity (called Intense)
▶ Inverse video (called Reverse)
▶ Both inverse video and high-intensity (called Intense-Reverse)

You can also make any part of the form blink, or remove blinking from an area that blinks. You choose a style by pressing the left- and right-arrow keys, pressing Enter when the name of the style you want appears in the upper-right corner of the screen.

210

With a color monitor, you pick a combination of foreground and background colors for an area from a palette that appears in the upper right corner of the screen. The eight possible background colors appear as horizontal stripes, with the 16 foreground colors as a series of small squares along each stripe. You choose a color combination by moving a cursor around the palette with the cursor keys.

The basic procedure is to select the area you want to style, and then select the attributes or colors for it. As you move through the choices, the selected area reflects the current attribute or color combination. Press Enter when the area looks as you want it to. (In monochrome, you add blinking to one of the other attributes by selecting the area a second time and choosing Blink).

Depending on the layout of the form, you can proceed in either of two ways: apply an attribute or color scheme to the entire area, and then go back and apply the default attribute to smaller portions of the area, or select each field in turn and apply the styling to it. In a form such as this one, where you want all the fields to have the same attributes and they are all close together, it's easiest to mark a rectangular area covering all the fields (the boundary of an area can't cross a field), and then change the attributes of the areas that shouldn't be included. If you want to use different attributes for different fields, or if the fields are widely separated on the form, it's better to style the fields one at a time.

Let's style the fields now. Move the cursor to the beginning of the First name field (not the text that indicates where it is). Press F10 and select the **S**tyle command. Select **C**olor or **M**onochrome, depending on the type of monitor you have. Now choose **A**rea. Press Enter to "anchor" one corner of the area. You'll be prompted to select an area with the cursor keys. Stretch the highlight so that it covers all the fields, plus one character beyond the Zip code field, and press Enter. At this point, the word Normal appears if you're using monochrome, or the palette appears if you're using color. If you're using monochrome, use the arrow keys to select Reverse. If you're using color, select any color combination that differs from the background. Press Enter when you've made the selection. Your screen should look like Figure 11.9.

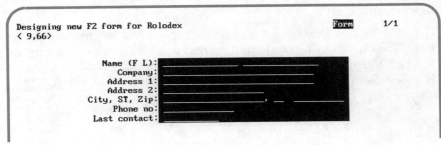

Figure 11.9: Adding styling to a form.

211

Now all the fields are highlighted, but some extraneous areas are highlighted as well. You'll remove the extraneous highlighting the same way you highlighted the entire area. When you're done, the screen should look like the central part of Figure 11.10.

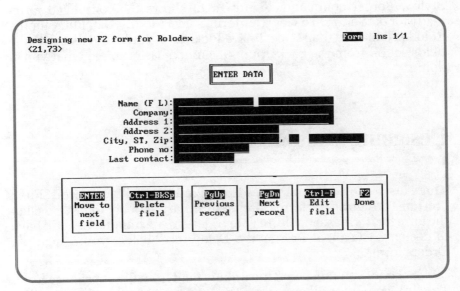

Figure 11.10: An entry form with styling and help information.

It's easiest to work with rectangular blocks, if possible. Move the cursor to the upper-right corner of the highlighted area, and execute the **S**tyle/.../**A**rea command again. Press Enter to anchor that corner, and move the cursor left so that it comes up to one space past the Last name field. Now stretch it downward three rows, and press Enter. The color or attribute you last used is still selected. If you're working with monochrome, change this area back to Normal. If you're working with color, change it back to the original default colors for the screen. Keep selecting areas and changing them back until your fields are highlighted as in Figure 11.10.

Notice that there's one highlighted space beyond the end of each field. The cursor will move to that space if you fill a field completely, and it's a bit less disconcerting to have that area marked in advance than it is to see the space change colors when the cursor moves to it.

Adding Help Information

Take another look at Figure 11.10. Notice that the form has a title and a group of keystroke guides. To enter this information, simply type it on the screen. To place the borders around the title and the various key help notes, use the **B**order/**P**lace command. To highlight the key names, use the **S**tyle/.../**A**rea command again. You can use styling on any area of the screen, not just on fields. You can even add styling to borders with the **S**tyle/.../**B**order command. Figure 11.11 shows the completed form, ready for data entry. To view this form, select **M**odify/**D**ataEntry for the Rolodex table and then select **I**mage/**P**ickForm. You'll find that with the fields set off from the background it's much easier to see what you're doing.

Designing Multi-Table Forms

There are some additional steps to designing multi-table forms. First, you *must* design all the forms for the subsidiary tables before you design the form for the master table. In your order-entry example, you will have to design a Customer form and a Detail form before you design the Orders form.

Second, you must *omit* the linking field from the subsidiary form. The linking fields will appear on the master form.

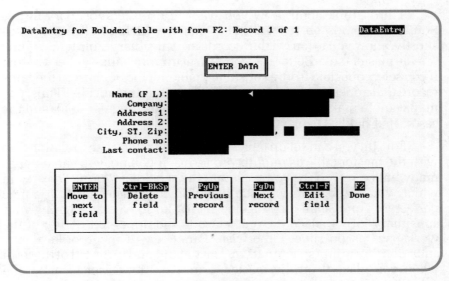

Figure 11.11: The completed data entry form.

Table 11.1: Cursor movement keys for designing forms.

Key	Effect
↑	Moves the cursor up a line; if the cursor is at the top of the screen, moves the cursor to the bottom of the screen.
↓	Moves the cursor down a line; if the cursor is at the bottom of the screen, moves the cursor to the top of the screen.
→	Moves the cursor right one column; if the cursor is at the right margin, moves the cursor to the left margin.
←	Moves the cursor left one column; if the cursor is at the left margin, moves the cursor to the right margin.
Backspace	Moves the cursor left one column, deleting the character to the left.
Del, Delete	Deletes the character to the right of the cursor.
Ins, Insert	Toggles between overtype (default) and insert mode.
Home	Moves the cursor to the top of the screen.
End	Moves the cursor to the bottom of the screen.
Ctrl-Home	Moves the cursor to the left margin on the current line.
Ctrl-End	Moves the cursor to the right margin on the current line.
Enter	Moves the cursor to the left margin on the next line.

Third, think about how you want to use the subsidiary forms. Some commands on the **ValCheck** menu, which you'll learn about shortly, allow you to look at the records in a subsidiary table while filling out the master table. Better yet, you can set up your validity check so that if you select one field from a subsidiary table, all the fields from the same record that appear in your form will be filled in automatically. Thus, you may want to make your principal lookup field a **R**egular field, and the associated fields, **D**isplayOnly fields.

Fourth, you can set up tables that have a one-to-many relationship with the master table as *multirecord* forms. If you do, you can enter as many linked records as you wish into the subsidiary form. The area in which you enter them will scroll within the master form. (Sounds perfect for your Detail records, doesn't it?) Fifth, when designing your subsidiary forms, place them as close to the upper-left corner of the workspace as possible. Otherwise, Paradox will incorporate in the subsidiary form any space that you leave above and to the left of the form when you place it on the master form. It's a lot easier to move the subsidiary form to an appropriate location when you don't have extra space to move around. These principles will become clearer as you work through the example.

Designing the Subsidiary Forms

First set up the subsidiary form for the Customer table shown in Figure 11.12. Choose **F**orms/**D**esign/**C**ustomer/**1**, and then type `Customer` as the form's name. Be sure to begin with the cursor in the upper-left corner. Follow the procedures you just learned for highlighting the entry form. Place all the fields as **R**egular fields. This allows you to make changes to a customer's address or phone number while taking an order, if necessary. Notice that the Cust. ID field is omitted. It will form the link to the Orders table.

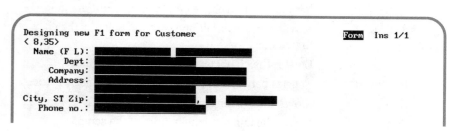

Figure 11.12: A simple subsidiary form.

Next, you'll set up the Detail form shown in Figure 11.13. This form requires a bit more explanation. As you can see, it's set up as though it were a table. Choose **F**orms/**D**esign/**D**etail/**1**, and then type `Detail` as the form's name. Type the field names where the column headings would appear, and then press Enter. To create the underline, select the **B**order/**P**lace/**S**ingleLine command. Press Enter to anchor one end of the line, press the left-arrow key three times, and press Enter again to draw the line.

```
Changing F1 form for Detail                                Form      1/1
< 4, 1>
Item no. Quant           Description              Price     Total

_____ ____  _____  _____  _____
```

Figure 11.13: Designing the Detail form.

Now place the fields. Below the Item no. heading, place the Stock no. field as a **R**egular field. This field is the link to the Inventry table. After it, leave a single space and place Quant as a **R**egular field as well. As you place the fields, adjust their widths to match the widths of the fields shown in Figure 11.13; otherwise, the form will be too wide. Leave another space, and place Description and Price as **D**isplayOnly fields with a space between them. They are DisplayOnly because your order clerks shouldn't alter anything in the Inventry table. Finally, leave another space, and create a Calculated field for Total, by entering the formula

```
[Quant]*[Unit price]
```

You can see this formula in the upper-right corner of the figure.

Next, create a *multi-record region* in this form. Again, move your cursor to the left edge of the screen, at the beginning of the Stock no. field. Execute the **M**ulti/**R**ecords/**D**efine command, and press Enter to anchor the region. Now press the left-arrow key until the entire row of fields, but none of the spaces after the Total field, is highlighted, and press Enter again. Press the down-arrow key twice to set up a region with room for three records, as shown in Figure 11.14, and press Enter. As noted, you can enter more than three records here, because the region will scroll.

215

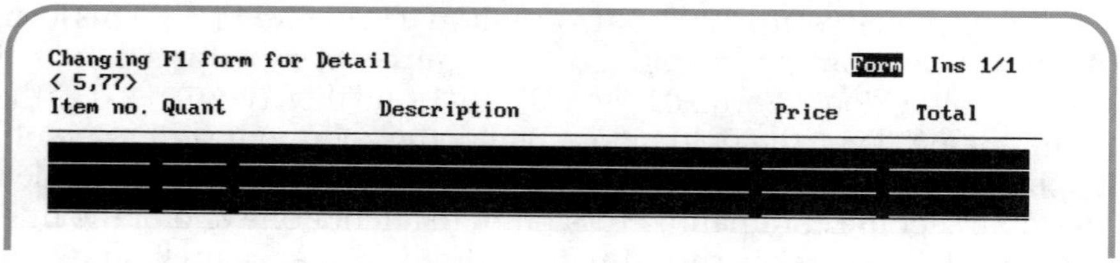

```
Changing F1 form for Detail                          Form   Ins 1/1
< 5,77>
Item no. Quant           Description           Price    Total
```

Figure 11.14: Placing the multirecord region.

Designing the Master Form

Finally, you must design the master Orders form. Set up the form shown in Figure 11.15. Leave seven blank lines before you set up the empty box. The Customer form you created will appear in that space. Eight lines below the Cust. ID field, press

Ctrl-Home	To move the cursor to the left edge of the screen.
F10	To display the Forms menu.
B	To select the **B**order command.
P	To select the **P**lace command.
D	To select the **D**oubleLine command.
↵	To anchor the line at the left margin.
→	To move the cursor to the right edge of the screen.
↓ (6 times)	To stretch the border.
↵	To anchor the opposite corner.

You will place the Detail form within this box.

If you wish, add the help information that appears at the bottom of the screen. The key caps were highlighted using the **S**tyle/**C**olor/**A**rea command, and the vertical lines were created using the **B**order/**P**lace/ **S**ingleLine command. You are now ready to link the Orders, Customer, and Detail tables using the forms you have created.

Execute the **M**ulti/**T**ables/**P**lace/**L**inked command. Choose Detail from the list of tables. Choose form 1 (Detail) from the list of forms. A prompt appears, asking you to select a link field. Select Order no. A rectangular shaded area will appear at the lower-right part of your screen. Use the cursor keys to center the shaded area in the empty box, and press Enter.

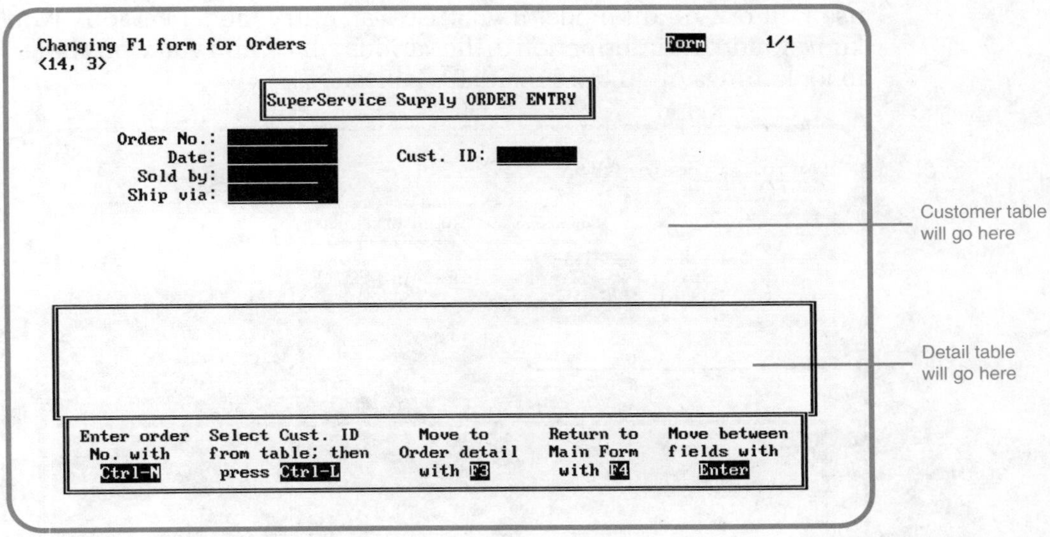

Figure 11.15: Designing a multitable form.

217

Now repeat the command choosing the Customer table and form 1 (Customer). Select Cust. ID as the link field. Again, a rectangular area will appear at the lower-right corner. Use the up-arrow key to move it up the form, so that it fits exactly between the upper border of the box containing the detail form, and the Cust. ID field, flush with the right edge of the screen. Press Enter when you've placed it. Your form should now look like Figure 11.16. If it does, press F2 to save it. If the shaded area for the Detail form extends beyond the borders of the box, you must go back to the Detail table and decrease the size of the fields. You can then try to link the forms again.

Now bring the Orders table to the workspace with the **View** command. Use the **Image/PickForm** command to select form 1 and the **Image/KeepSet** command to make it the default form. The Orders table should appear as shown in Figure 11.17. Mission accomplished!

Using Multi-Table Forms

In principle, there's no difference between entering data into a multitable form and entering data into a single-table form. However, you *must*

use Edit or Co-Edit mode. If you use DataEntry mode, Paradox won't
know to add the information to the various tables, and you won't be able
to look things up in the subsidiary tables.

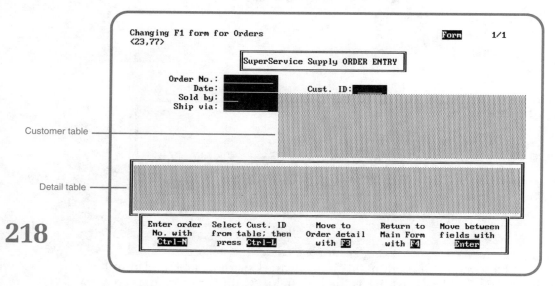

Customer table

Detail table

218

Figure 11.16: A master form with two embedded forms.

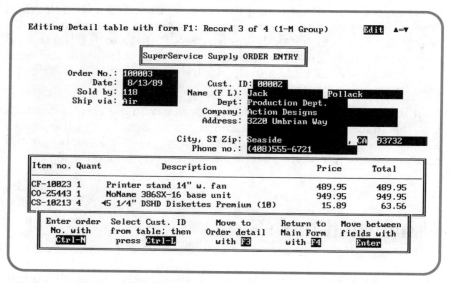

Figure 11.17: Using a multitable form.

Looking Up Values in Existing Tables

There are, however, a few tricks to simplify entering data into a form such as the order-entry form just described. Most important is the careful placement of validity checks. With multitable forms, you can look up data in existing tables to be sure that the values you enter are acceptable. For this purpose, you execute the ValCheck/TableLookup command. In the order-entry form, there are two fields where a table lookup is appropriate: Cust. ID and Item no. You'll want to use both the Customer and the Inventry tables as lookup tables. Press F9 to go into Edit mode. Move to the Cust. ID field, and execute the ValCheck/Define/TableLookup command. You'll be asked which table to use. Select the Customer table from the list. Having selected the table, you're given two options:

JustCurrentField   Allows you to look up the current value in the lookup table.

AllCorrespondingFields   Checks the value in the selected field for validity, and fills in any fields in the current table from the record in which the chosen value is found.

219

Obviously, the latter is the appropriate choice—it will fill in all the fields for each customer when you select the Cust. ID. Finally, you must choose from two more options

FillNoHelp   Paradox checks whether the value you entered exists in the lookup table, and displays an error message if it doesn't.

HelpAndFill   You can actually view the lookup table, and select an appropriate value.

Again, the latter is obviously the correct choice. There's no reason to hide the information from the order clerk; indeed, the only way to verify that the Cust. ID or the Item no. is correct is to view the name or description fields, respectively.

Repeat the procedure for the Inventry table. Press F4 to move into the embedded Detail form. You'll be in the Item no. column. Execute the ValCheck/Define/TableLookup command one more time. Select the Inventry table. Again, select AllCorrespondingFields and HelpAndFill. You now have access to all your customer and inventory data.

Using the Lookup Tables

Once you've installed these lookup features, Paradox displays the message

```
Press [F1] for help with fill-in
```

when your cursor moves to the appropriate field. If you press F1, (and you have selected the HelpAndFill option), Paradox displays the referenced table on the screen, with the cursor in the matching field of the first record, as shown in Figure. 11.18. As you can see, once you've selected the appropriate record, you simply press F2. The selected field is then filled in.

```
Move to the record you want to select
Press [F2] to select the record; [Esc] to cancel; [F1] for help
CUSTOMER┬Cust. ID┬═════Last name═════┬═════First name═════┬═════Department═════
    1  ║ 00001 ║ Jones          ║ Jonathan       ║ Purchasing Dept.
    2  ║ 00002 ║ Pollack        ║ Jack           ║ Production Dept.
    3  ║ 00003 ║ Bishop         ║ Walter         ║
    4  ║ 00004 ║ Franklin       ║ Howard K.      ║
    5  ║ 00005 ║ Grouch         ║ Oscar T.       ║
    6  ║ 00006 ║ Hernandez      ║ Andrew         ║
    7  ║ 00007 ║ Jameson        ║ J. Jonah       ║
    8  ║ 00008 ║ Jonas          ║ Jane           ║
    9  ║ 00009 ║ Jones          ║ James          ║
   10  ║ 00010 ║ Jones          ║ James          ║
   11  ║ 00011 ║ Jones          ║ James E.       ║
   12  ║ 00012 ║ Joy            ║ Anne           ║
   13  ║ 00013 ║ Khorajian      ║ Corey          ║
   14  ║ 00014 ║ Lathom         ║ Susan          ║
   15  ║ 00015 ║ Loquendi       ║ Norma          ║
   16  ║ 00016 ║ Osterlund      ║ Frank R.       ║
   17  ║ 00017 ║ Schocks        ║ Susan          ║
   18  ║ 00018 ║ Spencer        ║ O'Neil         ║
```

Figure 11.18: Using a lookup table.

Now comes a tricky part. The fields you want to fill are in an embedded table. Normally, you move to a form for an embedded table by pressing F4 or F3, "Down Image" or "Up Image", just as you would if the separate tables appeared on the screen in image format. As the legend at the bottom of Figure 11.17 indicates, this is how you fill out the detail items. You can move to the Customer data by pressing F4, but (as Figure 11.17 also indicates), if you press Ctrl-L while in the Cust. ID field, the associated fields from the same record will appear in the order-entry form automatically.

When you use the lookup feature in the Item no. field, you don't have to press Ctrl-L. The Item no. field is in the same table (Detail) as the associated fields (Description and Price), so they appear as soon as you insert the appropriate stock number. All you have to do is fill in the Item no. and Quant fields, and move to the next detail line. When you finish an order, press F2, "DO-IT!," and both the Orders and Detail tables will be updated automatically.

Notice that with this arrangement, you cannot actually change the Inventry table, even though you can look up items within it. That table is not in Edit mode.

Validity Checks

Additional validity checks can greatly simplify the use of complex forms. Below is a list of all the validity checks and number formats used in the order-entry form. To enter them, you bring the form to the workspace and press F9 to go into Edit mode. Place these validity checks *before* you enter any data into the form.

Table 11.2: Validity checks for the order entry form.

Field	Picture	Other Validity Checks
Order no.	######	Image/Format/General; 0 decimal places ValCheck/LowValue **100000** ValCheck/HighValue **999999**
Cust.ID		
Date		ValCheck/Default **today**
Sold by	###	ValCheck/TableLookup **Salesper** JustCurrentFields/HelpAndFill Image/Format/General; 0 decimal places
Ship via	1-day air, Ground 2-day air, Postal	ValCheck/Default **Ground**
Item no.		ValCheck/TableLookup **Inventry** AllCorrespondingFields/ HelpAndFill
Quant		Image/Format/General; 0 decimal places

Notice that you still have no way to derive the sales tax and grand total. These items will appear on the printed invoice. To produce that, you have to set up a report, and you'll learn how to do that in the next chapter.

A Note on Referential Integrity

Consider the ways using a set of linked tables protects your data and eases the entry of new data. First, by being able to look up your inventory and customer information, you minimize the chance of making errors. Paradox's **H**elpAndFill feature goes even further by automatically transferring the appropriate information into the order form.

In addition, the links you have established ensure that the detail records and customer data are securely connected to the master order form. If you're careful not to edit the Detail table on its own, then every record in it will be "owned" by a single record in the Orders table, linked to it by the Order no. Paradox won't let you delete a record from the master table without first deleting all the detail records that are linked to it. This ensures that there won't be any extraneous detail records for nonexistent orders.

Finally, you have stored the data with as little redundancy as possible. Although the Detail table has to duplicate the item descriptions from the Inventry table (because of the limits on hierarchy), the only other items stored in more than one table are the linking fields.

Creating and Using Reports

What You Will Learn

- ▶ Creating a Report from a Query
- ▶ Designing and Changing Reports
- ▶ Grouping Fields in Reports
- ▶ Calculating News Values in Reports
- ▶ Linking Tables Using Reports

Now you know several ways to get information into a database and to discover the relationships between various items. But you also need to be able to get the results on paper. For that, you need to generate reports.

It's as easy to create custom reports in Paradox as it is to do almost anything else. In this chapter, you'll learn the basics of report generation and see how to create a report that links information from several tables.

The Instant Report

The easiest way to produce a report is to select a table for viewing and press Alt-F7, the "Instant Report" key. The result is a simple columnar reproduction of the current image. The inventory listing you saw in Chapter 10 was such an instant report. If your table is too wide to fit onto your paper (which depends on your printer), the first 80 columns of all records will be printed, followed by a second series of pages with the next 80 columns of all records, and so on. You'll have to tape the pages from each series together horizontally to get the complete picture. You may also be able to change printer settings to fit more than 80 columns on a page. You'll learn how later in this chapter. When you create an Instant Report, its format, or `specification` is saved as report specification R, the default report.

The Standard Report

The **R**eport menu works rather like the **F**orms menu. You decide whether to design a new report or change an existing report, and then you are given a menu like the one shown in Figure 12.1. The Standard report, chosen by pressing **R**, is no different from what you get if you chose one of the other numbers. You can edit any of the 15 report formats to suit your needs. For now, however, let's look at what Paradox gives you by default.

Paradox has two quite different report formats—**T**abular and **F**ree-form. You'll examine one of each, and then design a couple of custom reports that take advantage of Paradox's advanced features.

Let's create the Inventory report you saw in Chapter 10. Press

F10	To display the Main menu if it's not already on the screen.
R	To choose the **R**eport menu.
D	To **D**esign a Report.
↵	To see a list of tables.
I	To choose the Inventory table.
R	To choose the Standard Report.

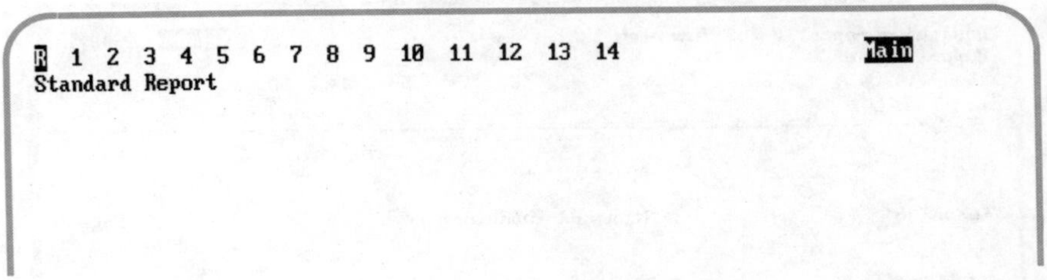

```
R 1 2 3 4 5 6 7 8 9 10 11 12 13 14          Main
Standard Report
```

Figure 12.1: Choosing a report form.

As with the Forms menu, you'll be asked for a phrase to describe the report when it appears on menus:

```
Report description:
Enter report description
```

Type

```
Standard Inventory Report
```

225

and press Enter. Press T to choose the **T**abular format.

You'll now see a screen similar to Figure 12.2.

The Report Screen

Notice that the screen is divided into *bands*. This report form has a *table band* at the center, which shows the fields in the report arrayed left to right, just as they are in the image of the table. It is set within the *page band*, which includes a standard header consisting of the system date, the description you typed, and a page number in the *page header band*. Bands are indicated by their name on a horizontal line. A small down-triangle indicates the margin of a band at the top of a page, and a similar up-triangle indicates the lower margin of a band. There is space in the page header band, and in the *page footer band*, below the table band, to enter additional information into the header or into a footer.

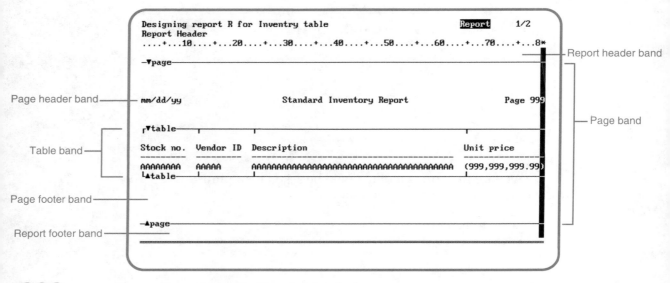

Report header band

Page header band

Page band

Table band

Page footer band

Report footer band

Figure 12.2: The standard Tabular report.

226

An additional, unmarked band—the *report header band*—is above the page header band. If you want your first page to have an additional header, type it there. Similarly, a *report footer band* follows the page footer band.

At the top of the screen is a ruler line, showing the character columns, to help you place information correctly onto the report form. At the right side of the screen is a thick vertical line, symbolizing the page margin. You can display a vertical ruler at the left margin by pressing Ctrl-V.

As you can see, not all of the report fits onto the screen. Like the Instant report, the standard Tabular report automatically prints what doesn't fit onto a standard page on additional sheets. Press Ctrl-right arrow, and the screen will move a half-page to the left, showing a portion of what will appear on the second set of pages.

The table band contains three rows of information. First, the field names appear on a single line, in the same order as they would in the table image. A series of dashes the width of each field underscores the field names. The third row contains the indicators that show where the data in your table will appear. The positions of the fields are indicated by rows of A's (for alphanumeric fields) or 9's (for numeric or currency fields). These are similar to pictures in tables and forms. In currency fields, the numbers are formatted with commas and decimal points as they are in the tables. Date fields are indicated by the dummy date format mm/dd/yy.

You can enter text anywhere on the screen that isn't occupied by a field, so you can add any information you need in the header and footer. You can reformat fields in a manner similar to using the **I**mage/**F**ormat command and the **F**ield/**F**ormat command in the **F**orms menu. As you'll see, you can change the format of any type of field.

In a tabular report, one row is printed for each record. The elements in the page band are repeated at the top of each page, as are the field names and dashes—or, indeed, any information you place in the table band above the actual row of fields. Anything in the page band at the bottom of the form is also repeated on each page.

Rearranging the Table Band

Figure 12.3 shows the Report menu for the Tabular report format. In this exercise, you'll be working primarily with the **F**ield and **T**ableBand submenus.

227

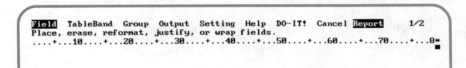

Figure 12.3: The main Report menu for Tabular reports.

In the following exercise, you're going to fit the fields on one page. It's a bit tricky, because you can't adjust the width of the columns until you adjust their contents. The place to start is to reformat the fields. You know the highest unit price is only in the thousands, so you can obviously reduce the size of that field. Move the cursor down to the picture of the Unit price field. Press

F10	To display the **R**eport menu.
F	To display the **F**ield submenu.
R	To **R**eformat the field.
↵	To select the current field.
D	To select the **D**igits command (the decimal places will disappear).
← (5 times)	To delete five integer places.
↵	To set the number of digits.
↵	To accept the default number of decimal places (two).

Now you've reduced the size of the field, but the text in the column is still as wide as the column. Use the space bar to space over the dashes below the words `Unit price`, after the final e.

Now you'll use the **TableBand** submenu to make adjustments to the columns in the table band. This submenu contains the following options:

`Insert`	Inserts a new column in the table band.
`Erase`	Erases a column from the table band.
`Resize`	Changes the width of a column.
`Move`	Reorders the columns, in a manner similar to the **I**mage/**M**ove command for tables.
`Copy`	Copies an existing column to another location in the table band.

228

Move to the line indicating the top of the table band, just before the vertical marker indicating the end of the Unit price column. Press

F10	To display the **R**eport menu.
T	To display the **TableBand** submenu.
R	To select the **R**esize command.
↵	To select the current column.
← (7 times)	To contract the column.
↵	To complete the operation.

▶ When you resize a column, the cursor can be anywhere in the column, so long as it's not directly above or below a field indicator. You must be at the right margin of a column to contract it, because you can reduce the width only up to the last character in the column.

You won't need the Vendor ID column in this report, so you can delete it. Move the cursor to that column. Now press F10 and then

T	To display the **TableBand** submenu.
E	To **E**rase the column.
↵	To confirm your choice.

All the other columns will move to the left, to fill up the vacated space.

Notice that the last column of the Reorder field is just off the screen. Delete one space each from the Stock no., Description, and On hand columns in the same manner as you did from the Unit price column, to make the rest of the report fit.

Now, just for a minor refinement, let's center the word Description over the field picture. Use the space bar to delete it, and type it in again in the appropriate position. Your report form should now look like Figure 12.4.

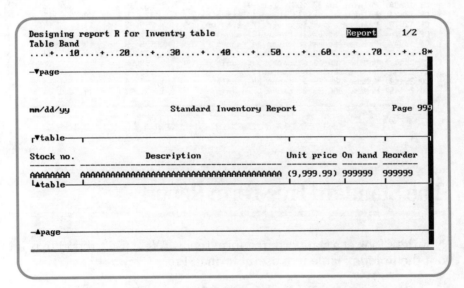

Figure 12.4: The Standard Inventory Report modified.

Checking Your Work

To see the result, use the **O**utput/**S**creen command. This displays the data on the screen as you have formatted it, as shown in Figure 12.5. Notice the legend at the top of the page. This indicates that if the report is wider than a page, the additional material will appear as Page Width 2. If you're satisfied, press DO-IT! to save your report. We'll come back to the Inventory report later, to add some more advanced features.

Legend

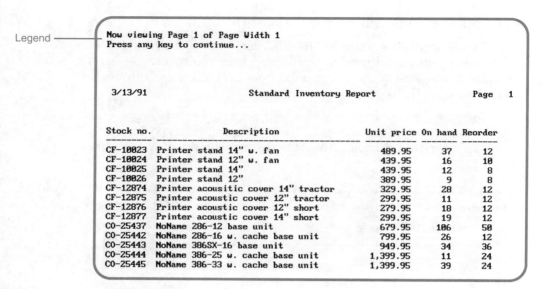

```
Now viewing Page 1 of Page Width 1
Press any key to continue...



  3/13/91                    Standard Inventory Report                 Page   1


  Stock no.            Description                  Unit price On hand Reorder
  ---------  ------------------------------------  ---------- ------- -------
  CF-10023  Printer stand 14" w. fan                   489.95      37      12
  CF-10024  Printer stand 12" w. fan                   439.95      16      10
  CF-10025  Printer stand 14"                          439.95      12       8
  CF-10026  Printer stand 12"                          389.95       9       8
  CF-12874  Printer acousitic cover 14" tractor        329.95      28      12
  CF-12875  Printer acoustic cover 12" tractor         299.95      11      12
  CF-12876  Printer acoustic cover 12" short           279.95      18      12
  CF-12877  Printer acoustic cover 14" short           299.95      19      12
  CO-25437  NoName 286-12 base unit                    679.95     106      50
  CO-25442  NoName 286-16 w. cache base unit           799.95      26      12
  CO-25443  NoName 386SX-16 base unit                  949.95      34      36
  CO-25444  NoName 386-25 w. cache base unit         1,399.95      11      24
  CO-25445  NoName 386-33 w. cache base unit         1,399.95      39      24
```

230

Figure 12.5: Viewing a report on the screen.

The Standard Free-Form Report

Now let's look at a standard free-form report. We'll use a report to print out the Rolodex table in a useful format. Press

F10	To display the Main menu if it's not already on the screen.
R	To choose the **R**eport menu.
D	To **D**esign a Report.
↵	To see a list of tables.
R ↵	To choose the Rolodex table.
↵	To choose Report R.

When asked for a report description, type

Address List

and press Enter. Choose the Free-form option. Your screen will look like Figure 12.6. Notice that, instead of a table band, the free-form report has a *form band*. In essence, the free-form format reproduces the default form created by the F7 key. In this exercise, you'll make this report resemble the viewing form you created in Chapter 11.

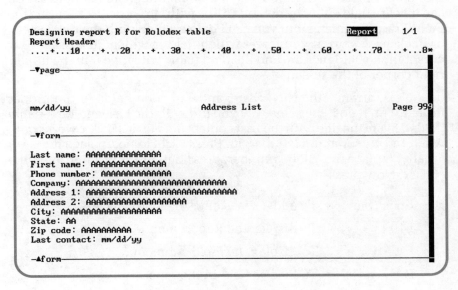

```
Designing report R for Rolodex table                    Report    1/1
Report Header
....+...10....+...20....+...30....+...40....+...50....+...60....+...70....+...8*

-▼page─────────────────────────────────────────────────────────────────


mm/dd/yy                          Address List                     Page 999

-▼form─────────────────────────────────────────────────────────────────

Last name: AAAAAAAAAAAAAAA
First name: AAAAAAAAAAAAAAA
Phone number: AAAAAAAAAAAAAA
Company: AAAAAAAAAAAAAAAAAAAAAAAAAAAAAA
Address 1: AAAAAAAAAAAAAAAAAAAAAAAAAAAAAAAAAA
Address 2: AAAAAAAAAAAAAAAAAAAAA
City: AAAAAAAAAAAAAAAAAAAAA
State: AA
Zip code: AAAAAAAAA
Last contact: mm/dd/yy

-▲form─────────────────────────────────────────────────────────────────
```

Figure 12.6: A standard free-form report.

Editing Text and Moving Fields

This report should be sorted in alphabetical order, so keep the Last name field first. However, you can recognize a last name, so move to the words Last name: and delete them by pressing the Del or Delete key. Now move down to the next line and press the Backspace key (you may have to press Ins or Insert key first). The text First name:, along with the First name field, moves up a line because you deleted the carriage return. Now delete the text First name:. Insert the comma between the last and first name fields.

Now move to the beginning of the line with the Phone number and press Ctrl-Y to delete the entire line. Press Enter to add a blank line. (This works only in Insert mode.) Try to use the Del or Delete key to delete the text on the following lines:

231

```
Company:
Address 1:
Address 2:
City:
```

You'll notice that when you reach a field picture, Paradox honks. You can delete a field either by deleting a line with Ctrl-Y or by executing the Field/Erase command, but you can't delete a field with the Del, Delete, or Backspace keys. If you forget which field is which, just place your cursor in the field picture, and the field name will appear in the upper-right corner of the screen.

Next, arrange the City, State, and Zip code fields in the proper format. You'll do it the same way you did with the Last and First name fields. Delete the line with the Last contact field on it. (Ctrl-Y works only when the cursor at the left margin. Press Ctrl-Home to place it there.) Finally, replace the Phone number. Press Enter to skip a line and type `Phone:`. Now press

Space bar	To add a space after the word `Phone:`.
F10	To display the **R**eport menu.
F	To display the **F**ield submenu.
P	To **P**lace a field in the report.
R	To select a **R**egular (i.e., data) field.
P	To select the Phone no. field.
↵	To indicate where you want the Phone number field to begin.
↵	To use the full width of the Phone number field.

As you could see when you placed the Phone number field, you needn't use the complete width of a field if you don't want to. (We'll look briefly at types of fields other than **R**egular before the end of the chapter.)

It might look a bit better if all the details for each individual were indented beneath the person's last name. To accomplish this, just move the cursor to the beginning of each line and press the space bar five times. Your screen should now look like Figure 12.7.

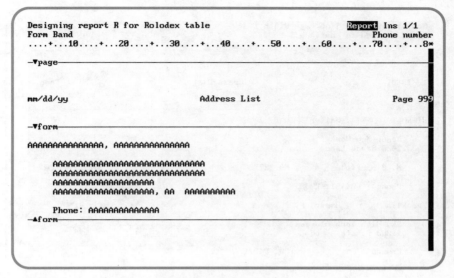

Figure 12.7: An edited Free-form report.

233

Checking Your Work

Again, test the results by executing the **O**utput/**S**creen command. As you'll see in Figure 12.8, the report doesn't look very good. There's too much space between the last and first names, and between the city and state. There are also blank lines in addresses that don't include a company name, or a second address line. As you might guess, you can use the **F**ield/**R**eformat command to reduce the field pictures, just as you can in designing forms. However, doing so will truncate values that are larger than the picture. Getting rid of the extra lines seems like even more of a challenge.

Fortunately, Paradox has a remedy—the **S**etting/**R**emoveBlanks command. It has two options:

LineSqueeze	Removes lines in which all the fields are empty.
FieldSqueeze	Removes spaces at the beginning and end of fields.

Use the command twice to select both.

```
Now viewing Page 1 of Page Width 1
Press any key to continue...



   3/13/91                          Address List                       Page   1


 Bishop          , Walter

       Major Key Works
       1420 Sandy Lane

       N. Bloomfield       , MD  22388

       Phone: (504)611-2300

 Franklin        , Howard K.

       Sky High Technologies
       11200 Dakota Avenue

       Fresno            , CA  94371
```

234

Figure 12.8: A trial run for the Address List.

LineSqueeze has an additional option. If you choose Fixed, each iteration of the form band in the final report will have the same number of lines. For any entry that contains blank lines, the requisite number of blank lines will be added to the end of the entry. If you choose Variable, the entries will not all be the same depth. Choose Variable. (Paradox won't split an entry between pages.) You'll see the message

    Settings changed

Now when you execute the **O**utput/**S**creen command, you'll see a noticeable improvement, as Figure 12.9 shows. Return to the Report menu and press F2 to save your work.

Mailing Labels

You may have noticed that one of the options on the **S**ettings submenu was **L**abels. You'll now use this command to set up a report to print mailing labels. Press

F10   To display the Main menu.

T   To invoke the **T**ools menu.

C	To select the **C**opy command.
R	To copy a **R**eport.
S	To copy the report to the **S**ameTable.
↵	To display a list of tables.
R	To choose the Rolodex table as the table to which the report is attached.
↵	To choose report specification R as the report to copy.
1	To copy report R to report specification 1.
R	To invoke the **R**eport menu.
C	To **C**hange an existing report specification.
↵	To display a list of tables.
R	To choose the Rolodex table.
1 ↵	To choose report specification 1.

235

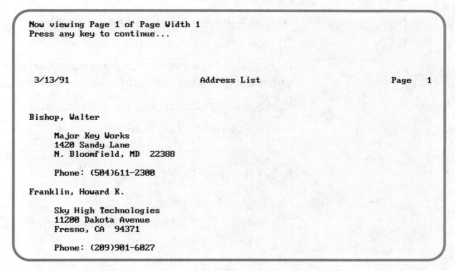

```
Now viewing Page 1 of Page Width 1
Press any key to continue...



    3/13/91                         Address List                    Page    1


Bishop, Walter

         Major Key Works
         1420 Sandy Lane
         N. Bloomfield, MD   22388

         Phone: (504)611-2300

Franklin, Howard K.

         Sky High Technologies
         11200 Dakota Avenue
         Fresno, CA   94371

         Phone: (209)901-6027
```

Figure 12.9: The improved Address List.

Use Ctrl-Y to delete all the lines in the report band, above the page band. Now move down to the page band, and use Ctrl-Y to delete all the lines above the form band. Next, move the cursor to the Last name field. Press F10 and then

F	To display the **F**ield submenu.
E	To select the **E**rase command.
↵	To erase the Last name field.

Keep pressing the Del or Delete key until the First name field is flush with the left margin. Move to the end of the First name field, press the space bar once, and use the **F**ield/**P**lace/**R**egular command to place the Last name field after the first name field.

Move to the following lines, and delete the leading spaces from each, until you come to the blank line before the Phone number field. Delete that line, and the line containing the Phone number, with Ctrl-Y. Keep moving down, until you reach the page band. Delete all but one line from the page band with Ctrl-Y. Delete everything from the lower report band, below the page band.

Now you'll use the Setting submenu to format the page to fit a label. Press F10 and then

S	To display the **S**etting submenu.
R	To select the **R**emoveBlanks command.
L Yes	To select the **L**ineSqueeze command.
F	To select the **F**ixed, command ensuring that each address label takes the same number of lines.
F10	To display the **R**eport menu.
S	To display the **S**etting submenu.
P	To display the **P**ageLayout submenu.
L	To set the page **L**ength.
Ctrl-Backspace	To erase the default of 66.
6	To specify a page length of 6 lines, the length of single 15/16" label.
↵	To confirm your entry.
F10	To display the **R**eport menu.
S	To display the **S**etting submenu.
P	To display the **P**ageLayout submenu.
W	To set the page **W**idth.

Ctrl-Backspace	To erase the default of 80.
40	To set the page width for one label on a 2-up label sheet.
↵	To confirm your entry.

Figure 12.10 shows how your screen should look for two-up mailing labels. Notice that you needn't place anything in the second page. When you've selected the Labels command, Paradox automatically formats the output so that one record appears on each label. The labels will be sorted as they are in the source table, with the second label in each row taking the record following the one on the first. Press F2 to save your changes.

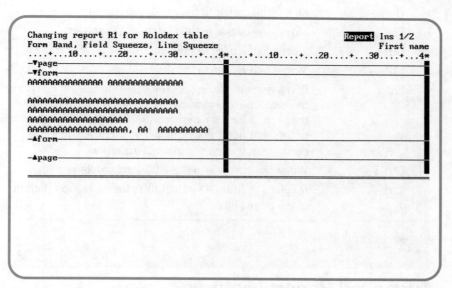

Figure 12.10: A report form for mailing labels.

For reference, Table 12.1 summarizes the effects of the cursor-movement keys in Report mode. Note that several keys behave very differently in insert and overtype modes.

Table 12.1: Cursor movement for designing reports.

Key	Effect
↑	Moves the cursor up a line
↓	Moves the cursor down a line
→	Moves the cursor right one column
←	Moves the cursor left one column
Backspace	In overtype mode, moves the cursor left one column; in insert mode, moves the cursor left one column and also deletes the character to the left of the cursor
Del, Delete	Deletes the character to the right of the cursor
Ins, Insert	Toggles between overtype (default) and insert mode
Home	Moves the cursor to the top of the screen
End	Moves the cursor to the bottom of the screen
Ctrl-←	Moves half a page to the left
Ctrl-→	Moves half a page to the right
Enter	In overtype mode, moves the cursor to the left margin on the next line; in insert mode, breaks the current line at the point where the cursor was when you pressed it unless that point is within a field picture; when the cursor is at the left margin, inserts a line
Ctrl-Y	When the cursor is at the left margin, deletes a line
Ctrl-V	Displays or hides a vertical ruler line at the left margin of the report form

Advanced Report Features

Now let's create a report to print out the invoices for the order entry application described in Chapter 10. First, I'll show you the finished product; then I'll explain how to arrive at it. In the process, you'll learn about several additional features of Paradox's report-generation mode. Figure 12.11 shows the complete report format.

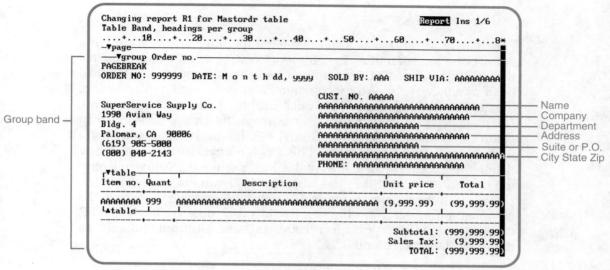

Figure 12.11: A multitable invoice report form.

To create this form, you'll generate a report for the Mastordr table. You created this table in Chapter 10 by renaming the ANSWER table generated by a query. Select the **R**eports/**D**esign command and choose the Mastordr table. Give your report the description Sales Invoice. Select the **T**abular report format. You'll see a table band containing all the fields from the table in a single line.

Obviously, this isn't the way the invoice should look. Begin by moving the cursor into the table band. Use the **T**ableBand/**E**rase command 16 times to delete all the fields that pertain to the order as a whole—the address information, shipping information, and so on. When you're finished, you should have a table band with only four fields: Item no., Quantity, Description, and Unit Price. This looks more like an invoice, but how do you get the rest of the information back, and why did you delete all those essential fields?

Well, you want all your detail records for a single order to appear on a single invoice, and you want only one invoice for each order. As you might surmise, if you left everything in the table band, you'd have all the information for the order included with each detail line—just the kind of redundancy you *don't* want. Obviously, you need some way of grouping the information so that the information for an order appears only once.

Grouped Fields

Fortunately, Paradox has a solution—grouped fields. Everything in a *group band* has something in common. Creating a group band ensures that the items sharing the common characteristic appear together. To put it another way, when the records embody a one-to-many relationship, the group band represents the "one," and the table or form band the "many." Everything that the records from the Detail table have in common—which is everything from the Orders and Customer tables—will appear once for each group. This yields a single invoice with many detail lines. Sounds like just what the doctor ordered. (Notice that only the detail items are still in the table band.) If you couldn't group the records in this manner, every detail record would have to include the complete information for the invoice, just as it does in the ANSWER table on which this report specification is based. Grouping thus solves the redundancy problem.

To create a group band, press

F10	To display the Report menu.
G	To display the **G**roup submenu.
I	To **I**nsert the group.

You then choose the basis for grouping:

Field	Groups all records having the same value in the field you select.
Range	Groups all records having the specified range of values in the field you select.
NumberRecords	Groups a specific number of records.

In this instance, you're grouping on the value in a given field—the Order no. field. You choose the field from the list on the screen after you select the basis for grouping. Since the cursor is in the right place, press Enter. Your screen should now look like Figure 12.12. Notice that the band is marked by the label

```
group Order no.
```

This tells you that the band is grouped by the values in the Order no. field. Since the value in this field is unique for each order, each invoice will contain all the detail records that match a given order number.

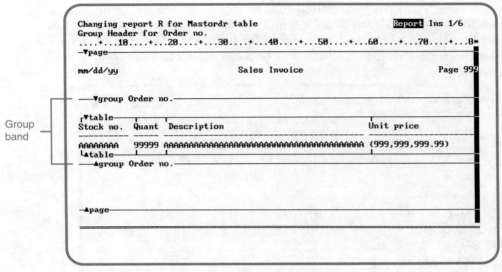

Group band

Next use the **S**etting/**G**roupRepeats/**S**uppress to ensure that the information common to all records comprising an order appears only once for each order.

Filling in the Group Information

Now we need to rearrange the report so that it looks like an invoice. Move to the left margin and delete all the blank lines from the Report band (unmarked, at the top and bottom of the report specification) and from the page band. Next switch to Insert mode, and type the text that you see in Figure 12.13. Next, you'll need to place all the fields that you deleted from the table band into the group band. Use Figure 12.11 to guide you. The Order No., Date, Sold by, Ship via, Phone no., and Cust. ID fields all go in the indicated locations. Skip a line after the text CUST. NO. and, on the line containing 1990 Avian Way, place the Company field. Below that, in order, place the following fields:

```
Department
Address
Suite no. or P. O. Box
```

You'll add the remaining two fields in the upper group band shortly after you learn about calculated fields. Finally, you'll need to rearrange the table band, as you did for the Reorder Report, to make room for the extension, which will be a calculated field as well.

```
Changing report R for Mastordr table                    Report    1/6
Group Footer for Order no.
....+...10....+...20....+...30....+...40....+...50....+...60....+...70....+...8*
─▼page─────────────────────────────────────────────────────────────────────██
  ──▼group Order no.───────────────────────────────────────────────────────██
PAGEBREAK
ORDER NO:           DATE:                    SOLD BY:        SHIP VIA:

                                      CUST. NO.

SuperService Supply Co.
1990 Avian Way
Bldg. 4
Palomar, CA 90006
(619) 905-5000
(800) 040-2143

 ┌▼table───────┬─────┬─────────────────────────────────────────┬──────────────
 Stock no.    Quant Description                                 Unit price
 ─────────── ───── ─────────────────────────────────────────── ──────────────
 AAAAAAAA      99999 AAAAAAAAAAAAAAAAAAAAAAAAAAAAAAAAAAAAAAAAAAA (999,999,999.99)
 └▲table───────┴─────┴                                                        ██
  ──▲group Order no.───────────────────────────────────────────────────────██
```

Figure 12.13: Type the text that you want to appear on every invoice.

Q Grouping Records in a Report Specification

1. Press F10.	Paradox displays the **R**eport menu.
2. Press **G**.	Paradox prompts you for the location where the group should be inserted.
3. Move the cursor to the appropriate location, and press Enter.	Paradox displays the **G**roup submenu.

4. Choose whether to group on the value in a **Field**, a **R**ange of values in a field, or a **N**umber of records.

If you choose **Field** or **R**ange, you are prompted for the field to use as the basis for grouping. If you choose **R**ange, you are then prompted for how many characters in the field should be used to define the range. If you choose **N**umberRecords, you are asked how many records should be included in a group.

5. If you enter a range or a number of records, press Enter to confirm your choice.

□

243

Calculated Fields

The invoice form includes several calculated fields of three types:

▶ Arithmetic calculations
▶ Concatenated Alphanumeric fields
▶ Summary calculations

First create a column for the Total field. To create this column, move the cursor to the right of the Unit Price field, and execute the **T**ableBand/**I**nsert command. Next, place the Total field in the table band by executing the **F**ield/**P**lace/**C**alculated command, and typing the expression

```
[Quant]*[Unit price]
```

As you can see, you create calculated fields the same way you do when designing forms.

The **R**emoveBlanks command doesn't exist in Tabular reports. However, you can achieve the same effect by concatenating the Alphanumeric fields, just as you did in Chapter 8. In place of the First name and Last name fields, use the **F**ield/**P**lace/**C**alculated command to create the calculation

```
[First name]+" "+[Last name]
```

directly under CUST NO.. Below the last line of the address fields, place the calculated field

```
[City]+" "+[State]+" "+[Zip or postal code]
```

This replaces separate City, State, and Zip code fields. (We placed a space, instead of a comma and a space, between the City and State to conform to the most recent postal guidelines.)

▶ To review the formula entered in a calculated field, move the cursor to it in the report specification. The formula appears in the upper right corner of the screen. To change a formula, use the **F**ield/**C**alcEdit command.

244

Summary Calculations

In the group footer band, below the table band, you will add three summary calculations by using the **F**ield/**P**lace/**S**ummary/**C**alculated/ **S**um/**P**erGroup command:

```
SubTotal:
Sales Tax:
TOTAL:
```

The fields should contain the following calculations, respectively:

```
[Quant]*[Unit Price]
[Quant]*[Unit price]*.065
[Quant]*[Unit price]*1.065
```

Because these are *summary* fields, the calculation *[Quant]***[Unit price]* reflects all the values in the group. This is accomplished by two steps: placing the summary fields within the group band instead of within the page footer band, and selecting the **P**erGroup option instead of the **O**verall option. The latter option summarizes all such values in the report up to the point where the fields appear. You might want to include such fields, for example, in the report footer band, below the page footer band, to get summary figures for the entire report.

Formatting Features

Three formatting features are worth noting. In the top line of the group band, you typed the reserved word

```
PAGEBREAK
```

This ensures that each group—that is, each invoice—appears on a new page. Second, notice the line of dashes and plus signs just below the table band. This provides a table footer similar to the table header within the table band. If it were placed *in* the table band, it would appear after each row of detail records. A sample invoice printed with this form appears in Figure 12.14.

```
ORDER NO: 100002  DATE:      March 28, 1991    SOLD BY: 104    SHIP VIA: Ground

                                          CUST. NO. 00002
SuperService Supply Co.                   Jack Pollack
1990 Avian Way                            Action Designs
Bldg. 4                                   Production Dept.
Palomar, CA  90006                        3220 Umbrian Way
(619) 905-5000
(800) 040-2143                            Seaside, CA 93732
                                          PHONE: (408)555-6721
Item no. Quant                Description              Unit price      Total
------------------------------------------------------+------------+----------
CS-10211  10   5 1/4" DSDD Diskettes Premium (10)         10.50       105.00
CS-10217  10   3 1/2" DSHD Diskettes Premium (10)         17.98       179.80
PP-79863   5   Roller Pens Fine Red                         .89         4.45
PP-79865   3   Roller Pens Fine Green                       .89         2.67
ST-21919   1   Fine folders 1/3 cut letter gross         21.99        21.99
ST-23122  12   Mailing envelopes tyvec 10x12 (12)          6.59        79.08
------------------------------------------------------+------------+----------
                                               Subtotal:    392.99
                                               Sales Tax:    25.54
                                               TOTAL:       418.53
```

Figure 12.14: An invoice generated by a report form and a query.

Finally, notice how the Today's date field is formatted in the top line of the group band. When you place a date field in a report, you have a choice of seven date formats:

```
mm/dd/yy
Month, dd, yyyy
mm/dd
mm/yy
dd-Mon-yy
Mon yy
dd-Mon-yyyy
mm/dd/yyyy
dd.mm.yy
dd/mm/yy
yy-mm-dd
```

In formats that separate the parts of the date by punctuation—virgules, periods, or dashes—the first part of the date will not have a leading zero, but the other parts will if it's appropriate. Thus, May 1, 1991 might appear as 5/01/91 or 1/05/91, depending on the format you choose.

Finally, note that the row of dashes in the table band is punctuated by plus signs. This helps to separate the columns in the detail records visually. Also, the line of dashes and plus signs appears again in the group footer. You'll see, when you print an invoice, that this creates a nice lower border for the detail records, and also helps to mark the columns.

Linking Tables in a Report

In the previous exercise, you prepared a report based on the data in three separate tables. You made the data available by creating an ANSWER table containing information from all three tables. There's a much simpler way to link tables in a report specification. However, it depends on certain conditions, which weren't met in the previous exercise. To link tables in a report specification, without combining the data in an ANSWER table, *every key field in the linked table must have an equivalent field in the master table.*

In the next exercise, you'll use this fact to create an inventory reorder report. This exercise reviews two important techniques you've already learned:

▶ Grouping of elements
▶ Basing a report on a query

The Reorder report will tell you what items need to be reordered, and from which vendor. To begin, set up the query shown in Figure 12.15. Use the **S**cripts/**Q**uerySave command to save the query as Reorder. Notice that in this query, all fields from the Inventry table are checkmarked; therefore, the ANSWER table will have the same structure as the Inventry table. We'll create the Reorder report specification as a report for the Inventry table.

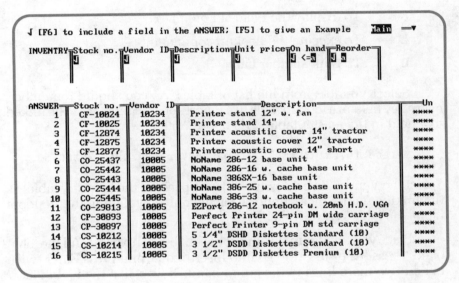

Figure 12.15: A reorder query.

 To checkmark all fields in a query, place the cursor in the first column, under the table name, and press F6.

To begin, use the **T**ools/**C**opy/**R**eport/**S**ameTable command to copy the Standard Inventory Report (Report R) to report specification 1. Now use the **R**eport/**C**hange command to edit this report specification. Call it Reorder Report when prompted for a report description, and enter that name in the page band.

The records in the report will be grouped by vendor, so you'll know from whom to reorder which items. To do this, insert a group band just inside the page band. Place your cursor in the upper page band, and use the **G**roup/**I**nsert/**F**ield command, and select Vendor ID as the field on which to group.

But the Vendor ID doesn't really tell you what you want to know, does it? To get that information, you need to link the Inventry table to the Vendors table. Press

F10   To display the **R**eport menu.

F   To display the **F**ield submenu.

L   To execute the **L**ookup command.

L   To **L**ink another table.

Select Vendors from the list of tables. As you should remember, every key field in a lookup table in a report specification has to be linked to a field in the master table. You're prompted to

```
Select INVENTRY field to match Vendor ID in VENDORS.
```

Select the Vendor ID field (which also appears in the Inventry table) as the linking field. Since Vendor ID is the only key field in the Vendors table, the table is now linked.

Place your cursor in the line between the group band and the table band. Press Ins or Insert to go into Insert mode, and press Enter twice to add two more lines to the group band. Now select the **F**ield/**P**lace/**R**egular command. At the end of the list of fields, you'll see

```
[Vendors->]
```

Move the cursor to that item and press Enter. You'll see a list of the fields in the Vendors table. Select the Company field. and press Enter three times. Rearrange the fields as needed, until the completed report specification looks like the one in Figure 12.16. Press F2 to save the report.

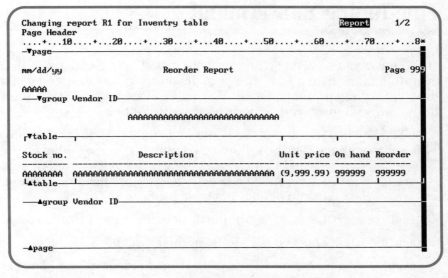

Figure 12.16: A report specification with a linked table.

249

To print the report, first use the **S**cripts/**P**lay command to execute the Reorder query shown in Figure 12.15. Then use the **T**ools/**C**opy/**R**eport/**D**ifferentTable command to copy your Reorder Report from the Inventry table to the ANSWER table. Use the **R**eport/**O**utput command to send the Reorder report to the screen, your printer, or a file. The latter option is especially useful when you need to incorporate the report into a word-processed document.) Your report should look like Figure 12.17.

```
   3/15/91                Reorder Report                    Page    1

   10005
   Stock no.           Description              Unit price On hand Reorder
   ---------  -----------------------------------  ---------- ------- -------

                   Micro Services Plus

   CO-25443  NoName 386SX-16 base unit             949.95      34      36
   CO-25444  NoName 386-25 w. cache base unit    1,399.95      11      24
   CS-10212  5 1/4" DSHD Diskettes Standard (10)    12.50     446     500


                   Sams Stationery Supplies

   PP-79868  Roller Pens Fine Black (12)             9.49    1124    1188
   ST-20381  Legal pads yellow 14"                   1.69    6902    7200
   ST-23123  Mailing envelopes tyvec 12x14 (12)      6.99     120     144


                   Great Office Furniture
```

Figure 12.17: A Reorder report.

Fine-Tuning Your Printout

Up to now, you've been setting up your report specifications so that everything fits on an 80-column page. If you're willing to spend some time with your printer manual, you can overcome this 80-column limitation, and make your reports look really spiffy.

The key lies in some of the commands on the **S**etting submenu. This submenu includes the following commands, among others:

Format	Lets you decide whether group headings belong before or after the table headers.
PageLayout	Lets you determine the length and width of the page.
Margin	Lets you set a left margin for the page.
Setup	Lets you send a *setup string* to the printer, or choose one from a predefined list.

Setting up your page is not as intuitive a process as it might be. The first step is to select a setup string. This is a sequence of characters that control how the printer prints. These sequences are often called *escape sequences*, because they begin with an escape character. In your printer manual, you might find codes that set your printer to print 12 or 15 characters per inch, instead of the usual 10. If the sequence begins with the Escape character, you enter it as

```
\027
```

which is the ASCII code for the Escape character. You can enter any characters whose ASCII code is below 32 or above 127 in this manner. You can enter the other characters just by typing them. If, for example, your printer were to print 15 characters per inch if you sent it the sequence ESC W 1 5, you would use the **S**etting/**S**etup/**C**ustom command, choose your printer port, and type

```
\027W15
```

This would give you a 120-column page, instead of an 80-column page.

(If you choose Predefined instead of custom, you can select from a series of descriptions of type styles for several different printers. If your printer appears on the list, you can select a setting from the list. If not, you can change both the names of the styles and the escape sequences themselves using the Custom Script as described in Chapter 1, and using the **R**eport/**S**etting/**S**etup command.)

Now you'd use the **S**etting/**P**ageLayout/**W**idth command and enter a width, of, say 110. This would leave a 10-column right margin. To set the left margin, use the **S**etting/**M**argin command, and enter a left margin of 10. This would center your report and still give you 100 columns in which to print your report. The result is certainly more salubrious than a string of taped-together page widths.

You might want to try the **S**etting/**F**ormat command on the Reorder report. This would place the table header after each vendor name, which would no doubt be a lot easier to understand.

If you're willing to experiment, and print out a dummy report several times, you can even place printer escape sequences directly into your report to control the way text appears in particular fields, or to format the text in the report specification itself. To do so, use the **F**ield/ **P**lace/**C**alculated command, and instead of a formula, enter a printer escape sequence. You might, for example, insert the code for boldfacing immediately before the report header and the code to turn boldfacing off immediately afterward. The possibilities are limited only by your imagination and your good taste.

251

Chapter 13

More About Scripts

What You Will Learn

▶ Automating Paradox Procedures
▶ Combining Scripts
▶ Editing Scripts

You've already been introduced to the Instant script, and to query scripts, in Chapter 8. In this chapter, you'll create a set of scripts to tie together and automate the order entry application. At the same time, you'll learn a bit about editing scripts, and learn a few other useful facts about scripts.

Automating a Procedure

The first step toward automating the order entry application is to record a simple script to start up our order entry procedure. Obviously, you'll want to start out in the order form, with a blank record ready. Begin your script by selecting the **S**cripts/**B**eginRecord command, and give your script the name

takeordr

Paradox will now record your keystrokes as you type them. Press

Alt-F8	To clear the workspace.
V	To select the **V**iew command.
↵	To display a list of tables.
O	To select the **O**rders table.
End	To go to the last record.
F9	To enter Edit mode.
F7	To switch to Form view.
PgDn	To move to the first blank record.

The PAL Menu

You can't stop recording at this point with the **S**cripts/**E**nd-Record command because you can't display the Main menu. Pressing F10 displays the Edit mode menu. You also can't use Alt-F3, the "Instant Script" key, because, as Paradox will inform you, there is a

```
Recording already in progress
```

Fortunately, there's an out. Press Alt-F10, and you'll see the PAL menu shown in Figure 13.1. This gives you a chance to stop recording your script at this point, before you enter the details of a particular order. Select **E**nd-Record from the menu, and your script is saved.

The next time you need to take an order, you can just play the Takeordr script by executing the **S**cripts/**P**lay command.

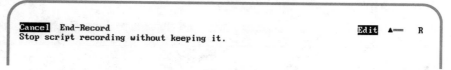

Figure 13.1: A way out of a script recording.

There's more to the PAL menu. When you're not recording, it appears as shown in Figure 13.2. You'll notice that some of the commands are the same as those on the regular **S**cripts menu. Thus, you can use this key as a shortcut to begin recording a named, rather than an Instant, script, or to play a script. One new command you may find useful is **V**alue. This command allows you to enter a calculation, and shows the result in the message area—just like having a little pocket calculator on-line. Moreover, you can reach it any time, because you don't have to go through the Main menu, which isn't always available. The other new commands are beyond the scope of this book.

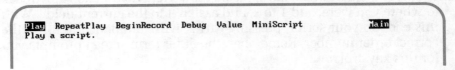

Figure 13.2: The PAL menu.

A Taste of PAL

Before proceeding, let's see exactly what Paradox recorded. If you view your script with the DOS TYPE command, or in an editor, you'll see the following:

```
ClearAll {View} {orders} End EditKey FormKey PgDn
```

255

This is actually a shorthand bit of code in PAL—the Paradox Application Language. As you can see, keys that have names, either on the keyboard or in Paradox, appear by name. Menu commands (such as **V**iew) are in curly braces. Since you select tables the same way you select menu commands, table names (and any other items you select from a list) will appear in curly braces. This is almost all you need to know to write scripts using an editor. It's also helpful for cleaning up scripts in which you pressed some wrong keys. Just load the script into your editor (which you can reach from the **S**cripts menu if you installed editor in using the Custom script), and delete the incorrect commands and key names.

For example, there's a bit of a problem with the Takeordr script. The order number should be the one after the last one in the table. It would be nice if you could get that into the first field automatically. You can, with a bit of PAL coding. Load the Takeordr script into the Editor with the **S**cripts/**E**ditor command, and then press the Ins key to type in insert mode. Press Enter and the up arrow, and type the following line:

```
SETKEY 14 CtrlPgUp x=[] CtrlPgDn []=x+1
```

This code requires some explanation. The SETKEY keyword assigns a set of commands to a key. The key is *14*—the ASCII code for Ctrl-N. This line of code says, "When the user presses Ctrl-N, act as though Ctrl-PgUp were pressed. Read the value in the field and assign it to *x*. (The square brackets represent the current field.) Then move back to where you were, add 1 to x, and assign it to the current field." With this code in your script, pressing Ctrl-N will automatically fill in the correct order number. Remember, the order form screen prompts you for this keystroke.

Recording a Script

1. Be sure your workspace appears as you want it to before you begin the script.

2. Press **S**.

    Paradox displays the **S**cripts menu.

3. Press **B**.

    Paradox asks you for the name of the script to record.

4. Type the name of your script, and press Enter.

    Paradox records every key you press, until you end the recording process.

5. When you finish, if you're at the Main menu, press **S**. If you're not at the Main menu, press Alt-F10.

    From the Main menu, Paradox displays the **S**cripts menu. If you're not at the Main menu, Paradox displays the PAL menu.

6. Press **E**.

    Paradox stops recording your keystrokes, and saves the keystrokes to that point to a script file with the name you specified. □

Embedding Scripts

I promised you a way to complete the day's work as well. This involves several steps:

- ▶ Copying the order records and detail records to history files.
- ▶ Deleting the noncurrent records from the Orders and Detail tables.
- ▶ Printing out invoices for all of today's orders.
- ▶ Decrementing the stock on hand in the inventory file.

First let's create the history tables. Use the `Create` command to create a table called *Ordrhist*, borrow the structure of the Orders table, and save it. Next, create a table called *Detlhist*. Borrow the structure of the Detail table, but delete the Description and Unit price fields. You don't need them in the history table. Save the table.

The next step is to move the data. Moving the orders is easy. Simply execute the **T**ools/**M**ore/**A**dd/**N**ewEntries command to add the records from Orders to Ordrhist.

As you'll see, you won't delete *all* the records from the Orders table—if you did, the Ctrl-N script wouldn't work because there'd be nothing from which to read the previous order number. Thus, when you update the Ordrhist table the next time, there will be some duplicate records. They will be moved to a KEYVIOL table, where you can safely ignore them.

To move the Detail records you need a query. The query appears in Figure 13.3. As you can see, all you're doing is creating a table that doesn't include the fields you don't want in the history table. Save this query with the **S**cripts/**Q**uerySave command. Call it

257

```
movedetl
```

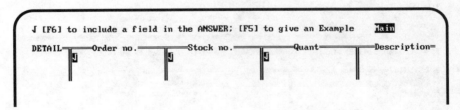

Figure 13.3: A query to create a reduced Detail table.

When you've executed this script with F2, the "DO-IT!," key, you'll have an ANSWER table with only three fields, just like the Detlhist table. Execute the **T**ools/**M**ore/**A**dd/**N**ew Entries command to move the records from the Answer table to the Detlhist table. Now execute the **T**ools/**M**ore/**E**mpty command to empty the Detail table.

Having saved all the records in the history tables, you can update the Orders table. Use the **D**elete query shown in Figure 13.4 to delete all but today's orders from the Orders table. Call this script

```
delorder
```

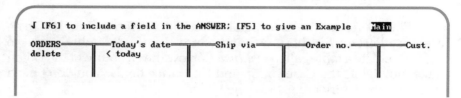

Figure 13.4: The delorder query.

The next step is to run the Mastordr query and print the invoices, as explained in Chapter 12. The final step is to update the Inventry table. To do so, set up the script shown in Figure 13.5. (The second table, whose name does not appear, is Inventry.) Save this script as

```
update
```

Your ANSWER table will contain all records from the Inventry table, but with the new figures in the On hand column. However, the On hand column will now be last, so you'll have to place the cursor in the Reorder column and press Ctrl-R to rotate the last two columns. To complete the job, execute the **T**ools/**M**ore/**A**dd/**U**pdate command to add the records from the ANSWER table to the Inventry table. Using **U**pdate ensures that the items that have been sold will be subtracted from the appropriate records.

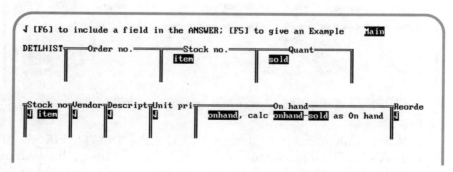

Figure 13.5: A query to update the Inventry table.

Embedding Scripts with the Scripts Menu

Now let's record a script that accomplishes all these steps. Use the **Scripts/BeginRecord** command, and call your script Finorder. Now press:

Alt-F8	To clear the workspace.
S	To display the **S**cripts menu.
P	To **P**lay a script.
↵	To see a list of scripts.
MO	To select the Movedetl query script.
F2	To execute the script.
F10	To display the Main menu.
T	To display the **T**ools menu.
M	To display the **M**ore secondary menu.
A	To **A**dd records to a table.
↵	To see a list of tables.
A	To select the ANSWER table as the source of the records to be added.
↵	To redisplay the list of tables.
D → ↵	To add records to the Detlhist table.
N	To make the records **N**ewEntries instead of modifications to existing records.
F10	To display the Main menu.
T	To display the **T**ools menu.
M	To display the **M**ore secondary menu.
E	To **E**mpty a table.
↵	To see a list of tables.
D → ↵	To select the Detail table to be emptied.
O	To select **O**K and confirm your decision.
F10	To display the Main menu.
T	To display the **T**ools menu.
M	To display the **M**ore secondary menu.
A	To **A**dd records.
O ↵	To select Orders as the source table.
O → ↵	To select Ordhist as the target table.

259

N	To make the records **N**ewEntries instead of modifications to existing records.
F10	To display the Main menu.
S	To display the **S**cripts menu.
P	To **P**lay a script.
↵	To see a list of scripts.
D	To select the Delorder query script.
F2	To execute the script.
Alt-F8	To clear the workspace.
S	To display the **S**cripts menu.
P	To **P**lay a script.
↵	To see a list of scripts.
MA	To select the Mastordr query script that was saved in Chapter 8.
F2	To execute the script.
F10	To display the Main menu.
T	To display the **T**ools menu.
C	To select the **C**opy command.
R	To copy a **R**eport.
D	To make a **D**ifferentTable the target of the copy.
↵	To see a list of tables.
MA	To select a report specification from the Mastordr table.
1	To choose report specification 1.
↵	To redisplay the list of tables.
A	To copy the report specification to the ANSWER table.
↵	To make the report specification the default.
F10	To display the Main menu.
R	To display the **R**eport menu.
O	To **O**utput a report.
A	To select the ANSWER table.
↵	To select the default report.
R	To select the **R**eport specification.

P	To send the report to the **P**rinter.
Alt-F8	To clear the screen.
S	To display the **S**cripts menu.
P	To **P**lay a script.
↵	To see a list of scripts.
U	To select the **U**pdate query script.
F2	To execute the script.
F10	To display the Main menu.
T	To display the **T**ools menu.
M	To display the **M**ore secondary menu.
A	To **A**dd records to the table.
↵	To see a list of tables.
A	To select the ANSWER table as the source of the records to be added.
↵	To redisplay the list of tables.
I	To select the Inventry table as the target.
U	To **U**pdate the records in the Inventry table in which the number of items on hand has changed.
F10	To display the Main menu.
S	To display the **S**cripts menu.
E	To select the **E**ndRecord command, and save these keystrokes to your Finorder script file.

261

That's quite a lot of keystrokes to complete the job! Aren't you glad you'll never have to repeat them? The result as it would appear in an editor is shown in Figure 13.6.

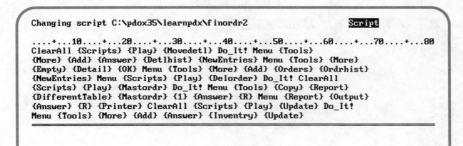

```
Changing script C:\pdox35\learnpdx\finordr2                    Script

....+...10....+...20....+...30....+...40....+...50....+...60....+...70....+...80
ClearAll {Scripts} {Play} {Movedetl} Do_It! Menu {Tools}
{More} {Add} {Answer} {Detlhist} {NewEntries} Menu {Tools} {More}
{Empty} {Detail} {OK} Menu {Tools} {More} {Add} {Orders} {Ordrhist}
{NewEntries} Menu {Scripts} {Play} {Delorder} Do_It! ClearAll
{Scripts} {Play} {Mastordr} Do_It! Menu {Tools} {Copy} {Report}
{DifferentTable} {Mastordr} {1} {Answer} {R} Menu {Report} {Output}
{Answer} {R} {Printer} ClearAll {Scripts} {Play} {Update} Do_It!
Menu {Tools} {More} {Add} {Answer} {Inventry} {Update}
```

Figure 13.6: The Finorder script as recorded.

If you viewed this script in an editor, all the commands would be run together in a single paragraph. Therefore, as shown in Figure 13.7, I've separated the script into sections, one for each procedure, so you can follow it more easily. I've also added a *comment* at the beginning of each procedure to help you follow the logic. These comments—the lines beginning with the semicolons—are ignored by Paradox, but they simplify things when you want to revise a script in an editor, because they remind you of what you intended the steps to accomplish.

```
; Move detail records to Detlhist file, empty Detail file
ClearAll {Scripts} {Play} {Movedetl} Do_It!
Menu {Tools} {More} {Add} {Answer} {Detlhist} {NewEntries} Menu
{Tools} {More} {Empty} {Detail} {OK}
; Update the order history file
Menu {Tools} {More} {Add} {Orders} {Ordrhist} {NewEntries}
; Delete all orders earlier than today's
Menu {Scripts} {Play} {Delorder} Do_It!
; Set up the query to collect the data for the Invoice report
ClearAll {Scripts} {Play} {Mastordr} Do_It!
; Print the invoices
Menu {Tools} {Copy} {Report} {DifferentTable} {Mastordr} {1}
{Answer} {R} Menu {Report} {Output} {Answer} {R} {Printer}
; Find the Inventory records that should be decremented,
Menu {Scripts} {Play} {Update} Do_It!
; Replace the On-hand figures with the updated figures
Menu {Tools} {More} {Add} {Answer} {Inventry} {Update}
```

Figure 13.7: The Finorder script separated into sections, with notes added.

> ▶ **Note:** When you execute the Finorder script (or any script),
> you won't actually see tables appearing and disappearing
> from the workspace. The script executes invisibly, unless
> Paradox encounters an error in the script. If you actually want
> to see the progress of the script, select the **S**cripts/**S**howPlay
> command instead of **S**cripts/**P**lay.

Embedding Scripts with an Editor

There is, however, a second way to set up this procedure: embed the
actual query scripts within this master script. The technique has
advantages and disadvantages. On the one hand, it's a little faster and
somewhat more elegant. On the other, if you've made mistakes, it may
be harder to find them. If your editor allows you to insert one file within
another one, you can embed the query scripts directly within this
master script. Search for

```
{Scripts} {Play}
```

When you find these words, delete them. The next word will be the
name of the embedded script. Start a new line, read the script into your
editor, and delete the script name. When you're finished, you can delete
all of the query scripts from your disk. A sample of what such a script
would look like appears in Figure 13.8.

This chapter has given you a brief taste of the power of scripts and
the PAL language. Once you master these tools, there is virtually no limit
to how far you can go with Paradox.

263

```
; Move detail records to Detlhist file, empty Detail file
ClearAll
Query
 Detail  | Order no. | Stock no. | Quant    |
         | Check     | Check     | Check    |
         |           |           |          |
         |           |           |          |
Endquery
Do_It!
Menu {Tools} {More} {Add} {Answer} {Detlhist} {NewEntries} Menu
{Tools} {More} {Empty} {Detail} {OK}
; Update the order history file
Menu {Tools} {More} {Add} {Orders} {Ordrhist} {NewEntries}
; Delete all orders earlier than today's
Menu
Query
 Orders    | Today's date    |
 delete    | < today         |
           |                 |
           |                 |
Endquery
Do_It!
; Set up the query to collect the data for the Invoice report
ClearAll
Query
```

Figure 13.8: An end-of-day script with embedded queries.

Graphs and Crosstabs

What You Will Learn

▶ Selecting Data for Graphing
▶ Using the Graph Menus
▶ Creating Cross-Tabulations

You have learned how to view data on the screen in a form designed for the purpose and how to create printed reports. In the process, you've learned ways of linking tables in order to gather the data to place into your forms and reports. Paradox offers you two additional ways of viewing your data—graphs and cross-tabulated tables.

Cross-tabulated tables, or crosstabs, are just what they sound like. You may find them helpful for getting a different view of your information or for gathering the information to present in a graph.

Paradox's graphing component allows you any degree of control and complexity that you like. If your table is properly set up, you can get a simple graph just by pressing Ctrl-F7, the "Instant Graph" key. On the other hand, you can customize your graphs to your heart's content. Paradox's graphing menus allow you to choose among nine types of graphs, plus combinations of them. You can customize the colors (for printing and for viewing on the proper equipment), the fill patterns, the titles and legends, the typefaces, and the page layout for printing. But you can get usable graphs just by accepting the defaults.

What Gets Graphed?

The most important issue in graphing is the data used as the basis of a graph. This has two aspects: gathering the data to be graphed and setting up your table so that Paradox reads it as you want it to be read.

Paradox always bases graphs on a single table. You may find that the information you want doesn't appear in a single table. If that's the case, you can create the table on which to base a graph by setting up a query. Sometimes you may have to set up a second query based on the ANSWER table. You'll see some queries to set up graphs (and crosstabs) before the end of this chapter. First, however, you'll learn how Paradox reads the data it finds.

How Paradox Selects Items to Graph

To begin with, Paradox (naturally enough) graphs only Numeric data. Chapter 7 referred to a table of sales figures, broken down by salesperson and by month. A portion of the table appears in Figure 14.1. (It includes additional columns for March through June, which are not visible in the figure.) This table happens to be perfect for producing a graph because, by default, Paradox produces a stacked-bar graph. Each bar can include up to six items, or *series*. The labels for the items along the X-axis—the line at the bottom of the graph—come from the items in the leftmost field. Thus, a graph of this table will be keyed to the Sales ID field. (In an unkeyed table, you can change this by rotating the fields. Last names would be more informative, for example. But this table uses Sales ID as a key field, so that won't work here.)

You determine what data is included in the graph by the order of the fields and the position of the cursor. When you press Ctrl-F7, the "Instant Graph" key, Paradox graphs all the fields to the right of the cursor, including the field in which the cursor is positioned. Thus, to graph all six months, you simply place the cursor in the Jan column. The resulting graph appears in Figure 14.2.

Compare the graph to the table on which it's based. You'll see that the title of the graph is the same as the name of the table. The labels on the bars are the items in the leftmost column, Sales ID, and the order in which the items appear within the bars is the same as the order in the table.

View	Ask	Report	Create	Modify	Image	Forms	Tools	Scripts	Help	Exit

View a table.

SALESPER	Sales ID	Last name	First name	Jan	Feb	
1	101	Garfield	Man	26690.63	21180.44	*
2	102	Marcias	Jose	29430.85	12808.81	*
3	103	Costa	Diane	19940.31	20280.62	*
4	104	Sayeed	Farouk	18890.82	20280.62	*
5	105	Bentley	Victoria	13780.85	10541.65	*
6	106	Mordo	Karl	6995.9	8301.1	*
7	107	Wolfe	Sara	29831	10029.34	*
8	109	Blessing	Morgana	20121.6	16987.3	*
9	112	Dormamma	Clea	21891.44	18186.67	*
10	118	Strange	Stephen	20003.45	13453.69	*
11	126	Wong	T	17432.02	18546.1	*

Figure 14.1: A table from which a graph can be drawn.

267

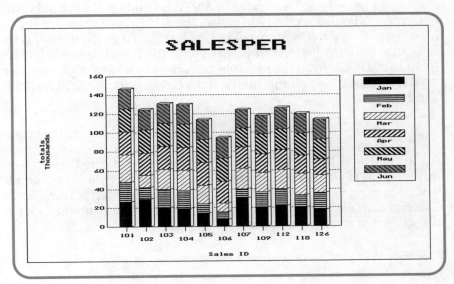

Figure 14.2: The default graph from the Salesper table.

You can change what's graphed by rotating the fields and by moving the cursor. Thus, for example, to graph only the March and April figures, you would rotate the fields until these two were the last two fields in the table and place the cursor in the March field before pressing Ctrl-F7, the "Instant Graph" key. To place the month with the largest overall figures at the bottom, rotate that month's field to the left.

The only way to change the bar labels in a keyed table is to create a sorted table with the field containing your preferred labels as the primary sort field. You can then base your graph on the sorted field. To change other items, you need to use the Graph menu, which you'll explore later in this chapter.

Setting Up a Graph Query

More often than not, the items you want to graph aren't all together in one table. For example, suppose you wanted to graph the relative sales by state from the data collected using your order entry application. You'd need to construct a query bringing together the following items:

▶ The State field from the Customer table.
▶ The Unit price from the Inventry table.
▶ The Quantity of each item sold from the Detlhist table.

To get this information, you'd have to set up a query such as the one shown in Figure 14.3. The resulting ANSWER table will have only two fields: the *State* field and a field called *Total*. However, there would be one record for each Stock no. sold in each state. To group the items by state, you have to clear the workspace with Alt-F8 (so Paradox doesn't include the items from the previous query) and set up a query on your ANSWER table. It's a simple query. Put a Checkmark in the State field, and type

```
calc sum
```

in the Total field. Figure 14.4 shows the resulting ANSWER table, sorted on the second field in reverse order. Figure 14.5 shows the default graph from that query. To give you a taste of Paradox's graphing power, Figure 14.6 shows a custom graph created with Paradox's Graph menu options, the subject of the next section.

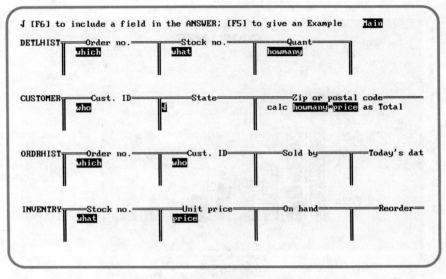

Figure 14.3: A query to gather data for a graph.

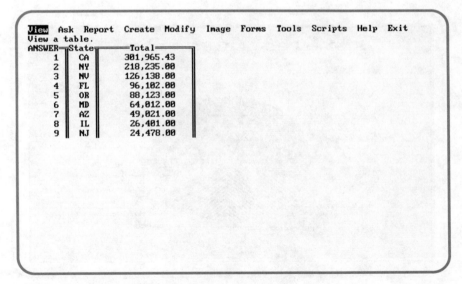

Figure 14.4: Data that can be graphed.

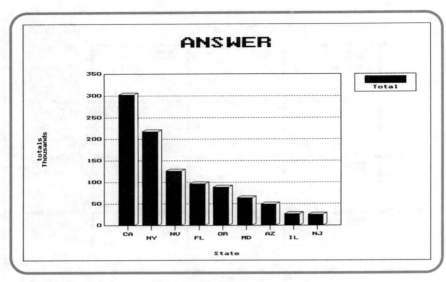

Figure 14.5: The graphic result.

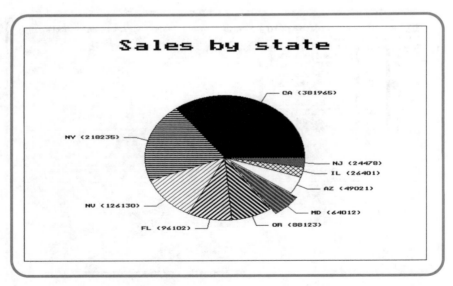

Figure 14.6: An enhanced graph.

The Graph Menus

You view the primary graph menu, shown in Figure 14.7, by executing the Image/Graph command. You must have an image on the workspace to execute this command. When you use the subsidiary menus to change the characteristics of a graph (with the Image/Graph/Modify command), you can then use this menu to determine which graph specifications will be used when you press the "Instant Graph" key, Ctrl-F7. The commands have the following effects:

Modify   Lets you change the characteristics of the graph to be displayed.

Load   Loads a previously saved graph settings file.

Save   Saves the settings you establish in a file with a name of your choice and the extension .G.

Reset   Restores the default settings, eliminating any changes you may have made with the Modify command; if you have loaded a graph file, its settings are canceled, but the file is not affected.

CrossTab   Changes the structure of a table in ways to be described later in this chapter.

ViewGraph   Displays the graph on the screen (the same as Ctrl-F7), or sends it to your default printer (IBM Graphics, unless you change your default printer with the Custom script), or saves the screen in a file that can be printed directly on the default printer.

271

```
Modify  Load  Save  Reset  CrossTab  ViewGraph                    Main
Modify the current graph specification.
```

Figure 14.7: The main Graph menu.

The Graphing Module

Paradox's graphing module, reached by executing the **I**mage/**G**raph/ **M**odify command, works quite differently from the rest of Paradox. Enter this command, and you are presented with a full-screen menu allowing you to choose the type of graph to be displayed. Press F10, and a second menu, which looks like a standard Paradox menu, appears at the top of the screen. This menu appears in Figure 14.8. From this point on, you return to the **G**raph/**M**odify menu with F10.

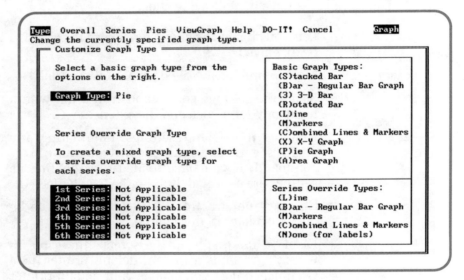

Type Overall Series Pies ViewGraph Help DO-IT! Cancel   Graph
Change the currently specified graph type.
┌─ Customize Graph Type ──────────────────────────────

Select a basic graph type from the
options on the right.

Graph Type: Pie

───────────────────────────────

Series Override Graph Type

To create a mixed graph type, select
a series override graph type for
each series.

1st Series: Not Applicable
2nd Series: Not Applicable
3rd Series: Not Applicable
4th Series: Not Applicable
5th Series: Not Applicable
6th Series: Not Applicable

Basic Graph Types:
(S)tacked Bar
(B)ar - Regular Bar Graph
(3) 3-D Bar
(R)otated Bar
(L)ine
(M)arkers
(C)ombined Lines & Markers
(X) X-Y Graph
(P)ie Graph
(A)rea Graph

Series Override Types:
(L)ine
(B)ar - Regular Bar Graph
(M)arkers
(C)ombined Lines & Markers
(N)one (for labels)

Figure 14.8: The graphing module menu, with the Graph Type menu.

▶ You can return from the Paradox submenus by pressing Escape, but you must always press F10 to return from the full-screen Graph menus.

The menu you see when you first enter the graphing module is the **T**ype menu. The other commands which you reach by pressing F10, all have standard Paradox submenus, each of which eventually leads to another full-screen menu on which you set or change graph specifications. Briefly, options on these menus do the following:

`Overall`	Lets you specify graph titles and colors, the background grid pattern, the scale and format of the axes, and the page layout for printing; also lets you choose one of four installed printers and the default file format or the Lotus .PIC file format for files.
`Series`	Lets you specify legends, labels, fill patterns, markers, and colors for each element in a series to be graphed (for example, each row in a stacked bar graph, or each line in a multiple-line graph).
`Pies`	Provides customization options for pie charts.
`ViewGraph`	The same effects as the `ViewGraph` command on the Image/Graph menu.

Creating Crosstabs

273

Paradox includes one more facility for viewing your data: crosstabs. Sometimes you may want to see one item broken down by another just to get a different view of your data. You also need to have your data in that format in order to create a *series graph*, if it isn't already in that format (as it was in the Salesper table).

Suppose, for example, you want to find out how much each member of your sales staff has sold in each state. To do so, you need a crosstab table. To get the crosstab table, you must have a table with three fields:

▶ The field with the items to appear as row labels.
▶ The field with the items to appear as column labels.
▶ The data to appear in the cells.

To get the information from the tables in your order entry database, you need a query such as the one illustrated as a query script in Figure 14.9. (I chose this format because the query involved so many tables that it wouldn't fit on the screen.) Notice that there are only two checked fields: the State field in the Customer table and the Last name field in the Salesper table. These are the items for the row and column headings. There will be a column for each state and a row for each salesperson. The third field is generated by the calculation

```
calc [howmany]*[price] as Total
```

The ANSWER table will have one record for each sale by each salesperson in each state. Once you have this table, you can press Alt-X to get an "Instant CrossTab"—*maybe*. It depends on the order of the fields in your ANSWER table. Rotate your answer table so that:

► The field containing the row labels is leftmost.
► The field containing the column labels is second.
► The field containing the values to be summarized is third.

```
Query

  Detlhist   | Order no.  | Stock no.  | Quant        |
             | _which     | _what      | _howmany     |
             |            |            |              |
             |            |            |              |

  Customer   | Cust. ID | State     |    Zip or postal code            |
             | _who     | Check     | calc _howmany*_price as Total    |
             |          |           |                                  |
             |          |           |                                  |

  Ordrhist   | Order no. | Cust. ID | Sold by |
             | _which    | _who     | _seller |
             |           |          |         |
             |           |          |         |

  Inventry   | Stock no. | Unit price |
             | _what     | _price     |
             |           |            |
             |           |            |

  Salesper   | Sales ID | Last name |
             | _seller  | Check     |
             |          |           |
             |          |           |

Endquery
```

Figure 14.9: A query to generate a table from which to derive a crosstab table.

If you see the message

```
Series field must be to the right of the key fields
```

execute the **I**mage/**G**raph/**C**rossTab command.

Your crosstab will present a *summary* of the data in your ANSWER table. You can choose the **S**um, **M**in(imum), **M**ax(imum), or **C**ount of the items. You are then asked to select the field containing the column labels, the field containing the row labels, and the column containing the crosstab values, in that order. (Thus, you needn't have a table with only three columns; however, you must have two label columns and at least one column of numeric data to tabulate.) If you see the message

```
Must choose a field to the right of the key fields
```

rotate your label fields and try again. Once the ANSWER table was properly rotated, it resulted in the CROSSTAB table shown in Figure 14.10. The default graph from the table appears in Figure 14.11. In the following section, you'll learn how to customize the graph to make it more meaningful and attractive.

```
 Editing Crosstab table: Record 8 of 13                        Edit  ▲═

 CUSTOMER┬Cust. ID┬═══Last name══════┬═══First name═══┬══════Department═════
      13 ║ 00013  ║ Khorajian        │ Corey          │
      14 ║ 00014  ║ Lathom           │ Susan          │
      15 ║ 00015  ║ Loquendi         │ Norma          │
      16 ║ 00016  ║ Osterlund        │ Frank R.       │
      17 ║ 00017  ║ Schocks          │ Susan          │
      18 ║ 00018  ║ Spencer          │ O'Neil         │


 CROSSTAB┬══════Last name══════┬═══════════CA═════┬═══════════FL═════┬═══════N
       1 ║ Bently              │     1,180.00     │    12,345.00     │*******
       2 ║ Blessing            │     2,244.00     │    31,310.00     │*******
       3 ║ Costa               │        32.00     │    39,854.00     │*******
       4 ║ Dormamma            │     9,876.00     │    26,581.00     │*******
       5 ║ Garfield            │    12,016.00     │    12,542.00     │*******
       6 ║ Macias              │     6,023.00     │    35,498.00     │*******
       7 ║ Mordo               │     1,231.00     │     5,432.00     │*******
       8 ║ Sayeed              │     8,583.00     │    56,473.00     │*******
       9 ║ Strange             │     8,340.00     │    34,091.00     │*******
      10 ║ Wolfe               │     2,233.00     │    23,987.00     │*******
      11 ║ Wong                │     5,839.00     │    22,986.00     │*******
      12 ║
      13 ║
```

Figure 14.10: A CROSSTAB table.

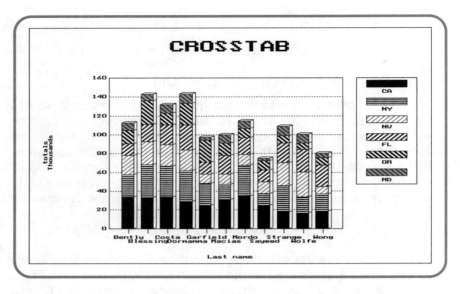

Figure 14.11: A default graph from a CROSSTAB table.

Enhancing Graphs

The first thing you'll probably notice is that the title isn't very helpful. The default graph takes its title from the name of the table. More significant, however, is the fact that Paradox automatically graphs the first six numeric fields. In this table, the numeric fields list sales by state, with the states in alphabetical order. It's generally more helpful to place the largest series at the bottom of a stacked-bar graph and arrange the others in diminishing order. To do that, rotate the various state fields so that they appear in the order shown in Figure 14.4.

Now let's take care of the title. Begin by entering the Graphing Module. Use the Image/Graph/Modify command. You'll be at the Graph Type menu. Press F10 to display the Graphing Module menu, and choose Overall/Titles. You'll see the screen shown in Figure 14.12. Notice that there is no title filled in on any of the lines.

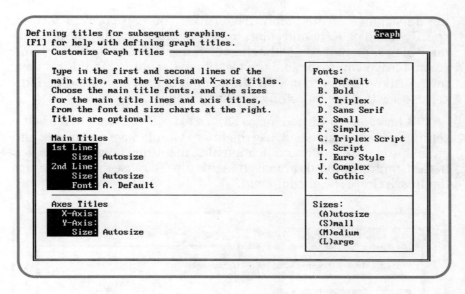

Figure 14.12: The Graph Titles menu.

On this screen, in the 1st line field, type in

`Monthly Sales by Salesperson`

Keep Autosize for this line. In the 2nd line field, type in

`States with greatest sales`

Now move to the next line and press **S** for **S**mall size. You can experiment with fonts as you wish. I chose Triplex Script, which is selected by pressing **G** when the cursor is in the Font field. You can check the results at any time by pressing F10 and choosing the **V**iewGraph/**S**creen command. Now go to the Axes Titles, and type

`Salesperson`

in the X-axis field.

Now press F10, and select the **S**eries/LegendsAndLabels menu, shown in Figure 14.13. Here you can replace the state postal abbreviations with full state names. Enter the states in order from Figure 14.4, until you have filled all six Legend fields. As you'll see from the graph in Figure 14.14, you will have already made a marked improvement in the appearance of the graph. If you like, you can go even further, specifying fill patterns and colors for each series, changing the arrangement of ticks on the axes, or the characters used to make up the grid, and so on. I leave you to explore the rest of the Graphing Module on your own. Just remember to use the **ViewGraph/S**creen command periodically to see that you're getting what you want.

When you're finished, press F2, "DO-IT!" If you want to reuse the settings you've established, use the **Image/Graph/S**ave command, and enter the name for your specification file. All settings currently selected in the Graphing Module are saved in this file. To reuse the settings, use the **Image/Graph/L**oad command.

278

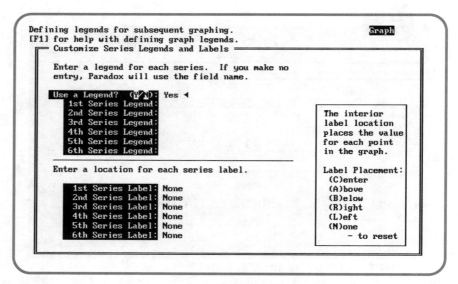

Figure 14.13: The Legends and Labels menu.

Printing Graphs

Now you can get some pretty fancy graphs on the screen. But you'd like to get them onto paper as well, wouldn't you? The obvious way to do that is to select the **ViewGraph/P**rinter command. But if you haven't told Paradox what kind of printer you have, you won't be able to proceed.

Defining Your Printer

To complete this step, play the Custom script, as described in Chapter 1. There, you used it to establish a default directory. This time, select the **G**raphs command. From the submenu, select **P**rinters.

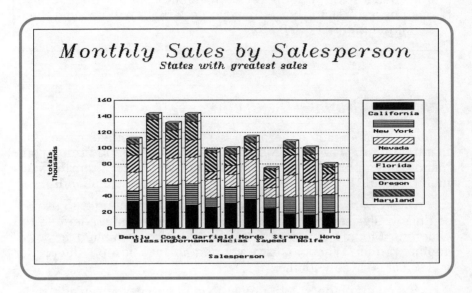

Figure 14.14: A custom graph generated from a CROSSTAB table.

Select the first printer. This one will be your default. (You can choose up to four printers, but they can be different print resolutions on the same printer rather than different printers.) You'll see a list of printer manufacturers. Select yours from the list. Select your printer model from the list that appears after that and a print resolution from the following list.

Next select the **D**evice command, and tell Paradox which port your printer is attached to. If you wish, you can repeat the procedure for the other printers. When you're through, select **R**eturn. Then select **DO-IT!**, and save your changes as directed. You'll be back at the DOS prompt. Next time you load Paradox, you'll be able to print a graph.

▶ Incidentally, you can change the default settings for any item in the Graphing Module menus using the **G**raph command of the Custom script. Each subcommand displays a menu screen exactly like those in the Graphing Module. Make any changes you wish in any of the menus before you exit the custom script, and the settings you establish will become the Graphing Module's defaults.

Sending a Graph to the Printer

You can print a graph either from the Graphing Module or the Main menu. From the Graphing Module, execute **V**iewGraph/**P**rinter command. The graph will be printed on your default printer. From the Main menu, execute the **I**mage/**G**raph/**V**iewGraph/**P**rinter command.

280

If you want your graph to go to a different printer (or to use the settings you've saved under a different printer number), go into the Graphing Module and use the **O**verall/**D**evice command to select another printer. When you save your graph specification, the printer you select is saved with it.

If your graph doesn't fit properly on the page, you can adjust the page layout with the **O**verall/**P**ageLayout command. You can adjust margins and dimensions and choose horizontal or vertical printing. Again, the changes you make are saved with the graph specification if you save one.

Installing Paradox on Your Computer

As mentioned in Chapter 1, you must have a hard disk to use Paradox 3.5. We'll assume that you do, and that your computer is not connected to a network. (Installation procedures are different if you will be using Paradox on a network.)

If your computer has both 5 1/4-inch and 3 1/2-inch drives, you already have a second usable copy of the Paradox diskettes. If not, before you install Paradox, make a backup copy of all the diskettes of the size appropriate to your computer. To do so, first make sure you have the same number of blank diskettes, or diskettes with data that you no longer need, as the diskettes you will copy. If you have one diskette drive, place your DOS system diskette into drive A, and type

```
DISKCOPY A: A:
```

(Note: If, as described in Appendix B, you have DOS on your computer's search path, you needn't use the DOS system diskette.) You will then see a message telling you to place the source diskette into drive A and press a key. Remove the DOS diskette and place one of the Paradox diskettes into drive A. You will be told to swap the source (that is, the Paradox diskette) and the target (the blank or reused) diskette several times until the copy is complete. You will then be asked if you wish to copy another. Press **Y** and press Enter, until you have copied all the diskettes.

If you have two diskette drives of the same kind, type

```
DISKCOPY A: B:
```

instead.

After you press Enter, you will see a message telling you to place the source diskette (one of the Paradox diskettes) into drive A and the target diskette (one of the blank diskettes) into drive B, and press a key. When the copy is completed, you will be asked if you wish to copy another. Press **Y** and press Enter, repeating the entire procedure until you have copied all the diskettes.

To begin installing Paradox, insert the Installation/Sample Tables disk into one of your diskette drives, and make that drive current. (If you don't understand these terms, read Appendix B before going further.) Paradox comes on both 3 1/2-inch and 5 1/4-inch diskettes and can be installed equally well from either drive A or drive B. If one of your disk drives is a 3 1/2-inch drive, you may find it somewhat simpler to use that drive, as you'll have to contend with fewer diskettes.

When the diskette is in your selected drive, make that drive current—that is, if it's drive A, type

```
A:
```

and press Enter. Then type

```
install
```

and press Enter. The Paradox opening screen will appear. Press Enter to continue. The Paradox Installation menu appears, as in Figure A.1. Press **1** for hard disk installation. (If you're going to use Paradox on a network, press **2**, and see your Network Administrator, before proceeding further. You will need some additional information that only your administrator can provide.)

You will be prompted to enter the letter name of the source drive, that is, the drive into which you placed the diskette. The current drive appears as the default, so you can just press Enter.

Next you will be prompted to enter the name of the drive on which you want to install Paradox. The default will be *C*, but you can change that to another hard drive if you prefer. (In the examples in this book, we'll assume that you have only one hard drive, and that it's drive C. If you have more than one hard drive, your work will go somewhat faster if you keep your program files on one drive and your data files on another.)

Next, you will be prompted to enter the name of the directory in which you want to install Paradox. The default

```
C:\PDOX35
```

is supplied. You can erase it by pressing Ctrl-Backspace and typing another directory name, if you wish. In this book, we'll assume you've used the directory name PDOX35.

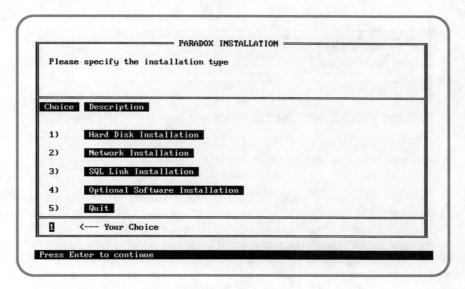

Figure A.1: The Paradox Installation menu.

Next, you must choose one of five country groups, as shown in Figure A.2. As that figure points out:

"To properly install Paradox, you must specify one of the five country groups below. This will tell Paradox which date and number formats to use and how to sort your alphabetic fields. After Paradox has been installed, you may change the date or number conventions by using the Paradox Custom Configuration Program." If you have ever worked with the COUNTRY= command and the alternate character sets supplied with DOS 3.3 and later, you'll recognize these options as conforming to the countries for which DOS includes character sets. If you're in the United States, press **1** and don't worry about the details.

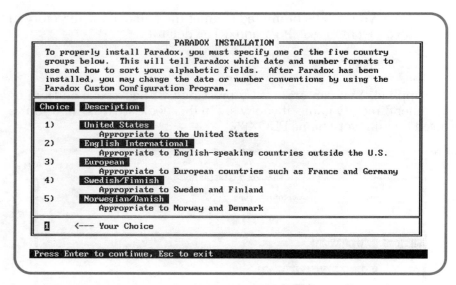

Figure A.2: Selecting nationality defaults.

284

Once you have made your selection, the installation program will copy some of the program files from the Installation disk. You will then be asked to insert System Disk 1 (if you are using 5 1/4-inch diskettes) or System Disk 1/2 (if you are using 3 1/2-inch diskettes) into your source drive. You'll then have to personalize your copy of Paradox by typing your name, company name, and the serial number of your copy of Paradox, as shown in Figure A.3. (The entry areas will be blank.) You'll find your serial number on the 5 1/4-inch Installation diskette. The program won't let you enter an invalid serial number. Although the serial number includes some uppercase letters, you can type them in lowercase.

When you've entered the information, the message

```
Copying files...
```

appears in a box in the center of the screen. Periodically, you'll be asked to insert various other diskettes, and to press Enter to confirm that you've done so. You'll also have to let Paradox tailor several sets of tables to the country default you selected, even if you're not planning to use those tables.

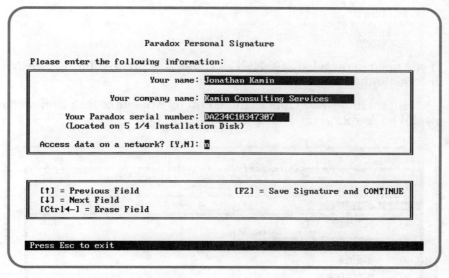

```
                    Paradox Personal Signature
    Please enter the following information:

                          Your name: Jonathan Kamin

                  Your company name: Kamin Consulting Services

           Your Paradox serial number: DA234C10347307
           (Located on 5 1/4 Installation Disk)

    Access data on a network? [Y,N]: n


    [↑] = Previous Field              [F2] = Save Signature and CONTINUE
    [↓] = Next Field
    [Ctrl◄─] = Erase Field


    Press Esc to exit
```

Figure A.3: Personalizing your copy of Paradox.

285

When these processes are finished, you will see the Optional Software Installation menu shown in Figure A.4. You can stop at this point by pressing **6** and then pressing Enter and Escape. However, if you want to work through the examples presented in the *Introduction* volume of the Paradox documentation, you should copy the sample tables and the sample application. (They will appear in the directories C:\PDOX35\SAMPLE and C:\PDOX35\SAMPAPP, respectively, unless you tell the program to place them elsewhere.) You may also want to install PPROG, the Paradox Personal Programmer. This subsidiary program allows you to create menus and help screens to go with your applications. However, unless you're a fairly experienced programmer, you can safely skip the Data Entry Toolkit and the Protection Generator. The former is quite advanced, and you can do everything the latter does through Paradox menu commands.

After installing each additional optional item, you'll be returned to the menu shown. When you are finished, press **7** and then press Enter and Escape to exit.

You may find when you're done that the installation program has modified your CONFIG.SYS file. If your CONFIG.SYS file had a BUFFERS command specifying fewer than 20 buffers, or a FILES command specifying fewer than 20 files, these are increased to 20. Your old CONFIG.SYS file is retained with the name CONFIG3.PDX. If you didn't have a CONFIG.SYS file, you'll now have one, containing the statements

```
FILES=20
BUFFERS=20
```

If you don't know what a CONFIG.SYS file is, you can safely ignore this information.

If you're new to computers, go on to Appendix B to find some useful background information.

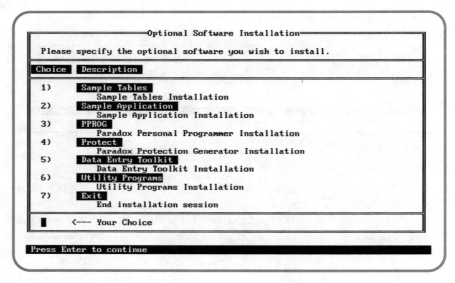

Figure A.4: The Optional Software Installation menu.

Useful Background Information

Without certain information, your computer can do nothing. Before it can run any programs or execute any commands, it must have an *operating system*. An operating system is a sort of "super-program" that tells the computer how to carry out such basic functions as reading information from your disks and displaying text on the screen.

Your computer's operating system is probably either PC DOS or MS-DOS. Paradox 3.5 can work only with these operating systems. (For simplicity, we'll refer to MS-DOS and PC DOS, which are closely related, simply as DOS.) The operating system organizes your data into *files*, which it keeps track of by listing information about them in *directories*.

If you have already run some application programs, you may have used DOS without knowing it, because you can execute DOS commands from within many applications programs. DOS is said to be *transparent* to these programs; that is, it is present, but invisible.

However, you need to know something about DOS to use your computer effectively. If you have never used DOS directly before, this appendix should give you enough information to get started.

You know DOS is present when you see the symbol

```
A>
```

or

```
C>
```

or something similar, on your screen. This symbol is the DOS *prompt*—its invitation to you to enter a command. The letter in the prompt represents the name of the drive that is *current*, a concept that will be explained shortly.

What Is a File?

As you no doubt know, information in a computer is stored in files. A file is a series of consecutive bytes (you might think of bytes as individual characters) of data with a specific name assigned to it. Every program that you run consists of one or more such files, and so are all the data files created by the programs you use.

288

File Names

You gain access to a file by means of its name. When you enter a command, you usually do so by typing the name of a file at the DOS prompt. Thus, for example, to start Paradox, you type

```
PARADOX
```

which is the main part of the name of the principal Paradox program file. (After you type a command, you must always press Enter, which signals DOS to execute the command.)

You gain access to data files by giving DOS their names, either as part of a command you type at a prompt, or from within a program. In fact, when you give a name to a table or script in Paradox, you are giving a name to the file in which it will be stored.

DOS imposes certain limitations on the names you can give to files. First, they must not be more than eight characters long. They may include any combination of letters and numbers, and the nonalphanumeric characters ~ @ # $ % ^ & { } - and _. No other characters can be used.

A file name may optionally have an extension of up to three characters. The extension is separated from the file name by a period (.) and may also have any combination of the acceptable characters, although certain conventions have developed regarding their use.

Program files all have the extensions .EXE, .COM, or .BAT. Some programs assign specific extensions to various types of data files, and others allow you to choose your own.

Paradox Objects and their Associated File Names

Paradox objects are grouped into *families*, based on the table to which they belong. All objects in a family have the same file name. They are differentiated by their file name extensions. The sole exception is scripts, which you name when you create them. The following list shows you the file name extension associated with each type of Paradox object.

Object	Extension
Forms	.F, .F2 through .F15
Graph print files	.GRF
Graph specifications	.G
Image settings	.SET
Lotus 1-2-3 graph files	.PIC
Primary indexes	PX
Reports	.R, .R2 through .R15
Scripts	.SC
Secondary indexes created by the **QuerySpeed** command	.X??,.Y??
Tables	.DB
Validity checks	.VAL

What Is a Directory?

Your computer's operating system keeps track of files by means of *directories*. DOS creates a directory on every formatted disk. A directory contains the following information about each file stored in it:

▶ The file name.
▶ The file name extension, if any.
▶ The length of the file in bytes.
▶ The date that the file was last created or modified.
▶ The time that the file was last created or modified.

To view a list of files in a directory, type the command

```
DIR
```

and press Enter.

Tree-Structured Directories

To help you manage hard disks, which can hold literally thousands of files, DOS allows you to create *tree-structured directories*. These are simply directories that have other directories, called *subdirectories*, subordinate to them. Subdirectories can hold any number of file names. Grouping related files in subdirectories makes it easier to find them.

Every subdirectory must have a name that follows the rules for file names. However, subdirectory names usually are not given extensions. In a directory that has subdirectories subordinate to it, the subdirectory names are displayed in the same form as the other file names, except that they are followed by the symbol

```
<DIR>
```

The main, or root, directory of a disk always has the name of the drive followed by \ (the backslash character).

What Is Currency?

When you use your computer, one drive is always the *current*, or *default* drive. To make a drive current, you type its name, followed by a colon, and press Enter. Thus, for example, to make your hard drive (or your primary hard drive, if you have more than one) current, you type

```
C:
```

and press Enter. To make your primary diskette drive current, you type

```
A:
```

and press Enter. When a drive is current, DOS always looks for things—programs to execute, or files to open, on that drive before it looks anywhere else.

If a drive has more than one directory, one directory on it is always the current, or default, directory. When a directory is current, DOS looks first in the current directory of the current drive first.

Directory Commands

There are three DOS commands to deal specifically with directories:

▶ MKDIR or MD creates a new subdirectory.
▶ RMDIR or RD removes an existing subdirectory.
▶ CHDIR or CD makes a different directory current.

To use these commands, you follow them with the name of the directory you want to create, remove, or make current.

On any drive, the last directory that was current remains current, even if the drive is not current. This means that, for example, if you last used the directory PDOX35 on drive C, and drive A is now current, any command you enter involving drive C will assume you want to use the PDOX35 directory. You can overcome this limitation by using a *path name*, described below.

What Is a Path?

You can refer to any directory by telling DOS the route to follow to find it. Such a description is called a *path* or *path name*. The path begins with the name of the drive, followed by the backslash (for the root directory), followed by all intervening directories, separated by backslashes. Thus, if you installed the Paradox Personal Programmer following the defaults supplied in the installation program, you would refer to its directory by using the path name *C:\PDOX35\PPROG*.

291

To refer to a file in a directory that isn't current, you precede it by the path name. The Personal Programmer itself would thus be called *C:\PDOX35\PPROG\PPROG*. (You might not be able to start the Personal Programmer by typing this path name on the command line, however. Many programs—Paradox among them—require that their directory be current before they can start.)

Directories and files can also be referred to by *relative path names*—that is, path names that relate to the current directory, rather than the root directory. Thus, if your current directory is *C:\PDOX35*, you could refer to the Personal Programmer directory simply as *PPROG*.

Extending DOS's Search Pattern

The DOS PATH command can help find the files you need. The PATH command tells DOS in which directories to search for the specified file. When a PATH command has been issued, you can execute a file in any of the directories specified in the path. The syntax is

```
PATH {drive}\PATHNAME;{drive}\PATHNAME;  . . .
```

where the drive name is optional, and *PATHNAME* represents the complete path from the root directory. Separate the path names with semicolons. There cannot be any spaces in the list of path names. The root directory, as usual, is indicated by a backslash. It's extremely useful to include the directory that contains your DOS files in the search path. You may also want to include your most frequently used software directories. Thus, you might want to include a PATH command such as

```
PATH C:\DOS;C:\PDOX35
```

If you do, you can make any directory current, and then start Paradox just by typing the program name. The directory you selected will remain current.

Backing Up Your Data

It's extremely important to have extra copies of your data files in the event that something goes wrong. To accomplish this, you have to be

able to format a diskette, and copy files to it. To format a disk, change
to the drive and directory that contains the DOS FORMAT file; type

```
FORMAT A:
```

and press Enter. (The Enter key tells DOS to accept what you have just
typed as a command.) You need not enter the commands in uppercase
letters. DOS commands are presented in uppercase letters here so that
you'll recognize them as such. You will be told to insert a disk and press
a key. Place a new diskette in the drive and press Enter. When the screen
reads

```
Format complete
```

the diskette is ready to accept data.

> ▶ If the directory containing the FORMAT file is on the
> search path, you needn't change directories first. You can
> simply enter the FORMAT command at any DOS prompt. Just
> be sure to specify a floppy drive letter, so you don't end up
> formatting your hard disk.

293

Next, you must copy your files from their current location to the
disk you have just formatted. To do so, use the COPY command. The
general form of this command is

```
COPY SOURCE TARGET
```

where *SOURCE* and *TARGET* may represent a drive, a path, a file name,
or any combination of them. You must give DOS enough information
so that it can find the files you want to copy and place the copies where
you want them. If either the source or the target is current, you can omit
it from the command. You can use the *wild-card pattern* *.* to refer to
all the files in a directory.

For example, if you create the directory *C:\LEARNPDX* for the
examples in this book, as suggested in Chapter 2, you'll want to copy the
files in that directory to your diskette. If that drive and directory are
current, type

```
COPY *.* A:
```

to copy all the files to the diskette in drive A. If drive A is current and \LEARNPDX is the current directory on the hard drive, you would type

```
COPY C:*.*
```

If \LEARNPDX is not the current directory and drive C is current, you would type

```
COPY C:\LEARNPDX\*.* A:
```

Starting Paradox with a Batch File

If you don't place Paradox's directory on your search path, you may find it convenient to start the program using a *batch file*. A batch file is simply a file containing a series of commands for DOS to execute in order. With a batch file, you can start Paradox with a single command instead of with two commands.

Make a directory current that's on the search path. (If you have a special directory for batch files, make that directory current.) Now type

```
COPY CON PDX.BAT
```

DOS is now prepared to create a batch file from what you type. Type the following commands, pressing Enter after each:

```
ECHO OFF
C:
CD \PDOX35
PARADOX
```

Now press Ctrl-Z. You should see the message

```
1 File(s) copied
```

The next time you start Paradox, just enter the command

```
pdx
```

at any DOS prompt and DOS will automatically make the Paradox directory current and start the program. The data directory will be Paradox's default data directory.

295

The Paradox
Command Tree

The diagrams on the following pages represent the Paradox menu structure. Not all Paradox commands appear in these diagrams—only those that are discussed in this book. Note that some commands can be reached following more than one path from the Main menu.

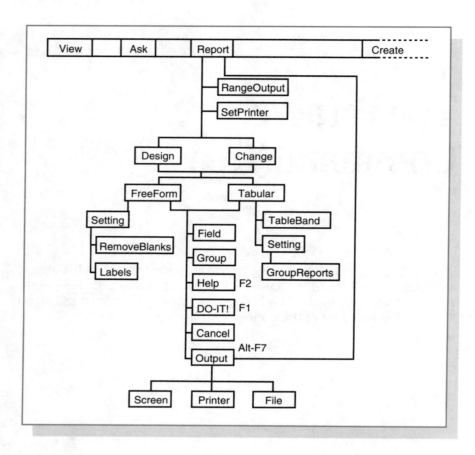

298

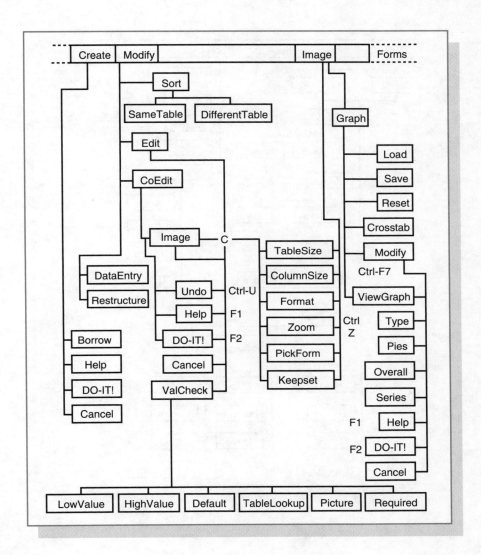

300

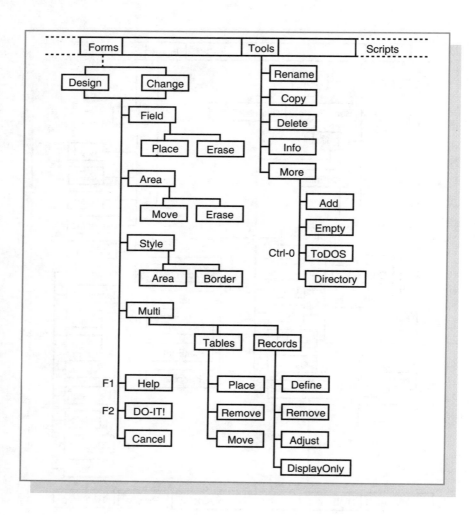

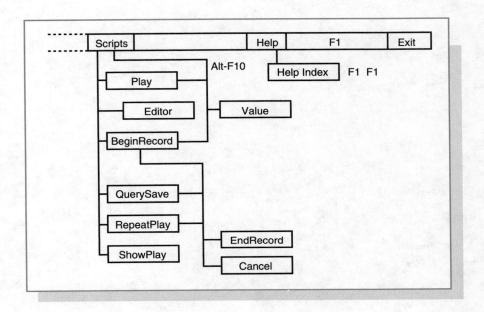

INDEX

304

307

308

309

313

Sams' First Books Get You Started Fast!

"The First Book Series ... is intended to get the novice off to a good start, whether with computers in general or with particular programs ...."

The New York Times

The First Book of WordPerfect 5.1
Kate Miller Barnes
275 pages, 7⅜ x 9¼, $16.95 USA
0-672-27307-1

Look For These Books In Sams' First Book Series

To Order Companion Disk

The companion disk contains all the files developed in *The First Book of Paradox 3.5*. The 5 ¼" disk is formatted to 360K, and the 3 ½" disk is formatted to 720K.

The disk may be purchased with cash, check, or money order. Purchase price includes shipping and handling. All orders will be shipped by first class mail. Make checks and money orders payable to *Kamin Consulting Services*. (No phone orders, please.)

Send this form with payment in U.S. funds to:

Kamin Consulting Services

528 Grand Avenue, Suite 100

Oakland, California 94610-3515

Overseas orders please add $1.00. California residents please add 6% sales tax, except residents of Alameda County, who should add 7% sales tax.

SAMS assumes no liability with respect to the use or accuracy of the information contained on these disks.

- -

Disk Order Form

Kamin, *The First Book of Paradox 3.5*, #27370

(Please print)

Name _____ Company _____

Address _____

City _____ State _____ Zip _____

County _____ Phone (   ) _____

Place of Book Purchase _____

5 ¼" Disk
Quantity: _____ @ $15 U.S.   Total: $_____

3 ½" Disk
Quantity: _____ @ $16 U.S.   Total: $_____

Method of Payment

Check # _____ Money Order # _____

All orders will be shipped U.S. Postal Service First Class.

Please allow six weeks for delivery.

Reader Feedback Card

Thank you for purchasing this book from SAMS FIRST BOOK series. Our intent with this series is to bring you timely, authoritative information that you can reference quickly and easily. You can help us by taking a minute to complete and return this card. We appreciate your comments and will use the information to better serve your needs.

1. Where did you purchase this book?

☐ Chain bookstore (Walden, B. Dalton)   ☐ Direct mail
☐ Independent bookstore   ☐ Book club
☐ Computer/Software store   ☐ School bookstore
☐ Other _____
_____

2. Why did you choose this book? (Check as many as apply.)

☐ ·Price   ☐ Appearance of book
☐ Author's reputation   ☐ SAMS' reputation
☐ Quick and easy treatment of subject ☐ Only book available on subject

3. How do you use this book? (Check as many as apply.)

☐ As a supplement to the product manual   ☐ As a reference
☐ In place of the product manual   ☐ At home
☐ For self-instruction   ☐ At work

4. Please rate this book in the categories below. G = Good; N = Needs improvement; U = Category is unimportant.

☐ Price   ☐ Appearance
☐ Amount of information   ☐ Accuracy
☐ Examples   ☐ Quick Steps
☐ Inside cover reference   ☐ Second color
☐ Table of contents   ☐ Index
☐ Tips and cautions   ☐ Illustrations
☐ Length of book
☐ How can we improve this book?_____
☐ _____

5. How many computer books do you normally buy in a year?

☐ 1–5   ☐ 5–10   ☐ More than 10
☐ I rarely purchase more than one book on a subject.
☐ I may purchase a beginning and an advanced book on the same subject.
☐ I may purchase several books on particular subjects.
☐ (such as _____)

6. Have your purchased other SAMS or Hayden books in the past year? _____
If yes, how many _____

7. Would you purchase another book in the FIRST BOOK series? _____

8. What are your primary areas of interest in business software? _____

☐ Word processing (particularly _____)
☐ Spreadsheet (particularly _____)
☐ Database (particularly _____)
☐ Graphics (particularly _____)
☐ Personal finance/accounting (particularly _____)
☐ Other (please specify _____)

Other comments on this book or the SAMS' book line: _____
_____

Name _____
Company _____
Address _____
City _____ State _____ Zip _____
Daytime telephone number _____
Title of this book _____

Fold here
- -

NO POSTAGE
NECESSARY
IF MAILED
IN THE
UNITED STATES

BUSINESS REPLY MAIL
FIRST CLASS   PERMIT NO. 336   CARMEL, IN

POSTAGE WILL BE PAID BY ADDRESSEE

SAMS

11711 N. College Ave.
Suite 141
Carmel, IN 46032–9839